DECOLONIZATION A SHORT HISTORY

DECOLONIZATION
A SHORT HISTORY

JAN C. JANSEN

JÜRGEN OSTERHAMMEL

TRANSLATED BY JEREMIAH RIEMER

PRINCETON UNIVERSITY PRESS
PRINCETON AND OXFORD

First published in German as *Dekolonisation* by Jan C. Jansen and
Jürgen Osterhammel, © Verlag C.H. Beck oHG, München 2013

English translation copyright © 2017 by Princeton University Press

Requests for permission to reproduce material from this work
should be sent to Permissions, Princeton University Press

Published by Princeton University Press
41 William Street, Princeton, New Jersey 08540

In the United Kingdom: Princeton University Press
6 Oxford Street, Woodstock, Oxfordshire OX20 1TR

press.princeton.edu

Jacket design by Chris Ferrante

Library of Congress Cataloging-in-Publication Data

Names: Jansen, Jan C., author. | Osterhammel, J?urgen, author.
Title: Decolonization : a short history / Jan C. Jansen and Jurgen Osterhammel.
Other titles: Dekolonisation. English
Description: Princeton : Princeton University Press, [2017] | Translated from
    German. | Includes bibliographical references and index.
Identifiers: LCCN 2016037948 | ISBN 9780691165219 (hardcover : alk. paper)
Subjects: LCSH: Decolonization—History—20th century.
Classification: LCC JV151 .J3613 2017 | DDC 325/.309—dc23
    LC record available at https://lccn.loc.gov/2016037948

British Library Cataloging-in-Publication Data is available

This book has been composed in Sabon Next LT Pro and Gotham

Printed on acid-free paper. ∞

Printed in the United States of America

10 9 8 7 6 5 4 3 2 1

CONTENTS

Preface   vii

1 Decolonization as Moment and Process   1

2 Nationalism, Late Colonialism, World Wars   35

3 Paths to Sovereignty   71

4 Economy   119

5 World Politics   139

6 Ideas and Programs   156

7 Legacies and Memories   171

Notes   193

Select Readings   225

Index   237

PREFACE

IF THE PRESENT is an unprecedented age of globalization, with all its contradictions and countervailing tendencies, we also live in the aftermath of earlier upheavals that marked the second half of the twentieth century. One of those upheavals was the rapid transformation of a handful of colonial empires into a plural world of sovereign states. A brief glance around the world reveals the lingering aftereffects of empire's demise: Australians arguing about replacing the British monarch as their sovereign; the North Korean government setting the clock back in 2015 as a means to eradicate a legacy of Japanese imperialism; Zimbabweans arguing about disinterring and repatriating Cecil Rhodes's remains to England; observers debating if the 2011 Tunisian revolution marked the last stage in the long decolonization of that country; social scientists and historians calling for truly "decolonial" analytical perspectives and mental attitudes; and a special committee at the

United Nations updating year after year a list of countries awaiting their release into independent statehood. Reverberations of decolonization such as these prompt us to remember that the contemporary world was built out of the ruins of European, and some non-European, intercontinental empires.

The pallid term "decolonization" refers to a particularly unwieldy process in twentieth-century history. A plethora of meanings, ambiguities, conflicting memories, and competing narratives makes it the focus of political and scholarly disagreements. Was decolonization essentially about obtaining national independence from alien rule, or at least to the same degree about economic or cultural self-determination? Is it tied to colonialism as a system of rule, or does it also apply to noncolonial contexts? When did it start, and when, if ever, did it end? Can it best be understood through a *longue durée* approach going back to the beginning of the twentieth century, or is it rather the baffling rapidity of imperial collapse in the decades after 1945 that claims our primary attention? And, in hindsight, was it a failure or a success? Are a great deal of the current problems in the world to be blamed on a botched or incomplete decolonization?

This book does not claim to settle these controversies once and for all. Rather, it presents the issues as clearly as possible and outlines the most important arguments. In place of a detailed and full-blooded story, it seeks to provide a concise and comparative interpretation of decolonization that inserts this dramatic process of global change into the wider history of the twentieth century. Even if decolonization's most dramatic and decisive hot phase is to be found in the short period of roughly three decades following the Second World War, it cannot be understood without the longer history of anticolonial unrest and late-colonial transformations since the First World War, nor can it be fully appreciated without the various reverberations leading up to the present. Along with this long-term approach, we regard decolonization as a multifaceted process that stretched across various fields in addition to politics, such as the economy, culture, or the normative foundations of the international community. Instead of giving primacy to a single perspective on the course of events, we believe that one needs to combine local, regional, imperial, and international levels of analysis. In developing our own understanding of what is a potentially boundless topic, we are happy to draw on an enormously rich treasure of historical scholarship coming from many different countries. However, the huge variety of detailed research on the end of empires has rarely been accompanied, at least during the past two decades, by new attempts at interpretation and synthesis.

This brief book grew out of the collaboration of the authors on a book on colonialism, published in Germany in 2012. Originally intended merely to be the subject of a concluding chapter in that book, decolonization assumed a life of its own and seemed to merit a separate and more comprehensive treatment. Our *Dekolonisation* came out in German in 2013. For the present English language edition, we revised the entire text and expanded its length by roughly a quarter. Still, the book retains much of its original character. Part introductory survey, part historical essay, it is analytical rather than narrative in its overall design. This implies that it does not offer an exhaustive or encyclopedic country-by-country or empire-by-empire treatment of decolonization. While we seek to bring out the various trajectories and patterns of decolonization in the different parts of the world, most of the chapters delve into systematic aspects. This approach allows us to discuss more methodically, for instance, evolving norms of international legitimacy and different explanatory models; the nature of anticolonialism and late colonialism, and their impact on the decolonization process; the economic dimensions of decolonization; the place of decolonization in world politics; the intellectual history of decolonization; and the manifold legacies and memories it left both in former colonizing and colonized societies—fields where a lot of exciting work is currently in progress. The format forces us to be selective with the cases studied and restrictive with regard to the level of detail presented to the reader. While, for example, the decolonization of Cyprus leading to the Mediterranean island's independence in 1960 triggered a serious and violent international crisis with lasting consequences for the country and the European Union, it cannot possibly be discussed in its full complexity. Likewise, there will only be sketchy material on the leading historical figures and characters, on the celebrated heroes and villains of decolonization who still populate the popular memory of this epoch.

For this edition, we have thoroughly revised and supplemented the original book and updated and revised the bibliography and references so as to make the book more accessible for English-speaking readers. Some first-rate references in languages other than English have been retained, though, reminding us that the history of decolonization cannot be a monolingual enterprise.

Even a short book like this one incurs a long list of debts. Mischa Honeck, Valeska Huber, and Martin Rempe have read parts of the German or English version, and we have greatly benefited from their comments and criticism. At Princeton

University Press, we are especially grateful to Brigitta van Rheinberg, who early on expressed her interest in bringing out this book and skillfully navigated it through a long process of revision and production. While revising the manuscript for the English language edition, we were also fortunate to draw on several anonymous reviews solicited by Princeton University Press. Jeremiah Riemer provided a draft translation of the German original that formed the basis of our revision; Molan Goldstein made our revised and expanded manuscript a readable text. In preparing the two editions of the book, we were lucky to rely on the help of student assistants Wolfgang Egner and Agnes Gehbald for the German edition and German Historical Institute interns Sascha Brünig and Cora Schmidt-Ott for the American edition. Finally, this book is indebted to the work of generations of scholars from various disciplines and countries who, over the past decades, have broadened and sharpened our understanding of decolonization. Among them, a special tribute is due to Dietmar Rothermund who has published a great number of books, over half a century and both in German and in English, on this historical process in South Asia and elsewhere, always inspiring models of scholarship and insight.

DECOLONIZATION A SHORT HISTORY

1

DECOLONIZATION AS MOMENT AND PROCESS

"DECOLONIZATION" is a technical and rather undramatic term for one of the most dramatic processes in modern history: the disappearance of empire as a political form, and the end of racial hierarchy as a widely accepted political ideology and structuring principle of world order. One can pin down this historical process by using a dual definition that, instead of keeping the process chronologically vague, anchors it unequivocally in the history of the twentieth century. Accordingly, decolonization is

(1) the simultaneous dissolution of several intercontinental empires and the creation of nation-states throughout the global South within a short time span of roughly three postwar decades (1945–75), linked with

(2) the historically unique and, in all likelihood, irreversible delegitimization of any kind of political rule that is experienced

as a relationship of subjugation to a power elite considered by a broad majority of the population as alien occupants.[1]

Decolonization designates a specific world-historical moment, yet it also stands for a many-faceted process that played out in each region and country shaking off colonial rule. Alternative attempts at a definition accentuate this second dimension. The historian and sinologist Prasenjit Duara, for example, puts less emphasis on the breakdown of empires and more on *local* power shifts in specific colonies when he defines decolonization as "the process whereby colonial powers transferred institutional and legal control over their territories and dependencies to indigenously based, formally sovereign, nation-states." He, too, adds a normative aspect: the replacement of political orders was embedded in a global shift in values. This dissolution signifies a counterproject to imperialism in the name of "moral justice and political solidarity."[2]

It is equally possible to ask, quite concretely and pragmatically, when the decolonization of a specific territory was completed. A simple answer would be: when a locally formed government assumed official duties, when formalities under international law and of a symbolic nature were carried out, and when the new state was admitted (usually within a matter of months) into the United Nations. A more complex (and less easily generalizable) answer would weave these trajectories toward state independence into more comprehensive and intricate processes of ending colonial rule and extending political, economic, and cultural sovereignty.

Decolonization can thus be described at different levels, and even its exact time frame may vary according to the thematic or regional focus. Vagueness and ambiguity are part of the historical phenomenon itself, and they cannot simply be defined away. From a global perspective, decolonization has its "hot" and most decisive phase in the middle of the twentieth century during the three decades following the Second World War. The core period of decolonization, however, needs to be incorporated in a longer history with less sharply defined chronological margins. This long history of decolonization harks back to the years following the First World War, when anticolonial unrest took on a new dimension and colonial rule itself was subject to major transformations, and it extends to the many aftershocks palpable up to the present.

People all over the world have used different words to describe these dramatic transformations and the world they thought would supplant a world of empires. Compared with concepts such as "self-determination," "liberation," or "revolution" (and their many linguistic and cultural variations)—and also to other popular categories applied to contemporary history, like "Cold War" or "globalization"—it is a somewhat anemic word derived from administrative practice that has become the most common term for this process. "Decolonization" is not a category that historians or social scientists thought up in retrospect. Traces of the concept may be found before 1950. The term, which can be attested lexically since 1836, found some theoretic elaboration in the writings of the German émigré economist Moritz Julius Bonn in the interwar period. Yet, we only find it used with any significant frequency beginning in the mid-1950s, that is (as we know in hindsight), at the apex of those very developments the term describes.[3]

Initially it was a word from the vocabulary of administrators and politicians confident of being able to keep abreast of the unfolding historical dynamics. What now appears to us as its cool and technical character actually reflects a political idea that was widespread at the time. Following the Second World War, the political elites of Great Britain and France, the last remaining colonial powers of any consequence, believed that they could engineer the transfer of power to "trustworthy" indigenous leaders in the colonial territories previously under their control, and that they could manage this transfer in accord with the colonial ruling elites' own ideas. It was hoped that these transitions would be long and drawn out—in other words, lasting decades rather than a few years—and that they would take place peacefully. There was also the expectation that the newly independent states, not without gratitude for many years of colonial "partnership," would cultivate harmonious relations with their former colonial powers. With this in mind, decolonization was understood as a strategy and political goal of Europeans, a goal to be reached with skill and determination.

Only in a few instances did the actual course of decolonization bear much semblance to this kind of orderly procedure. The confidence to keep the exit from empire under firm control was called into question by historical reality, the momentum of numerous self-reinforcing tendencies, speed-ups, unintended consequences, or mere historical accidents. While a number of colonial experts faced the inevitable end of colonial rule in Asia after 1945, almost all of them were united in believing that colonial rule in Africa would last—an erroneous belief, as would soon become apparent. For them, decolonization was thus a constant disappointment of the imperial illusion of permanence. It marks a historical juncture at which the exact outcome was anything but certain from the outset.

Competing options were considered, negotiated, overtaken by events, and sometimes swiftly forgotten. This presents historians today with a great challenge: how, in hindsight, to avoid trivializing this openness to the future as experienced by contemporaries into a superficial impression that everything had to happen the way it did.[4]

Even if it may have proceeded peacefully in some cases, the process of decolonization on the whole was a violent affair. The partition of India in 1947 (at about 15 million refugees and expellees, the largest forced migration condensed into any comparable twentieth-century time period), the Algerian war of 1954–62, and the 1946–54 war in Indochina are among the most conspicuous instances of violence in the second half of the twentieth century. Between 1945 and 1949, a bloody chaos held sway on the islands of Indonesia.[5] In all these cases, it is practically impossible to give a precise count of the number of victims. The picture becomes even more dismal when we add the Korean war (1950–53) and the war the United States waged against Vietnamese national communism (1964–73) as follow-up wars of decolonization, and when we also include those civil wars that took place immediately or shortly after decolonization (in the Congo, Nigeria, Angola, Mozambique, etc.). The confrontation between rebels and colonial powers was often conducted with extreme brutality. State archives—many of them lost, deliberately destroyed, or still inaccessible— often provide only fragmentary evidence of this brutality.[6] In some cases—for example, Kenya—its extent has only come to light recently, partly accompanied by spectacular court cases over the European states' responsibility.[7] Other episodes of large-scale violence, such as the gruesome (and successful) repression of a major uprising in French Madagascar in 1947–49, have vanished almost completely from public memory outside the country concerned.[8]

As a political process, decolonization has by now passed into history. If in 1938 there were still approximately 644 million people living in countries categorized as colonies, protectorates, or dependencies (not counting the British dominions), today the United Nations registers only seventeen populated "non-self-governing territories" having a total population of about 2 million inhabitants "remaining to be decolonized."[9] Not all of these remaining colonial subjects—for example, the 32,000 inhabitants of Gibraltar—feel a strong urge toward full national self-government. Even while this great transformation was still under way, the concept of decolonization broke loose from the illusions harbored by European actors at that time and acquired a broader meaning. As a shorthand label, it designates what the historian Dietmar Rothermund has called "perhaps the most important historical process of the twentieth century."[10]

SOVEREIGNTY AND NORMATIVE CHANGE

From another perspective, the vanishing of colonialism represents the end of Europe's overseas empires. Even if not synonymous with it, decolonization is at the center of what has been dubbed "the end of empire." Decolonization thus meant more than a profound rupture in the history of formerly colonized countries; it was more than a mere footnote in the history of Europe. As the "Europeanization of Europe," decolonization led to "Europe falling back on itself,"[11] altered the position of the continent in the international power structure, and interacted with the supranational integration of Europe's nation-states, which reached its first culmination in 1957 with the establishment of the European Economic Community (EEC), the forerunner of the present European Union (EU).

Overseas empires in which white-skinned Christian Europeans dominated nonwhite non-Christians had been gradually built up since around 1500. They were hardly ever systematically planned, and they were usually expedited by an interplay of hazy vision and improvised exploitation of opportunities.[12] All these empires were patchwork, and none was consistently organized down to the last detail. The non-European territories were subordinated to their respective European metropoles as "colonies" in a wealth of different legal constructions. The political idea of nationalism with its goal of the independent nation-state changed little about colonial realities during the nineteenth century. Only in Spanish-speaking South and Central America was a large empire replaced by a multitude of independent states.

On the eve of the First World War, the British Empire was the only true world empire, since it also included Australia and New Zealand, in that it was represented on every continent. Three additional features made it unique. First, within the geographic boundaries of Europe, it also ruled over Europeans: Malta (since 1814) and Cyprus (since 1878) were British colonies; Corfu and the Ionian Islands had been so from 1815 to 1864. Ireland had an independent special status within the United Kingdom that was viewed as colony-like by Irish nationalists. Second, within the British imperial structure, there were several countries that were self-governing, that is, they regulated their political affairs themselves in democratic institutions and procedures under loose supervision by the British Crown. Starting in 1907, the generic term "dominions" became customary for these countries.[13] Ever since several individual possessions were bundled together into the Union of South Africa in 1910, the "dominions" became the four proto-nation-states of Canada, Australia, New Zealand, and South Africa; in South Africa, however, the black majority was excluded from political participation, a tendency that was aggravated even more around the middle of the twentieth century. Third, alone among all the European colonial powers, Great Britain had the military resources (especially at sea) and economic strength (especially as the center of world finance) to exercise a preponderant international influence even beyond its colonies or outside the "protectorates" it administered somewhat less directly. It is possible to speak of such an "informal empire" on the eve of the First World War, especially in China, Iran, the Ottoman Empire, and parts of Latin America. The term "British world-system" has been suggested to designate this conglomerate of "formal" plus "informal empire."[14]

The other empires were smaller, based on area and population. The French Empire was present in Southeast Asia, North and West Africa, the Caribbean, and Polynesia. Portugal laid claim to control over territories in southern Africa (especially Angola and Mozambique); Belgium, over the heart of the African continent with its share of the Congo. The German flag waved over a collection of colonies scattered among Africa, China, and the South Seas, and the Italian flag flew over Libya since 1911, while the Netherlands possessed in the "East Indies" (today's Indonesia) one of the most population- and resource-rich colonies in the world. Only the Spanish Empire, once powerful and extensive, had been reduced to mere remnants of its early modern self since the loss of Cuba and the Philippines that followed its defeat in the war of 1898 between Spain and the United States. With the exception of the

German colonial empire, all these empires survived the First World War and even saved themselves, however battered, for a time beyond the Second World War.[15] By 1975, they had disappeared. The oldest of the European overseas empires, the Portuguese, was the last to dissolve.

Decolonization came at the end of widely differing imperial trajectories and timelines. In the case of Spain and Portugal, it put the seal on a protracted, though unevenly phased, history of imperial contraction. France experienced a second major colonial breakdown after a first period of defeat overseas from 1763 to 1804. Britain was used to a long and complex history of imperial metamorphosis; nowhere else did decolonization come as less of a surprise. The Dutch, symbiotically tied to what they saw as a huge model colony of considerable stability, clung with particular tenacity to their own illusion of permanence. The much more short-lived Japanese Empire collapsed during the final apocalypse of the Second World War, leaving not even scope for a decision to retreat. For the United States, decolonization confirmed an already existing preference for tools of informal empire, temporary military occupation, and a worldwide string of enclaves and military bases over formal territorial rule.[16]

From out of a world of imperial blocs and dependency relations there emerged in the "short" twentieth century a mosaic of politically autonomous states, each of which jealously defended its "sovereignty," even if with symbolic gestures alone. The concept expressed negatively as *de*-colonization, as the removal of foreign rule, can also be reinterpreted positively: decolonization as an apparatus for the serial production of sovereignty, as a kind of sovereignty machine that produces political units, standardized according to templates of international law: a series of states, each with a defined national territory, its own constitution, legal order, government, police, flag, and national anthem. Seen this way, decolonization is comprehensible as a statistical trend: on the one hand as a reduction in the number of colonies from 163 in 1913 to sixty-eight in 1965 and to thirty-three in 1995,[17] and on the other hand as an upward curve showing the quantitative increase in subjects of international law, in other words, of states that were recognized by the already existing community of states as having equal rights and subject to no higher authority.

The League of Nations was founded in 1919 by thirty-two such sovereign states, nine of which were from Latin America; in all of Asia, only Japan, China, and Siam (Thailand since 1939) were represented; in Africa, only South Africa and Liberia (the latter was a de facto US protectorate). Strictly speaking, founding members Canada, New Zealand, Australia, and South Africa, as British dominions, did not constitute fully sovereign nation-states; this is what they would first become in 1931 via the Statute of Westminster.[18] And the fact that the classic colony India figured among the League of Nation's founding members should be understood, in part, as a symbolic way of honoring India's military service, and partly as a concession awarding Great Britain, the strongest power in the new international organization, a second vote in disguise.

In 1945, the United Nations was founded by fifty-one states, not many more than the number of original members in the League of Nations from 1919.[19] This indicates that, in the meantime, there had not been any drastic change in the po-

litical map of the globe. Africa and large parts of Asia—
especially Southeast Asia, almost completely colonized—were
still without a voice of their own on the world stage. By 1957,
the number of members had reached eighty-two, owing
above all to the entry of Asian countries and those European
states that had not yet taken part in 1945. Then, in 1960 alone,
eighteen new memberships were added. By 1975, the number
of members had reached 144. Today, it has 193 members,
including mini-states like the island republic of Nauru in
the Pacific with 10,000 inhabitants. The Olympic world movement in the form of the International Olympic Committee
(IOC)—one of the most extensive global organizations—goes
so far as to recognize 206 "national" committees.

Since new states seldom emerge ex nihilo, in almost every
case they owe their existence to separation from a larger political entity, generally an empire or a federation. Usually the
metropole survives the loss of its peripheries and shrinks
back to its core: the "hexagon" is what remains of the French
global empire; the Turkish Republic, of the Ottoman Empire;
the Russian Federation, of the Soviet Union. In rarer cases
(the Habsburg monarchy in 1918, Yugoslavia after 1991), the
empire disintegrates and disappears completely, leaving nothing more than nation-states behind. The formation of new
nation-states by joining together smaller elements was already rather rare in the eighteenth and nineteenth centuries
(the most important examples are the United States, Italy, and
Germany, and to some extent, also Canada and Australia); in
the twentieth century, this has occurred only in exceptional
cases. The twentieth century was an era of geopolitical frag-
mentation. The vast majority of the 193 members of the United

Nations are postcolonial or post-imperial states. These states and societies have a colonial or imperial past, which never remains without any impact on their self-image and identity today.

On the international scene, there were—and still are, to this day—hierarchies and dependencies of all kinds. In many cases, the sovereignty once so highly coveted remains incomplete, since many states would be unable to protect their territory with their own military resources in cases of conflict, and some of them would not be economically viable without transfer payments from abroad. And yet, in today's world there are no longer those obvious structures of subordination between societies culturally alien to each other that have been labeled "metropole" and "colony."[20] If, around 1913, there was nothing unusual in Asia, Africa, the Caribbean, and the Pacific about the status of a territory as a distant power's possession, by 1975 colonies had not only factually disappeared— with the exception of Hong Kong, Rhodesia/Zimbabwe, and Southwest Africa/Namibia, as well as a few small territories with tiny populations—but had also become scorned, both morally and in terms of international law and also with deep repercussions on historical narratives and judgments. With decolonization, international hierarchies and power relations had to adapt to a world of sovereign nation-states as the primary component of the international system.

Colonialism ended for a variety of reasons. One of the most important causes of its dissolution was that it gradually lost its raison d'être in the eyes of a growing number of people both in the colonies and in the metropoles. This transformation in the worldwide climate of opinion had already become apparent and legally binding in 1960 when the General

Assembly of the United Nations declared, in its epoch-making Resolution 1514: "All peoples have the right to self-determination; by virtue of that right they freely determine their political status and freely pursue their economic, social and cultural development."[21] At the same time, the "subjection of peoples to alien subjugation, domination and exploitation," which included colonialism, was declared a crime against international law. It was then and still remains, however, a major question as to what is being understood by "alien."

Decolonization, by way of summary, has a structural and a normative side. It means a radical restructuring of the international order. And by proscribing colonialism—and the racism that accompanies it—decolonization simultaneously means a reversal of those norms that shaped the relationship of peoples and states to each other through the middle of the twentieth century. In that way, decolonization sent shock waves that went far beyond the dissolution of formal colonial rule.

TIMES AND SPACES

In its narrowest possible construction, decolonization may be reduced to an isolated change of sovereign ruler in a particular country. There were different ways in which such a change could take place. In the most peaceful case, government power was handed over to indigenous politicians in general agreement with the colonial power. A transfer of power of this kind happened in the British Empire, for example, by way of a law passed by Parliament in London. In a ceremony that with time became a well-rehearsed routine, an envoy of the government presented a gracious letter in which the king or (since 1952) queen offered the newly independent state best wishes for the future.[22] The flag of the colonial power was lowered and that of the new state raised in its place. The military took leave with a musical band playing (most of the soldiers were, however, not British). The erstwhile governor completed his last official business. In less harmonious situations, independence was proclaimed one-sidedly with triumphant gestures and a seizure of power by victorious nationalists. Colonial officials and foreign citizens fled the country. In these cases, the change of power had nothing in common with a "transfer."

The symbolism and the ceremonies associated with this crucial constitutional moment, however, were similar. To this day, every nation that underwent this emotion-laden rite of passage celebrates its independence day—following the model of the Fourth of July in the United States. Decolonization in this sense is a moment that can be captured precisely in historical time. One need not be a devotee of a narrative history of political events in order to appreciate how fruitful it can be to take a close look at those glorious moments of independence. These snapshots offer historians a useful vantage point. One can investigate how the colonial power and the colony arrived at this turning point and, looking into the future, inquire into what became of the dramatic replacement of a coercive political order with the institutions and the spirit of independence and freedom.

An approach focusing on the history of events—which is always indispensable, even if rarely sufficient—will concentrate on reconstructing political developments and concomitant ideologies and narratives within the chronological framework of a few years, months, or even days before independence. From documents, media reports, memoirs, and oral history interviews, a detailed picture can be obtained in many cases. But a broader history of decolonization cannot be constructed from building blocks like these alone. Decolonization does not limit itself to a series of "flag histories"—as important and hard-fought as they may have been. The colonizers did not simply turn off the light and vanish into the night.[23] Any colony's formal-legal independence was integrated into broader processes of disentanglement and re-entanglement that were political, economic, social, and cultural in nature. On closer inspection, this was a complicated, often long-drawn-out affair: property relations had to be sorted out; the political, economic, and cultural aspects of foreign relations had to be rebalanced; citizenship regulations for the different population groups had to be developed; and archives had to be divided up. In addition, these processes were subject to very different temporalities: a quickly acquired external political sovereignty was not necessarily—in fact, was rarely—accompanied by an effective control of borders or local government, by economic self-reliance and control of natural resources, or the rupture of academic exchange relationships.[24] Histories interested in these changes choose longer time frames beyond formal independence and tend to delve into one subprocess (economic, cultural, etc.). While broadening the temporal scope, this approach still confines itself to the immediate relationship between the colonial power and indigenous power elites in narrowly defined situations.

With a different calibration of the historical optics, decolonization can be fitted into more comprehensive contexts. As a matter of fact, decolonization was enmeshed in various macro-processes and threads that shaped the twentieth century. It intersected with other fundamental changes in the international sphere, such as the Cold War and international bloc formation; the rise of international organizations and NGOs and the emergence of a global public; the history of human rights and human rights activism; and European unification. It evolved in a world shaped by economic booms and busts (the Great Depression, the postwar economic boom, and subsequent economic crises), by urbanization and global population growth, and by new social movements and civil rights activism. It was more than a footnote to the histories of asymmetric warfare and proxy wars, of global economic and forced migration, and of international development and aid. It reveals multiple connections to the worldwide spread of literacy, mass consumerism, and mass media; the post-1945 rise of social welfare states, hygiene, and living standards; and the rise of the social sciences and social engineering. To be sure, all these processes did occur in contexts remote from decolonization—modernization theory and interventionist social and economic policy, to name but two examples, reached a peak of popularity at the same time in many totally uncolonized places. Yet decolonization conferred on the processes their specific shape in many parts of the world. They would be experienced in close relation with the end of colonial rule.

Zooming out even further enables us to place twentieth-century decolonization in the millennium-old history of empires. It is clichéd to say that every empire eventually comes to an end, sometimes suddenly through a military defeat or revolution, otherwise in a protracted process of weakening and decline. The paradigm for this in European history has always been the fate of the Imperium Romanum. Only in quite rare cases—China would be the best example—have empires merely experienced metamorphoses in form without completely disappearing. A historian or historical sociologist with an interest in the history of empires occasionally searches for patterns or even regularities of a cyclical kind in the "life" of empires. For example, "thresholds" are postulated that every empire crosses sometime, and phases that the empire inevitably has to go through are distinguished. Such an approach broadens our perspective in space and time, but it also allows details to disappear and makes it hard to identify features peculiar to a specific era.

From a *spatial* point of view, imperial history, which has experienced a significant upsurge in the last several decades, reminds us that the modern seaborne empires of the Portuguese, the Spanish, the Dutch, and the British by no means represent the historical norm. Rather, as the early modern Europeans embarked on their imperial ventures from what was hardly a position of military strength and economic supremacy, they were entering into a much older history, one that was shaped by the old Eurasian empires.[25] Ever since the conflicts between the naval power of Venice and the expanding empire of the Ottomans, different types of empire collided with each other in the Mediterranean. China's "opening" during the Opium War (1839–42) was also this kind of collision between empires organized in different ways. In the nineteenth century, the dominant political entity in the north and east of the Eurasian continent was the Tsarist Empire, which had all the characteristics of a hierarchically ordered multiethnic empire, spread out in territorial contiguity. It was revived, after a crisis-ridden transitional period following the October Revolution of 1917, in the shape of the federal Soviet Union.

There has been a long and inconclusive debate about whether decolonization also extends to the dissolution of the Soviet Union. There were aspects that made the Soviet Union both similar to and different from the West European (and Japanese) overseas empires. During the decades in which the latter dissolved, the Soviet Union remained territorially intact; it outlasted the global moment of decolonization. But when, in 1989–90, the "steel frame" that kept the empire together broke and, from the Baltics to Muslim Central Asia, the non-Russian Soviet republics (with the exception of Chechnya) became independent in a process that was remarkably low in violence, this was frequently *experienced* in the new states as liberation from the Russian "yoke." Certain parallels to the foregoing process of West European decolonization cannot be overlooked, whereas the ethnic violence that engulfed Yugoslavia from 1991 onward accompanied the breakup of a fragile federation that few of its inhabitants had ever considered to be an empire.

In the process leading to independence of the non-Russian Soviet republics, however, it is the differences that stand out. These republics were not part of a worldwide movement and did not profit from long-lasting international support; the "détente process" of the 1970s was aimed more at liberalization in the eastern Central European satellite states than at the destruction of the Soviet Union itself. The theme of racism hardly played a role at all, and in its place the factor of religion—especially in Central Asia—assumed an even greater significance. The Soviet Union was much more strongly integrated at the elite level, mainly through the Union-wide organization of the Communist Party, than the West European colonial empires had ever been. The power establishments in the republics possessed a much higher degree of indigeneity than was the case in any of the overseas empires, and this was an important precondition for their relatively smooth path to independence. On the whole, we find good grounds for not assimilating the dissolution of the Soviet Union too closely to the historical model of decolonization. The concept of the "global Cold War" offers an interpretive framework much better suited to accounting for the post-Soviet experience.[26]

A different role was played by the Japanese Empire, which lasted exactly half a century, from 1895 to 1945.[27] From a geographic perspective, this was an overseas empire held together by a strong navy and maritime trade. Since the Japanese imitated many of the colonial methods of the West Europeans, certain similarities were apparent from the outset. In its later phase (starting around 1932), the Japanese Empire bore a closer resemblance to the fascist empires of Italy and Germany. Much like the collapse of the Soviet Union, the end of the Japanese Empire was not preceded by any lengthy process of resistance and political mobilization. Prior to the end of the war in 1945, there was not a single case of any national liberation organization being able to challenge the Japanese in their colonies and the territories later conquered and occupied by the Imperial army. The empire was brought down by the military power of the United States, ultimately by US atomic bombs. Japanese imperialism was, however, closely intertwined with the status of all the European powers in Asia; they were all elements of an imperial system of competition that self-destructed in 1945 and was never restored in Asia. For that reason, Japanese imperialism can hardly be ignored even if the definition of decolonization is more narrowly construed.

Overall, developments in the twentieth century may be distinguished from earlier collapses of empires throughout world history by the way they discredited any kind of alien rule. Until then, it had been taken for granted by all concerned that the place of one disappearing empire would be occupied by a new one. The twentieth century's imperial collapses thus have a certain emphatic finality about them. In this, they resemble the prior secession of the thirteen North American colonies from Great Britain, with the utopian hope for the dawn of a new era that event invoked.

From a long-term perspective, twentieth-century decolonization appears as the last stage in a series of emancipations from the European colonial empires. One can distinguish two earlier proto-waves of decolonization: *first*, the revolutions that took place in the New World between the 1770s and 1820s, in each case linked with freedom struggles conducted by military forces and militias, leading to the establishment of independent republics in North and South America and in the former French colony of Saint-Domingue (which became a sovereign state in 1804 as Haiti); *then* the gradual and less violent expansion of political scope for the white inhabitants of the British Empire's settler colonies (especially Canada, Australia, and New Zealand), which led at the beginning of the twentieth century to dominion status.

This is not to say that earlier patterns were only repeating themselves in the twentieth century. With the important exception of Haiti, these proto-waves terminated colonial rule of Europeans over Europeans or Creoles of European descent. Over long periods, the newly created states in the Americas and the dominions did not end forms of dispossession, discrimination, or rule over their non-European inhabitants. In South Africa, the racial exclusion and systematic segregation of the black majority even peaked at a time when the country was no longer governed as a British colony. Twentieth-century decolonization, by contrast, was in almost all cases about dismantling colonial rule over non-Europeans and peoples formerly regarded as essentially inferior and incapable of self-government.

This also informed the way these earlier emancipations reverberated in the twentieth century. At the beginning of the century, the colonial powers had long since convinced themselves of the unassailability of their own position of dominance. Even in the British Empire, there was no occasion to fear a repeat of the settler revolts that had brought down British rule in eighteenth-century North America. The constitutional mechanisms applied to the countries that were emerging as the dominions defused the potential for serious conflict. The only one-sided declaration of independence by white settlers in the empire took place with the secession of Southern Rhodesia in 1965, that is, at a very late date. On the side of the colonized peoples, by contrast, the separationist legacy of the United States played a larger role. Thomas Jefferson and George Washington became role models for independence fighters everywhere in the world. When the Vietnamese leader Ho Chi Minh proclaimed the Democratic Republic of Vietnam on September 2, 1945, he quoted from the 1776 Declaration of Independence.[28] Until the Cold War became globalized sometime after 1950, at which point revolutionary movements all over the world could expect to be opposed by the United States, that former rebel state, in spite of its own imperial ambitions and adventures, retained remnants of its image as an anticolonial great power. In the British Empire, however, there emerged an alternative model, in part from the lesson learned when the American Revolution created the independent United States: the model of a step-by-step, constitutionally safeguarded convergence toward domestic self-government and external sovereignty. Dominion status became an important (interim) goal not only for white settlers in the British Empire (and beyond) but also for many Asian and African nationalists. Yet the eighteenth- and early-nineteenth-century independences in the Americas mattered in a rather nonrevolutionary way as well. They provided a model for a conservative interpretation of the principle of self-determination that would leave most borders created during the colonial era untouched during twentieth-century decolonization.[29]

ANALYTICAL PERSPECTIVES

In the literature, there are different analytical perspectives on decolonization. Each of them shifts attention to different contexts and factors shaping (and possibly also explaining) the decolonization process. They may be systematized—rather schematically—according to three different levels of decolonization: imperial, local, and international.

Nowadays, the *imperial* perspective is not meant as an apologia for empires; that kind of conservative viewpoint is hardly found any longer in the scholarly literature. Rather, this perspective proceeds from the ascription of historical subjecthood to a particular empire and then inquires into how the last stage fits into the long-term evolution of that empire. In books about British, French, or Portuguese (etc.) decolonization, special attention is paid to political developments in the relevant metropole, to strategies that concern the empire as a whole, to shifts in the relative weight of different parts of the empire, to the interaction between decision makers in the center and those in the periphery of the empire, to how these decision makers reacted to liberation movements and in general to changing circumstances overseas. This literature is also inclined to link the end of empires to the enfeeblement of the metropole ("the decline of Britain," etc.), even if this decline tends to be viewed without nostalgia. A more in-depth assessment of the ways in which decolonization impacted the metropoles has become a booming research field. As another recent trend, the imperial perspective has proved particularly receptive to comparative (inter-imperial) approaches to the end of empires.

The *local* perspective adopts the viewpoint of a single colony or of a particular region—for example, French West Africa (Afrique Occidentale Française, or AOF)—that traverses the process of decolonization. It concentrates on on-site developments, sometimes in a comparative fashion. Originally, histories of liberation movements and wars as well as biographies of their leading personalities were characteristic of this perspective. The successes of anticolonial resistance were depicted as the emergence of a new nation. Another type of local approach looked into the shrinking ability of the colonial state to establish and sustain stable relationships with local collaborators.

In recent years, a new kind of historical writing has arisen, one previously reserved for novels or memoirs: reconstructing in the greatest possible detail what is admittedly often hard to capture in the sources, namely the everyday experiences of ordinary people in a period of upheaval and uncertainty. For example, the 1947 partition of South Asia, into India and what was then disaggregated into the two disconnected territories of the country Pakistan, did not appear solely as the outcome of strategic moves undertaken by a few key actors, but also as a humanitarian tragedy of major proportions.[30] Even the easily demonized colonial "masters" acquire a human face if we think about repatriated "empire families."[31] Such a history of decolonization "from below," which sometimes tracks the fates of individuals beyond the historical borderline separating independence from the colonial era, inevitably clashes to some extent with the heroic narratives of victorious anticolonialism or a regulated transmission of power. Not infrequently, it shows how the transition was disorderly and chaotic, and how political acumen and moral responsibility cannot be neatly assigned to heroes and villains.

The *international* perspective chooses a framework that surmounts the individual colony and the single empire. Its classical subject matter is made up of diplomatic-military crises that include not only the dyad of colonizers and the colonized, but also "third-party" governments and international organizations, such as the 1954 Geneva Indochina conference, the 1956 Suez crisis, the Congo crisis of 1960–63, and most recently, the crisis surrounding East Timor (1999–2002). There is a growing interest in the role of world public opinion, especially in the United Nations as a critical forum, and in the mutual perception and support of liberation movements in different colonies, often across imperial borders as well. Today, historical investigations undertaken from this perspective tend to belong more to a "new international history" than they do to colonial history.

The three analytical perspectives are not mutually exclusive. Rather, they complement each other when it comes to describing and understanding specific cases and paths of decolonization. Only by combining a variety of factors on the local, imperial, and international levels, and their articulation, can justice be done to the complexity of historical cases and reductionism be avoided that may result from locking oneself into a single perspective. An analytical checklist like the following shows how the three perspectives can be integrated. This list may serve as a flexible tool kit, applied to specific historical cases.[32]

Characteristics of the Late-Colonial Era

- Which type of colony is being examined (colony of exploitation, settler colony, military base colony, etc.)? What was the position and status occupied by the colony within the overall imperial structure?
- What was the demographic share of the colonizing population, and what was its internal composition (administrators, soldiers, merchants, missionaries, etc.)? How extensive or limited was its influence within the different sectors of the colonial state and economy?
- How and to what degree was the colonial economy dependent on the world market? How important were export enclaves, and who controlled them (including control by third-party groups, e.g., Chinese in Southeast Asia)?
- What was the class and gender structure of the indigenous population, its ethnic and religious composition, and its geographic distribution with special regard to the proportion of the urban and the rural population?
- In what way was colonial rule organized (political decision-making, administration, and police)? How directly and how intensely was colonial rule exercised on the ground?

- What was the legal position of the colonized (segregated law codes and special jurisdiction, explicit religious or ethnic discrimination, etc.)?
- To what extent did the colonial power intervene in local society through cultural and educational policy (directed by both the state and missionaries)? What difference did colonial intervention make at the primary education (as indicated, for example, by the degree of literacy) and secondary education levels? Did it contribute to the emergence of Western-trained and Western-educated groups among the colonized population?
- Which were the main movements of anticolonial resistance: their activists, supporters, and social substratum; their motives and goals? How did the colonial state respond to anticolonial challenges?

External Conditions

- At what point in time did a process of decolonization begin to take hold? How important were the influence and legacy of preceding decolonization events in the vicinity or further away?
- How relevant was pressure from third parties (United States, Soviet Union, United Nations, nonaligned movement, world public opinion, etc.)?
- Was there a decolonization strategy among politicians and colonial experts in the metropole?
- How significant were colonial issues in the public arena of the metropole, and how did they relate to party divisions?
- Did colonial interest groups (settler lobby, trade and mining interests, missionaries, etc.) exert a significant influence on the political process in the metropole?

- What was the real and perceived significance of the colonial tie for the economy of the metropole?

The Course of the Decolonization Process

- How, to what degree, and with which results was violence used by liberation movements as well as by the colonial state, by settler militias, and so on?
- Did other (e.g., ethnic-religious) conflicts complicate the picture of a binary confrontation of liberation movements and the colonial state?
- How much room for maneuver was left to "proconsuls" commissioned by the colonial state?
- What were the goals, programs, and political idioms of liberation movements?
- In what constitutional form was independence achieved? Who prepared and decided on a constitution?
- Which regulations regarding citizenship were implemented in the new nation-state?
- What kind of elections were held after independence? Was there genuine competition?
- In what way did external borders and internal divisions characterize the political geography of the new state?
- What kind of treatment was meted out to the expatriate ex-colonizers and their property (e.g., expropriation, expulsion, toleration)?

Short- and Medium-Term Consequences

- What kind of political (including military and security policy) ties were maintained between the new state and the former colonial metropole (e.g., Commonwealth membership, military bases)?

- Similarly, what kind of economic ties were maintained (e.g., currency relations, tariff preferences, trade and investment before and after independence)?
- How durable were the political institutions created at independence?
- What role did the military play before and after independence?
- How did the colonial past impact the cultural situation after independence (retention of European languages or promotion of national languages, promotion of nationalistic versions of history, etc.)?
- What were the consequences of decolonization in politics (e.g., triggering of a systemic crisis), in the economy, and in society (e.g., return of settlers, immigration of the new nation's citizens) in the metropole?

EXPLANATORY MODELS

Contemporaries of decolonization inquired about the causes and driving forces behind the events and broader transformations they were witnessing or actively shaping. Since the late 1940s, there have been lively debates about how to *explain* decolonization. Many historians of decolonization have also set this as their goal. But in so doing, it is not always clear exactly *what* should be explained. The question of why overseas empires came to an end *at all* would be absurd for its naïveté. It is only meaningful to pose more specific questions—and it is often best to do so in a comparative context: Why did the dynamic of decolonization set in at a specific time? Why did it slip away from the control of the colonial power, or why (to the contrary) was this a dynamic that the colonial power was able to shape? Why did one process of decolonization take a more violent course and another take a more peaceful one? Why did the process unleash specific kinds of conflicts (ethnic, religious, social, etc.)?

In the literature, we find various ways of explaining decolonization. For the sake of clarity, we distinguish five general models providing different explanations of why colonial rule came to an end.[33] These explanatory models occasionally show up in pure form. More commonly, however, they are combined with one another in different ways from case to case. Historians make use of them in their works as arguments they freely deploy and combine. Even when the question of explaining decolonization is not explicitly evoked, such models tend to structure and undergird the historians' accounts and narratives of the events.

(1) The *transfer of power* model. Decolonization is conceived as the purposeful fulfillment, rationally implemented by European administrators in cooperation with "moderate" indigenous politicians, of a reforming tendency already inherent in colonialism, namely to send non-European peoples who came of age thanks to their colonial education on their way into "modernity" based on self-determination. This model thus puts emphasis on metropolitan decisions and plans as the motor of change. It found its classic expression in the British literature. In its extreme versions, it sets a self-congratulatory tone, stressing a liberal tradition within British colonial policy ever since the violent separation of the North American colonies. The dissolution of the British Empire is described accordingly as a gradual and freely chosen extension of self-government rights across the different colonies: from Canada, through the white settler colonies, South Asia, to Africa and the Caribbean.

(2) The model of *national liberation*. Decolonization is viewed here as the toppling of alien rule based on violence by native liberation movements aiming to unite their nation and availing themselves of a broad spectrum of means, from peaceful negotiation to boycott to armed struggle. This model is, to a certain extent, the mirror image of the transfer-of-power-idea. It stresses the need and urge of the colonized peoples to free themselves from colonial rule. Liberal or reform-oriented tendencies or a readiness on the part of the colonizers to relinquish control are generally considered as secondary or as a means to defuse anticolonial resistance.

(3) The *neocolonialism* model. Decolonization is presented as the colonial powers' voluntary renunciation of coercive colonial structures that have become obsolete once they realize, in the age of powerful multinational corporations (who, in turn, depend on indigenous collaborators), that they can achieve their goal of economic exploitation just as well and more cheaply without direct domination of a state. In a broader (not only economic) sense, this model describes decolonization as a strategy to retain geopolitical and economic influence in a world in which nation-states have become the norm and to shield these spheres of influence from nationalist pressure and international interference or scrutiny.

(4) The *unburdening* model. Decolonization in this view is a deliberately planned effort at modernization by abandoning overseas positions whose military and strategic value has become increasingly doubtful, fiscally costly, politically risky, and damaging to the colonizer's international reputation, and that are also less and less supported by the public at home—in other words, an attempt at unburdening usually linked to a shift in global priorities (e.g., from empire to Europe). This

model thus prioritizes metropolitan reactions to changing situations in the colonies (e.g., the rise of anticolonial activism, costly modernization, or repressions), in the international arena (i.e., the increasing delegitimization of colonialism), and at home (e.g., economic decline, diminishing domestic support). Following such cost-benefit calculations, clinging to the burdensome and loss-making enterprise of maintaining colonial rule seemed increasingly irrational.

(5) The *world politics* model. Decolonization is seen as the inevitable consequence of the newly emerged bipolarity between the post-1945 nuclear superpowers, which no longer leaves any room for the old European strategies of securing power by colonial control over the widest possible expanse of territories and devalues the possession of conventional colonial empires as a guarantee of top billing on the world political stage. This model addresses the changing patterns of the international power structure and the inevitable decline of the European colonial powers and their traditional imperial instruments. In a strong version, decolonization amounts to no more than a footnote to the Cold War; weaker versions consider the new international order as the ineluctable framework to which liberation movements and colonial governments had to adjust their activities.

Even if all these models combine and prioritize elements from the three analytical perspectives (local, imperial, international), each model tends toward one of them. The models reveal their differences above all when the question of agency is addressed: in the transfer of power and unburdening models, it is the political elites—parliamentary politicians and the administrative top cadres embodying an "official mind"—of the colonial powers, while in the model of national liberation it is the national movements of the colonized that have agency. In the Marxist neocolonial model, big business interests are presumed to be the puppet masters behind the policy of the metropole. Finally, the world politics model stresses unavoidable adjustment to preexisting objective constraints and limitations on action, thus shifting agency to the outside and leaving to the authorities in the imperial capitals only some tactical leeway to react. In a weaker form, the other models, too, use the idea of diminishing decision-making options for the colonial powers.[34]

The five models of explanation emerged parallel to the actual course of decolonization, and we already find them in the literature before 1980 or thereabouts. They are in some respects mirror images of the "theories of imperialism" that were the subject of a lively discussion at the time.[35] Those theories, mostly developed in the early 1900s by liberal or Marxist social scientists, tried to explain the driving forces behind imperial and colonial expansion. The models or theories of decolonization, in turn, account for the reversal and end of that historical process. Whoever, for example, believes that colonies had been acquired for economic reasons is inclined to suspect that the end of empires is also explicable in economic terms. Since the 1980s, a wealth of empirical studies have refined and aptly combined the established models of explanation. Yet, there have hardly been completely new models for explaining decolonization as such and its varying paths. The new cultural history has pursued different goals. Historiographic interest has shifted from causes to effects. This reflects an extended time horizon. The history of decolonization a few years after the event[36] was written differently from how it is being envisaged from the distance of half a century. Only across a temporal distance of several decades was it possible for postcolonial studies to emerge. They arose from the disturbing observation that "colonial" habits of thinking have not automatically gone away with the loss of colonialism's importance as a political institution.

Today, three points are more clearly apparent than they were three or four decades ago.

First: With the end of empires and colonies and the formal proclamation of a "right of self-determination" for nations, a condition of hierarchy-free coexistence among peaceful nation-states has by no means been achieved. Although much more difficult to legitimize than in the past, imperialistic patterns of behavior by the strong toward the weak still exist and have even reappeared in new shapes, adjusted to a world of formerly sovereign nation-states; imperialism after empire is being revived in attenuated forms, and in the language of world politics, "spheres of influence," "interventions," and "protectorates" have gained unexpected currency.

Second: The European continental powers and Japan have not been thrown into ruin by the loss of their empires. They have withstood their own decolonization well, both economically and politically, sometimes *with* (as in the case of France and Portugal) and sometimes *without* major domestic political upheavals (Great Britain, the Netherlands). Today's problems of integrating immigrants and refugees are not necessarily a direct legacy of the colonial past: Afghans or Syrians in Germany or Moroccans in Belgium do not come from the former colonial empires of these countries.

Third: There is no direct correlation linking the colonial situation, the decolonization process, and the current situation of states. Former colonies can be very poor, but they can also be prosperous (e.g., South Korea, Taiwan, Singapore, Brunei); regions in Asia and Africa that were never colonized in the nineteenth and twentieth century are among the poorest (e.g., Liberia, Nepal, Haiti) and the richest (e.g., Saudi Arabia) countries in the world. Neither an especially repressive colonial rule (like that of the Japanese in Korea) nor a notably violent decolonization process leads inevitably to extraordinary burdens in the era of independence. Kenya, where the withdrawal of the British was associated with enormous violence, is economically no worse off than neighboring Tanzania, where decolonization—or more precisely, the release from a League of Nations mandate/UN trusteeship—took place quite smoothly.[37] To be sure, an undramatic transition to independence has never been a disadvantage. Conversely, the one country that suffered the longest from a sequence of imperial interventions during the age of decolonization, Vietnam, was cruelly damaged in the fulfillment of its potential. Elsewhere in Asia, the two halves of Korea are like a laboratory experiment in how one and the same colonial point of departure—in this case, the collapse of Japanese rule in 1945—can lead to extremely different paths being taken.

2
NATIONALISM, LATE COLONIALISM, WORLD WARS

WHEN DID DECOLONIZATION TAKE PLACE? The three post-1945 decades distinguish themselves as the core period of imperial demise. While this moment may be pinned down chronologically, there is less of a consensus about when the momentum of decolonization began. Attempts at periodization vary considerably from region to region. For some cases, scholars have rightfully retraced the push toward decolonization back to the 1920s, the First World War, or even the late nineteenth century; other cases may suggest a much shorter time frame, starting as late as in the 1940s or after. Looking beyond specific cases, there are good reasons to hark back to the period comprised by the two world wars. In these roughly three decades, many elements that shaped the post-1945 course of decolonization and most of the political programs to be implemented later already had taken form. Anticolonial and nationalist movements intensified in many parts of the colonized world, as did international arguments about colonialism and efforts at reforming colonial policymaking and practice. All these tendencies fed into a fundamental legitimation crisis of colonialism. In some regions—in particular in South and Southeast Asia—the Second World War unleashed dynamics that directly lead into the imperial endgame.

Even if major seeds of decolonization were sown during the years since the First World War, this period should not be limited to a mere prelude to post-1945 imperial demise. Like the core period between 1945 and 1975 itself, the larger era of decolonization was full of paradoxes, contradictions, and countervailing tendencies. Late-colonial attempts at modernizing colonial rule, for instance, both served to redefine and relegitimate colonialism *and* contributed to its decline. Neither was it clear—in 1918, 1939, or even 1945—that the colonial empires would crumble with such rapidity, nor was there any certainty about what the world replacing them would look like.

THE SIGNIFICANCE OF THE FIRST WORLD WAR

According to conventional wisdom, the First World War ended the "Age of (High) Imperialism." Such a perspective ignores the continuing importance of empires beyond 1918. Even if colonial conflicts were only of secondary importance for the outbreak of World War I, this was a war of empires.[1] To be sure, the colonial territories—with the exception of East Africa and, indirectly, the British and French colonies where Muslims were targeted by German-Ottoman propaganda[2]— rarely became theaters of war. Yet the colonial powers, above

all Great Britain and France, drew on the military and economic resources of their empires during the war on an unprecedented scale. There were more than 2.5 million soldiers
participating in the war from the British dominions and
India alone, which corresponded to more than a third of the
men (6.7 million) conscripted in the metropole. France mobilized more than 600,000 soldiers and over 180,000 workers
from its colonies, predominantly North and West Africans.
French colonial troops were also deployed in Europe fighting
white-skinned enemy troops—a fact that triggered reactions
of outrage from other colonial powers, even from the British
who were allied with France.[3] From the vantage point of imperial history, the war between 1914 and 1918 was embedded
in a larger cycle of imperial military confrontations and post-
imperial violence between 1911 (Italian invasion of Ottoman-
controlled Tripolitania, 1911–12; Balkan Wars, 1912–13) and 1923
(demobilization, post-Ottoman war in Anatolia, 1919–23; post-
imperial violence in Central and Eastern Europe).[4]

Likewise, the Paris peace provisions of 1919–20 did not, by
any means, point the way toward a post-imperial age. To be
sure, the peace settlement sounded the death knell for some
long-established multiethnic empires. With the end of the
war, the Habsburg Monarchy and the Ottoman Empire disappeared, Germany lost its overseas colonies and significant
parts of its continental empire in Europe, and the Russian
Empire went through a deep crisis and transformation. Yet
the colonial empires of Great Britain, France, the Netherlands, Belgium, and Portugal either emerged from the war
without losses or even made territorial gains. Germany's African and Pacific colonies, as well as the Arab provinces of
the Ottoman Empire, remained under alien rule and became

"mandated" territories of the newly established League of Nations. Major beneficiaries of this new system were Great Britain and France, under whose quasi-colonial trusteeship most of these territories were placed. The mandate system also allowed some British dominions, especially Australia and South Africa, themselves not nominally independent political entities, to act as quasi-colonial powers. Colonial rule had also not lost its international legitimacy as a matter of principle in 1918; after all, the Covenant of the League of Nations committed itself with pathos to the Western nations' "sacred trust of civilization" to guide the development of "those colonies and territories... inhabited by peoples not yet able to stand by themselves under the strenuous conditions of the modern world."[5] Even the revisionist challenge to the postwar order on the part of the Italians, Japanese, and Germans assumed the form of new imperialistic expansionism, to some extent mimicking the empire-building by the senior imperial powers. On a global scale, thus, empires remained the dominant political form until 1945.

Why is it nevertheless advisable to begin a history of decolonization with the First World War? There are a number of reasons for this approach.

(1) *Anticolonial unrest.* Starting in 1917–18, the colonial powers increasingly came under pressure from anticolonial protest movements. The frequently cited idea that the Great War and its horrors had permanently swept away the aura of Europe's civilizational superiority justifying colonial rule is certainly plausible, yet it is difficult to prove in any particular case.[6] One may even argue that this myth had, at least in Asia, already shown deep cracks since Japan's victory in the Russo-Japanese war (1904–05).[7] Aside from such sweeping statements,

anticolonial unrest during the war manifested itself in some local and regional insurrections that were directed against mobilization in French West Africa and in Algeria; imperial mobilization also fed confessional and ethnic conflicts in several British dominions, particularly in South Africa and Canada. Colonial authorities in a number of French and British colonies—particularly in North Africa—were also concerned about pro-German movements among the local population (a sort of short-lived "Wilhelmian moment").

Viewed globally, however, colonial rule emerged relatively unscathed from World War I, which in some regions went along with stronger repression, such as the application of martial law. The final phase of the war and the immediate postwar period saw an intense phase of anticolonial mobilization. Oppositional and nationalist groups from different parts of the colonial world (e.g., Vietnam, Tunisia, Algeria, and Egypt) tried to influence the Paris peace negotiations with petitions or delegations.[8] At the same time, a wave of anticolonial unrest in 1919–20 shook the imperial order in Ireland, Egypt, Afghanistan, India, Korea, Syria, and Iraq and reached into regions that were not formally colonized, such as China. For the British Empire, in particular, the postwar years have been characterized as a "crisis of empire," marked by anticolonial unrest and the overexpansion of an empire weakened by the war efforts.[9]

(2) *The internationalization of colonialism.* At the level of international politics, the colonial powers saw themselves confronted with demands for an internationalization of colonial affairs, most prominently in the Fourteen Points outlined by US President Woodrow Wilson on January 8, 1918, and his subsequent public interventions. When Wilson set out to stress

that "national aspirations must be respected" and that "people may now be dominated and governed only by their own consent," the idea of national "self-determination" had already been advanced by V. I. Lenin and the Bolsheviks as the basis for the postwar order.[10] Yet, it was Wilson who became, in the final phase of the war and bolstered by US war propaganda, internationally perceived as the champion of self-determination. Even if he explicitly referred this right to Central and Eastern Europe, Wilson's liberal program proved attractive to anticolonialists in different parts of the world. From China to Korea to India to North Africa, protest movements, each with its own particular reading, invoked the Fourteen Points and sought contact with the United States. This "moment" was less unified or coherent than the synchronous utilization of the Wilsonian agenda and language in various parts of the world may suggest.[11] The different movements rested on lengthier, often decades-long histories of protest, each with its own local roots, actors, and forms. They integrated Wilson's language into their programs, which did not themselves originate in the US president. What these different movements did make apparent for the first time on a large scale, rather, was a strategy to internationalize anticolonial protest that would go on to shape the course of decolonization in the following decades.

The most tangible outcomes resulting from American skepticism about European colonialism showed up in the mandate system of the League of Nations. Supported by the idea of an internationally sanctioned trusteeship that was limited in time, the mandate system was a compromise between the advocates of an internationalization of imperial rule and the Great Powers. Although they were formally accountable to the League of Nations, the mandatory powers managed their territories like protectorates and sought to shield them, in most cases successfully, against international interference. To be sure, with its commissions, inquiries, petitions, and publications, the mandate system was far less controllable than the imperial powers wanted it to be. Yet, while it turned at times into "the site and stake of a great international argument over imperialism's claims,"[12] the League of Nations was no forum for anticolonial criticism of the kind that the United Nations would slowly become after 1945.

(3) *Projects and expectations of reform.* Reacting to local and international pressure, the colonial powers saw themselves compelled during the war to promise reforms. These reforms were mostly motivated by the intensified mobilization of imperial resources starting in 1917. In light of the substantial and largely voluntary contribution to the war made by Australia, Canada, New Zealand, and South Africa, the British government called an Imperial War Conference in 1917, whose final declaration held out the prospect of a more far-reaching autonomy for the dominions. In a gesture to India, too, there followed in August 1917 a declaration containing a vague promise of political reforms heading in the direction of responsible government. In the French colonial empire in 1916, a West African deputy to the French Chamber of Deputies, Blaise Diagne, got the French government to award citizenship rights for a portion of the Senegalese population as a quid pro quo for military service; the government also committed itself to reforms for Algeria. This wartime zeal for reform lapsed with the end of the war: the measures undertaken in 1919 in India and Algeria fell well short of general expectations in both countries. Yet, the reforms promised during the war—

along with the international debates about a new liberal world order—opened up a horizon of expectations that became an important point of reference for protest movements in the decades to follow. Moreover, the growing armies and veteran groups constituted important lobbies responsible for driving up costs inside the colonial empires.[13] In the Middle East, the postwar order of 1919–20 brought about another momentous disappointment. The Arabs who had sided with the Entente powers under the leadership of the sharif of Mecca, Hussein, waited in vain for a state of their own, vaguely promised to them during the war.

The First World War did not shine a beacon illuminating a universal pathway to decolonization. It did, however, allow the first signs of a fundamental legitimation crisis in colonial rule to surface, a crisis that erupted openly in the decades to follow. The war cleared the stage for that conflict-laden interplay of anticolonial mobilization and "late-colonial" policies that was to shape the interwar period.

ANTICOLONIALISM AND NATIONALISM

After the First World War, local unrest was on the increase in the colonial world. A wave of anticolonial protests and, in the wake of the Great Depression, social unrest on an unprecedented scale seized a growing number of European overseas territories. This was particularly true, in the interwar period, for Asia and North Africa. Political movements now took the place of what had been sporadic resistance. In India, the preeminent British colony, the most powerful national movement in the empire took shape under the leadership of the lawyer Mohandas K. ("Mahatma") Gandhi. Gandhi's doctrine of nonviolence (as part of his theory of *satyagraha*), his organizational activities, and his campaign of boycott and civil disobedience turned the Indian National Congress, which had existed since 1885, from a rather loose federation of regional associations into a tightly led mass organization. In French-controlled Vietnam, which had a longer tradition of resistance, the end of the 1920s saw the start of intensified anticolonial activities by nationalists and communists, who also supported peasant revolts at the beginning of the 1930s. In the gigantic colony of the Dutch East Indies, at the same time, a multifaceted national movement arose, most visibly in the youth movement led by Sukarno. In both cases, France and the Netherlands, respectively, responded to the political and social movements with massive repression.

In the Middle East and North Africa, too, anticolonial protest took on a new quality. In Egypt, formally independent since 1922, liberal nationalists fought against continuing British de facto control of the country; starting in the 1930s, more radical nationalists and the Muslim Brotherhood emerged as new actors. In the newly created mandated territories of the Middle East, Arab nationalism, still a marginal and relatively unpoliticized phenomenon in the Ottoman period, became a mass movement. In Iraq (1920), Syria (1925–27), and Palestine (1936–39), uprisings could only be suppressed with significant military deployments. Mandatory Palestine was marred by a basic conflict of a specific kind, with Britain's commitment to the Zionist project of a Jewish "homeland" being difficult to reconcile with the simultaneous guarantee of the rights of the native Arab population. A spiral of violence between the Arab inhabitants and the growing Jewish population made interwar Palestine, alongside India, the hottest trouble spot of the British Empire.

The French colonial empire was especially shaken in the Maghreb. In Morocco, it was not until the late 1920s that France and Spain gained the upper hand militarily against uprisings, for which Abd al-Karim al-Khattabi became the symbol in the Rif rebellion (1921–26); at the same time, religious and nationalist circles in the cities organized and demanded reforms, also by way of mass protests starting in 1936. In the settler colony of Algeria, a multifaceted protest movement took shape. Here, for a long time, it was reform-oriented activists who dominated until, starting in the mid-1930s, decidedly nationalistic forces (reimported from emigrant circles in metropolitan France) also made their presence felt. In Tunisia, by the end of the First World War, nationalists were demanding independence for their country. As of 1934, Habib Bourguiba began expanding nationalism into a mass movement.

In sub-Saharan Africa, anticolonial and nationalist movements became a mainspring of resistance after the Second World War. More than political movements, a wave of labor unrest rocked many British colonies in West and Central Africa (as well as in the West Indies) from the mid-1930s. In South Africa, black trade unions started to emerge even earlier than that. Additionally, since 1912, the African National Congress (ANC) existed as a political agent of the educated black elite; only in the 1950s, however, did the ANC become a mass movement. The relative calm that prevailed south of the Sahara misled European politicians as late as 1950 into assuming that a flourishing colonial future still awaited Africa. Yet many core elements of later African nationalist movements had already been formulated on the eve of the Second World War. An important role was played here by ties to black activists in the United States and the Caribbean and their pan-African movements.[14] In different versions and degrees of radicalism, these movements linked the struggle against worldwide racism and imperialism with a nostalgic reference to Africa. Paris became the birthplace of Negritude, a literary-artistic movement of African and Caribbean intellectuals, notably Aimé Césaire, Léopold Senghor, and Léon Damas. These intellectuals were unsparing in their critique of colonialism, racism, and Eurocentrism, while promoting a reevaluation of Africa and African culture within a framework of persistent Franco-African ties.

Anticolonial protest always arose out of a concrete colonial situation. It extended widely to include a diverse spectrum of forms: from critical intellectual debate and analysis, via political protest, labor struggles, tax revolts, and boycotts, to spontaneous disturbances, acts of sabotage and terror, and armed uprisings. Its constituency also varied. In most cases, representatives of the new Western-educated strata (lawyers, physicians, teachers, journalists, civil service clerks) played a prominent role. These groups did have a deep knowledge of the workings of the colonial state but found their professional, social, and political aspirations blocked. Yet, depending on the context, other social groups—such as veterans, business elites, religious reformers, and women's organizations, as well as organized workers and small farmers—became leading supporters of anticolonial movements. Although traditional elites, notables, and leaders frequently clashed with nationalists, the boundary between traditional and modern elites should not be drawn too neatly: some collaborating traditional or neo-traditional elites successfully transformed themselves into anticolonialists or—like the sultan of Morocco, the kabaka of

Buganda (in Uganda), or the king of Swaziland—even placed themselves at the head of national movements. Quite a few nationalists, in turn, were ready to cooperate with the colonial state to a certain extent.

National movements and anticolonial protest were anything but homogeneous. They did not always prove to be as diverse as they were in Algeria and Indonesia, where several currents competed for leadership.[15] Yet almost everywhere, especially in their incipient phases, fragile alliances and rivalries between different groups of actors characterized anticolonial movements. Even in cases of armed "people's wars," as in Angola and Rhodesia (later Zimbabwe), there were frequently several rival guerrilla factions. This diversity was matched by numerous internal conflicts and debates.

From the outset, both the ends and the means were highly contentious and malleable. While anticolonialism and nationalism did overlap, their alliance was by no means self-evident.[16] National identity and imperial solidarity were not necessarily mutually exclusive but could, for instance in Canada, coexist and coalesce. The anticolonial demand for a completely independent nation-state was actually a relatively late development. It only rarely surfaced in early anticolonial movements, as in Vietnam in the early twentieth century.[17] Far more typical was a protracted phase of intellectual critique and mobilization, part civic and part violent, that aimed at the removal of abuses and discriminatory structures within the existing political framework.[18] This renegotiation of colonial rule often unfolded within the institutions and ideologies that justified the colonial state itself, such as the legal system, representative boards, the press, clubs, and associations. Demands for equality were not limited to the political sphere but included socioeconomic and cultural issues as well. The labor struggle became an important arena for anticolonial activities in regions with the rudiments of industrial production and in mining centers, as well as in the area of infrastructure (above all, among rail and dock workers).[19] In India, Tunisia, the Caribbean, and West and South Africa, trade unions were important actors in the emerging national movements.

Even as campaigns for equality proved largely ineffective and were increasingly replaced by demands for self-government or independence, the fully "sovereign" nation-state did not remain uncontested as a model for the future. The alternatives confronting the nation-state were models of layered sovereignty, such as partial autonomy resting lightly under a Commonwealth-like roof or some kind of federal union. In the Middle East, the Maghreb, and sub-Saharan Africa, in particular, regional and transregional (pan-Arab, pan-Maghreb, pan-African) ideas of political unity or federation existed in a tense relationship with nationalism. But almost everywhere, in the end, anticolonial protest identified with the quest for a sovereign nation-state, which was identified with the colonial state in its existing borders. Only a few national movements (such as in Vietnam, Burma, Morocco, Tunisia, Egypt, and Madagascar) were able to invoke precolonial state structures. The great majority, however, had recourse to political formations that were newfangled—often multireligious, multiethnic, and multicultural—and were thus very different from the normative model of a homogeneous nation-state.

Along with the ends, the means used to achieve them were also contested. Hardly a single anticolonial movement was able to avoid the crucial questions of whether it should seek cooperation or confrontation with the colonial power, and whether colonialism was to be overcome through peaceful political mobilization or armed struggle. Also subject to debate were whether independence needed to be accompanied by a social revolution and how far-reaching such a revolution had to be.

At different moments and to different degrees, the history of anticolonialism was thus marked by long experimental phases, in which a multitude of aims and strategies were pursued, tested, and debated. In some regions, particularly in sub-Saharan Africa, this period reached well into the post-1945 era. While it is often told as a story of radicalization of their goals and means, the history of anticolonial movements provides many instances of moderation and accommodation as well. If we were to flesh out an overarching dynamic, it would probably be the reduction of alternative options that marked the specific paths toward a nation-state.

In terms of their worldviews, the emancipatory elites tended to be either modernists or traditionalists, though in most cases without things coming to a complete breach between the two. The modernists frequently acquired a liking for socialism, later for the planned economy of the Soviet type, and occasionally even for what appeared to be a moderate brand of fascism, at least until fascism revealed its true face in the 1935–36 war against Ethiopia. The traditionalists were seldom simply conservatives of the European type. They did not want to set the clock back to precolonial times and did not shy away from resorting to modern media and forms of mass mobilization. Yet, they did not envision a model for their own future in the social reality of the West as they perceived it. Hardly anyone embodied this kind of complex position better than Gandhi, whose ideas about an agrarian, nonindustrial

India did not, however, meet with approval from Jawaharlal Nehru and other modernists in the Indian liberation movement.[20]

Religion was often the central motif of neo-traditionalist self-discovery, yet the national movements were political and not primarily religious movements. The spectrum of religious references was broad and contradictory: in North Africa, reformist Islamic scholars played an important role; in Indonesia, ties were established between Islamic and socialist movements; after 1945, Christian Reformed churches, sometimes with a millenarian character, played an important role in many sub-Saharan countries, while in others this role was assumed by graduates of missionary schools with their own conception of Catholic or Protestant religiosity. The religious connection might fluctuate or even disappear: in Tunisia during the mid-1930s, Bourguiba made a mark for himself as a defender of Islamic identity, twenty years later as a secular modernizer. Religious community-building was, furthermore, not always integrative: in multireligious contexts, such as in Cyprus, Lebanon, Palestine, and most dramatically India, it was capable of unleashing a violent and disintegrative dynamism.

Conflicts about regional or "ethnic" affiliation are often invoked as a characteristic of national movements in southern Africa. But a strong regional dominance could also emerge in other places. In Tunisia, for example, the nationalist elite was primarily recruited in the eastern coastal region (the Sahel); in Indonesia, predominantly on the island of Java. Almost everywhere, urban-rural differences played a role: most nationalist elites came out of an urban environment, yet this did not inevitably mean they had no ties to rural majorities.

In the case of armed conflicts such as those that engulfed Indochina, Malaya, Kenya, and Algeria, the rural population was both main actor and chief victim. Sub-Saharan Africa was not the only region where "ethnic" classification could turn into a problem: Malay nationalists fought for their primacy over Chinese and Indian minorities; in Morocco and Algeria, Berber population groups, in spite of their substantial involvement in the liberation struggle, would eventually have to subordinate themselves to an Arab-defined nationalism; and members of the various coastal ethnic communities resented highland Merina dominance within Malagasy nationalism.

Quite often in the course of a liberation struggle, tensions showed up between nationalist elites and their mass followings, frequently in connection with social and generational conflicts. In Indonesia in 1945, for example, Sukarno was increasingly challenged by the youth movements allied with him. Arab notables in the Middle East had been able to salvage their leadership positions from the Ottoman era and extend them into the mandate period, but they now found their moderately nationalistic course of limited compromise under pressure from more radical groups.[21] A similar constellation emerged after 1945 in West Africa, where nationalist politicians saw the position they had only recently established as negotiators with the colonial power imperiled by more far-reaching demands from the movements of workers, students, and youth.

Gender constituted a specific field of social conflict and division within the anticolonial movements. While these movements were, generally speaking, dominated by males, women were never entirely absent. The specific positions of women in these struggles, however, varied considerably from one context to the next. In many anticolonial movements, individual women, women's rights organizations, and other associations run by women (e.g. professional organizations of market women in West Africa) did play a conspicuous role, including in cases of armed struggle. Independently from the actual involvement of women, gender and family issues were often at the core of national self-assertion.[22] In some cases, questions of gender norms, women's emancipation, and neo-traditional role models became an important arena of confrontation between the colonial power and national movements.[23] By and large, feminist activists were often sidelined after independence and could only partially influence nationalist agendas, with Tunisia being a rare example of a post-independence state committed (to a certain extent) to women's rights. Female equality in family relations, in education and production, and sometimes in the fighting forces was a crucial programmatic point in a few Asian movements of revolution and resistance. In most cases, these demands were directed at "feudal" rather than "imperialist" oppression. In China, for instance, Westerners and Japanese were blamed for many different things but not for propping up patriarchy. The pathbreaking Chinese Marriage Law of 1950 was a quintessentially domestic affair.

Hence the picture painted all too readily in hindsight of a nation unified in a common struggle against foreign rule is, as a rule, a historical fiction. Almost everywhere in the colonial world, nationalism entered into competition with a variety of alternative affiliations and belongings. Local, "tribal," religious, regional, even imperial solidarity and loyalty did not simply disappear with the emergence of nationalist movements. The various currents of nationalism also often formed an entire field of competing positions. The campaign against colonial rule was closely tied in with the struggle over the prerogative of interpreting nation and state—a struggle over political authority that was not only directed against traditional and moderate elites but also pitted nationalists against each other. Sometimes these conflicts within the anticolonial camp were carried out no less acrimoniously than the confrontation with the colonial power. In many cases—and frequently with the active participation of the colonial administration—the hegemony of one particular actor or group of actors within the national movement had already emerged at the moment of independence. In other cases, most dramatically in India, the Belgian Congo, Nigeria, and Angola, the conflicts escalated *after* independence.

The anticolonial protest movements, finally, were characterized by numerous international—and trans-imperial—ties and transfers of ideas and concepts. Nationalist leaders had frequently spent long periods of time abroad, usually in the metropole of their respective colony, later in the United States or the Soviet Union as well.[24] From there, they brought home new ideological orientations, forms of organization, and contacts. As a rule, it was Western-educated elites, frequently students, who established these kinds of exchanges and interconnections between metropole and colony, yet they were by no means restricted to these elites. Algeria's first nationalist party (the Etoile Nord-Africaine around Messali Hadj, founded in 1926) arose in the milieu of North African migrant workers in France. And Nguyen Ai Quoc (later known as Ho Chi Minh) worked during his extensive travels as, among other things, a gardener, cook, sailor, and photo retoucher. The horizon of anticolonial movements was by no means confined to the imperial centers. These movements also maintained contacts with one another. Even if they did not produce an organized "international" of colonialism's opponents (with the League against Imperialism quickly disintegrating after its foundation in 1927), they were observing one another, learning from one another, exchanging experiences, and supporting one another logistically and materially. Long before his assassination in 1948, Gandhi rose to become an international icon of emancipation.

The protest movements were also frequently in contact with representatives of an international anticolonialism that took shape beyond the colonies. They held ties with transnational networks of pan-Africanists, pan-Asianists, and exiles. They received support from anticolonialists in the metropoles—including in Japan—who were in the tradition of humanitarian critics of colonialism and of public campaigns against colonial misrule (especially in the Congo Free State of Leopold II) in the nineteenth and early twentieth centuries.[25] Finally, many of them stood, at least for certain periods, in contact with international communism. The Third International (the Comintern) embraced an anti-imperialist course in Asia from 1919 to the mid-1930s; from 1927–28, however, it was weakened by colonial repression, the growing orientation to antifascist united fronts, and the Soviet Union's turn toward the development of "Socialism in One Country." The interwar period saw a series of congresses in which anticolonialists and anti-imperialists of different stripes and from different parts of the world met and mobilized for their cause, foreshadowing later efforts at institutionalizing cooperation in the global South.

LATE COLONIALISM AND "DEVELOPMENT"

When the territorial reorganization of the Paris Peace Treaties went into effect in the 1920s, the colonial world—so long as one includes the British dominions—attained the greatest expansion in its history. After their wartime experiences, Great Britain and France seemed to be convinced that they could assert control of their colonial possessions even against local resistance. The exclusive access to colonial areas for exploiting resources, selling goods, and settling emigrants seemed like a way to compensate for the decline in the world's economic integration, in other words, in a period of deglobalization following the First World War. The colonial empires—including the dominions under way toward complete independence—became more important than ever before for the metropoles.

Nowhere did the heightened importance of the colonial empires appear as clearly as in the economy.[26] After the volume of trade inside most of the colonial empires had slowly increased during the 1920s, the world economic crisis after 1929 strengthened autarkic tendencies and the creation of trade blocs in imperial economic policy. Great Britain and France were now aiming for the first time at the economic integration of their empires, and to this end they resorted to preferential tariffs, currency unions, and higher (mainly public) investments.[27] Many of the economic policy instruments created in this period persisted beyond the Second World War.

But in other areas, too, the colonial empires gained in importance. Scholarly research about them was given a cross-country and cross-disciplinary impetus, accompanied by the intensified institutionalization of some subdisciplines (such as ethnology, colonial geography, or colonial economics). Especially in the British Empire, moreover, the interwar era was also a phase of growing (and officially promoted) migration to the dominions. Via propaganda in the media and popular culture, the colonial empires around 1930 gained an unprecedented public presence in the metropoles. The largest colonial exhibitions of all time took place during these years (1924–25 in Wembley; 1931 in Vincennes).[28]

Parallel to this, there was also a change in the approach of the Europeans to their colonial empires. These empires—in different ways and at different paces—entered into their "late-colonial" phase: a phase of exploitative maturity and of empire after imperialism. No longer was continued expansion the focus, but instead consolidation, improved efficiency, professionalization, and even efforts to make colonial rule and the utilization of colonial resources more scientific.[29] There were signs of such a departure from purely extractive colonialism as early as around 1900, especially evident in the early infrastructure and economic programs undertaken in the East Indies by the Dutch, who did not take part in the late nineteenth-century race for new colonies. But only after 1918 did this turn into a broader movement, which was then accelerated once more by the Great Depression. Politicians in the metropoles, leading colonial civil servants, internationalists, and experts now engaged in debates on colonial reform and a "humane" colonialism, on uniform imperial constitutions, and on the colonies' economic integration and development. Active or former colonial officials, like A.D.A. de Kat Angelino, Albert Sarraut, or John S. Furnivall, assessed the pros and cons of colonial policy and stimulated thinking about their reorientation.[30] Investigative commissions visited different parts of the British and French colonial empires and the League of Nations–mandated territories, accompanied by countless reports and proposals for solving the problems they had diagnosed. In France, the leftist Popular Front government (1936–37) worked on colonial reforms, many of which, however, remained stuck in first gear.[31] The Japanese Empire and US control over several Pacific and Caribbean territories were too young for terms like "early" and "late" colonialism to make much sense. At the same time, they too, for a brief moment in the 1920s and early 1930s, shared these tendencies toward civil stability and a rationalized *mise en valeur.*

Across the different empires, late-colonial planning efforts extended to two fields, though these were not necessarily linked to each other or integrated in any kind of overarching plan: (1) political reforms and constitutional changes and (2) socioeconomic development programs.[32] Starting in the interwar period, there was an upsurge in political reforms intended to cautiously expand the opportunities for the colonized population to participate in local government. Occasionally, these reforms were accompanied by an easing of restrictions in the laws of assembly, association, and the press, and by initial steps in opening up administrative posts to local educated elites. Even if these did not touch the elementary power structure of the colonial state, reforms like this did signal a new approach: they stood for a departure from the ideal of administering the colonies free of politics.[33]

In the British Empire, India constituted the most important field of experimentation for this kind of policy. As of 1919, elected Indian politicians participated in government at the local level and, to a limited extent, also at the provincial level. In this system, known as a "dyarchy," or dual government, certain political issues were "transferred" to Indian authorities, while finance and the maintenance of law and order remained in the hands of British colonial officials. Key legislation continued to be under the control of the British Parliament in London and the viceroy in New Delhi. In 1935, this dual rule was abandoned at the provincial level in favor of Indian governments under parliamentary control, although British provincial governors retained emergency powers. Parallel to this constitutional liberalization, Great Britain started an "Indianization" of the colonial civil service apparatus in 1919. In other parts of the British Empire, local and regional representative bodies were strengthened during the interwar period, but nowhere were steps undertaken in the direction of governments beholden to elected parliaments ("responsible government") comparable to what was done in India. Here, reforms were usually related to advisory legislative councils, which already existed in many Crown colonies (like Ceylon and Jamaica) since the nineteenth century but which elsewhere, above all in southern Africa, were newly created. The main starting points for these reforms were the step-by-step opening of such councils to elected indigenous representatives, their endowment with new responsibilities, and a wider local franchise. The reforms went furthest in Ceylon, where a general and equal suffrage for men and women was introduced in 1931.

Other colonial powers also increased efforts to reconstruct and expand local and regional representative bodies. Their influence and composition varied by region and colonial empire: while a governing system tailored to the US model gradually took shape in the Philippines, the Indonesian People's Council (Volksraad) established in 1918 primarily remained a representation of local Europeans and some moderate nation-alists. A special case existed in the French colonial empire, where "assimilated" territories like the old possessions in the Caribbean, the four Senegalese *communes* (Saint-Louis, Dakar, Gorée, and Rufisque), Cochin China, and Algeria sent dele-gates to the French Parliament. In Senegal and Algeria, con-sequently, reform initiatives were strongly oriented toward ex-panding citizenship rights and parliamentary representation to these colonies' Muslim majorities.[34] Partially successful in Senegal, these kinds of demands were blocked by European settlers in Algeria. Here, representative bodies at the local, re-gional, and central level also remained in the hands of settlers, notwithstanding the Muslim electorate's expansion. While Japan pursued an even more ambitious policy of legal integra-tion and cultural assimilation of its colonial territories, this policy did not entail a significant increase in political represen-tation on the part of its colonial subjects.[35] Likewise, through the Second World War and even beyond, Belgium and Portu-gal proved disinclined to strengthen political participation in their colonial territories.

These trends continued following the end of the war. After 1945, two different approaches to political reform stood out, each designated for simplicity's sake according to their leading exponents as the "British" way and the "French" way (without implying that there had ever existed any coherent imperial policy). A policy of decentralization or devolution was domi-nant in the British Empire: individual territories were treated as specific entities in which, depending on the situation, con-stitutional reforms were implemented and distinctive institu-tions for political participation and self-administration were created in usually tough negotiations. This may be contrasted with a policy of intensified political integration of metropole and empire, pursued most ambitiously in the French case. Parallel to the negotiations for the constitution of the Fourth Republic in 1945–46, and to a large extent due to the political activism of West African leaders, measures were undertaken with the aim of narrowing the gap between metropole and colonies in the newly created French Union.[36] The legal code applying only to the colonized populations (*code de l'indigénat*) was abolished, forced labor prohibited, and the "old" colonies of Martinique, Guadeloupe, Guiana, and La Réunion were declared *départements*. From then on, most colonies were represented in Parliament and in a newly created consultative assembly of the French Union, even if the composition of the delegations did not correspond to the real proportions of the population groups in the territories. Moreover, all inhabitants of the colonial empire then counted as equal "citizens," though it remained unclear which concrete rights were associated with this status. Only in the mid-1950s did France begin to move away from this imperial integration policy and turn increasingly to self-administration for smaller regional entities. Ironically, this coincided with the only occasion when the closer political integration of a colonial territory was ever seriously considered in the British Empire—with regard to the small Mediterranean archipelago of Malta.

Other colonial powers proved more open to experimenting with elements of imperial integration. Elements of an integration policy can be found in Portuguese and Spanish late colonialism, even if the Iberian empires' efforts were not nearly as ambitious and in part more rhetorical. Thus, while Portugal transformed its colonies into "provinces" in 1951 and promoted a specific ideology of "lusotropicalism," the specific legal regime governing most of the colonized population (*estatuto do indigenato*) and forced labor remained in place until the early 1960s.[37] The Netherlands tried to strike a middle path with their 1954 Statuut (charter), linking the remainder of their colonies (Suriname and the Netherlands Antilles) as internally autonomous territories in a form of "voluntary" association to the metropole; with Indonesia already outside the Dutch realm, this kind of imperial integration did not seem as ambitious as it may have been in 1945. The United States applied a broad array of strategies to different territories, ranging from full incorporation (Hawaii, becoming the fiftieth state in 1959) to the granting of a hedged independence (Philippines).

In spite of the fundamental differences between the decentralizing (British) policy and the integrating (French) policy, both approaches contained a potential for developing a momentum of their own. Both contributed to the politicization of ever wider population groups. They were taken up and reshaped by Asian and African political leaders. In the British case, the result was a "spiral of constitutional concessions";[38] in the French case, an ever broader and more diversified catalog of demands raised by the "citizens" of the empire.[39]

Alongside political reforms, questions of socioeconomic development and "modernization" increasingly moved into the focus of colonial policy debates during the interwar era.[40] For the first time now, the colonial powers were considering making larger investments overseas, above all for the construction and expansion of infrastructure projects such as streets, railway lines, and harbors. Prior to 1939, most of these projects existed above all on paper. By way of import substitution, a certain degree of initial industrialization did take place in some regions; until the outbreak of the Second World War, however, investments and development measures remained far behind the often ambitious plans.

In this respect, the Second World War marked a turning point and the dawn of the main "development era."[41] Under wartime conditions, the prewar trends toward more interventionist economic policies gained widespread acceptance. The British war economy introduced numerous elements of state-run economic management, such as the marketing boards that traded African agricultural commodities at prices fixed by the state. In July 1940, the Colonial Development and Welfare Fund, a new investment fund for development and social welfare projects in the empire, was created. Colonial development plans drawn up in Europe lagged significantly behind the massive modernization policy that Japan was pursuing in its possessions. On the Chinese island of Taiwan, which fell into Japanese hands in 1895, an exportable sugar industry was systematically built up; and in southern Manchuria, starting in 1905, a heavy-industry region meant to complement the raw-materials-poor economy of the Japanese archipelago was developed. Starting in 1931, all of Manchuria became one giant field of experimentation for Japanese colonial economic policy, while in Korea some latitude remained for native entrepreneurs. Japan was the only colonial power prior to 1945 that saw an opportunity for strengthening the metropole in a planned industrialization of the imperial periphery. After the withdrawal of the Japanese, the infrastructure and industrial plant they created remained in place, though some of it was removed from Manchuria by the Soviet Union.[42]

The measures, instruments, and plans from the war era reached far beyond the year 1945. Sub-Saharan Africa in particular now moved into the focus of late-colonial modernization, whereas the prevailing policy had been oriented toward using and preserving (supposedly) "traditional" structures in (supposedly) static societies.[43] Increasingly, colonial development plans included components of social welfare policy.[44] By exporting achievements of the welfare state in health care and public assistance, higher pay settlements and labor rights, better educational opportunities, and "modern" living, colonial rule would now contribute to improving living standards worldwide. A pioneer in this kind of colonial development policy was the United States, which invested massively in a vocationally oriented elementary school system in the Philippines. On the eve of the Second World War, literacy rates there were higher than in all other colonies of the region.

The timing, manner, and intensity of late-colonial reforms varied strongly. Just like the emerging anticolonial and nationalist movements, the exponents and planners of late-colonial policy—both in the metropoles and on the spot—were divided over what course to take, how to apply available methods, and which goals and strategies to pursue. Neither socioeconomic development programs nor political-administrative reforms followed a plan of *de*-colonization. Experimental and frequently reactive, these programs were by no means embedded in some comprehensive strategy. Above all, they were intended to help channel and render controllable the protests that were taking shape and therewith place colonial rule on a new foundation of legitimacy.

Contrary to the intentions of its planners, late-colonial policy created important preconditions for the end of colonial rule. The rulers' promises of modernization were seized on by the ruled, who actively used their new political opportunities and freedoms. The late-colonial policy of defensive conciliatoriness spurred the rise of new elites and tended to undermine the position of the colonial rulers' traditional partners. But, above all, late colonialism promoted a buildup and centralization of state activity.[45] The late-colonial "developmental state" took shape. In many parts of southern Africa, the colonial state made itself felt really for the first time. In light of the enormous growth of a European presence in the form of administrative officials and technical and political experts, as well as of settlers (especially in the case of Angola, Mozambique, and Southern Rhodesia), the period after 1945 is often referred to as the "second colonial occupation" of Africa.[46] The far-reaching activity and regulation of the late-colonial interventionist state frequently stirred up new kinds of resistance. Yet, the source of its decline must not inevitably be located here; after all, the colonial state had even earlier exhibited a tendency to intervene in many areas of society.

In spite of its emphatically "modern" and more human face, the colonial state remained a repressive state even in its later mutation. Developmentalist colonialism pursued its goals—including, for example, those of environmental protection—in no less an authoritarian manner than its predecessors.[47] Forced labor remained a matter of routine in many colonies until 1945 and beyond. Late colonialism witnessed expansion and improvement in the institutions of state repression: aerial surveillance and larger intelligence and security apparatuses were to guarantee a more efficient use of physical force.[48]

NEW IMPERIALISMS AND THE SECOND WORLD WAR

As opposed to the consolidation course undertaken by the old colonial powers, new and decidedly expansive types of imperialism emerged during the interwar era. Fascist Italy, Nazi Germany, and Imperial Japan, each in its own way, pushed aggressively for a reordering of the postwar imperial order. The clash of these new revisionist and hypernationalist imperialisms with the old colonial empires and with the rising anticolonial-minded, even if no less imperial in behavior, powers of the United States and the Soviet Union turned the Second World War into what was a truly global war of empires. As with the First World War, the war between 1939 and 1945 was preceded by years of imperial warfare, this time in East Asia. In contrast to the Great War, the history of events during the Second World War mattered hugely for the history of decolonization.

Shortly after Mussolini came to power in 1922, Italy sought to resume the relatively disappointing colonial expansion it had started in the prewar era. While they issued an ideological challenge to France's status as a colonial Mediterranean power as well as to the selective British naval presence there, the Fascists initially concentrated on other regions in North and East Africa. They pushed ahead with the reconquest of the three Libyan provinces largely lost in the First World War (Tripolitania, Cyrenaica, and Fezzan). In the 1930s, Libya became an experimental field for Italian settler colonialism and a Fascist prestige object. Through 1939, over 100,000 Italian immigrants settled there.[49] In October 1935, Italy attacked Abyssinia (Ethiopia), a member of the League of Nations, which by May 1936 was conquered with extreme brutality, including the use of poison gas.

Germany's revisionism took on various forms after 1919. During the short period of membership in the League of Nations (1926–33), German diplomats and experts pushed the international oversight of the mandated territories, many of which had been German colonies. Continuing where the German overseas empire left off in 1914 played only a subordinate role in the *Lebensraum* doctrines of the Third Reich from 1933 on, even if the colonial revisionists of the Weimar Republic did initially pin great hopes on the new regime. After the step-by-step implementation of "Greater German" territorial claims, the focus was instead on expansion to the east, where, after the Soviet Union had been subjugated, a continental equivalent to the British world empire was to emerge. Nazi occupation and territorial reorganization in Central and Eastern Europe between 1939 and 1944 bore recognizable features of an empire.[50] The Reich's brutal settlements and resettlements were largely inspired by preceding Fascist experiments in North Africa.[51] Yet its systematic policy of exploitation, enslavement, and extermination toward major population groups, its dispensing with any kind of reformist paternalism, and its ideological fueling by an exterminatory racism made the short-lived German war empire into a phenomenon sui generis that was clearly distinct from its imperial proto- and countertypes.

Neither Italy's nor Germany's imperial ambitions and actions intruded so deeply into the sphere of European and North American colonial empires as did Japan's.[52] Between the annexation of Taiwan in 1895 and the military invasion of the core Chinese provinces that began in July 1937 and that marked the early start of the Second World War in Asia, Imperial Japan had expanded almost exclusively at the expense of its East Asian neighbors China, Korea, and Russia, thus leaving Western interests in "semicolonial" China largely untouched. Japan itself had practiced classic methods of informal economic penetration in China until 1937, and in its possessions (Taiwan, Korea, Manchuria) it had created colonial structures that were not fundamentally distinct from those of the Western powers. Its seizure of Southeast Asia between 1940 and 1945 rested on what had become the unchallenged dominance of the military in Japanese politics and followed a somewhat different logic. In an international economic climate that was generally perceived as extremely competitive and crisis-ridden, Japan was also seeking its salvation in the autarky of a greater region under its direct control. This extended region was something Japan believed it had to secure from a position of relative weakness vis-à-vis the United States and the Soviet Union. Of special interest here were the European colonies in possession of raw materials: Indonesia (oil), Malaya (tin), and Vietnam (coal). An additional factor ideologically enhancing this expansion was the resumption of older "pan-Asian" ideas that awarded Japan a "natural" leadership role for all of Asia and wished to see it as a spearhead for liberating the continent from European-American colonial rule; the new empire would become a "Greater East Asia Co-Prosperity Sphere."[53]

As early as the summer of 1940, Japan had granted wide-ranging military and economic privileges to the Vichy authorities in Indochina. With the attack on the US fleet in Hawaii on December 7, 1941, there ensued a blitzkrieg against all American, British, and Dutch positions in Southeast Asia. In February 1942, the military stronghold of Singapore that the British had been fortifying at great cost since 1921 fell to the Imperial Japanese Army. These military advances raised hopes among nationalist Japanese intellectuals that the Euro- and US-centric world order had definitively come to an end.[54] Almost everywhere—especially in Burma and Indonesia—the Japanese were greeted as liberators by at least some groups in the population. Inevitably, though, they forfeited such sympathies because of an occupation that was insensitive at best but gruesome on the whole. Secret police terror, forced labor, forced prostitution, and the plunder of food supplies took place to an extent unknown in the region's earlier colonial history.

Other parts of the colonial world were also drawn deeply into the war. Italy's attack on Somalia and Egypt (starting in June 1940) and the Wehrmacht offensive under Rommel (starting in March 1941) made North Africa a key theater of war until October 1942. Like Japan, the Western colonial powers fell back heavily on their imperial resources. Great Britain was supported both militarily and economically by all four of the "Old Dominions"; even in South Africa, pro-British forces maintained the upper hand against strong political resistance.[55] India, without its own politicians being consulted, was enlisted on a large scale in the defense of the metropole. The Indian army grew to 1.8 million men during the war years. Owing to a personnel shortage, thousands of Indians were commissioned as officers. Like the other colonies in Africa and Asia, India was used for war production. And, as was also the case in the colonies of other European colonial powers, forced labor acquired greater importance again. The war effort of the British Empire showed up in the high level of debt that Great Britain had amassed to its own colonies, with India leading the way, by 1945.

While the Belgian Congo, rich in raw materials, was on the side of the Allies, the French colonial empire became divided with the surrender to the Third Reich in June 1940.[56] The majority of colonies (North and West Africa, Madagascar, and Indochina) initially backed the collaborationist Vichy regime, while a minority (with French Equatorial Africa [Afrique Equatoriale Française, or AEF] at the forefront) joined the Free French resistance movement under Charles de Gaulle. The advance of the Resistance began with a battle for the colonial empire, to which both French warring parties attached enormous importance. Like the colonial powers in Southeast Asia, Free France depended heavily on outside support. The capture of Syria, Madagascar, and North Africa was essentially a triumph of British and US army units. Even if the impact here was not as great as that of the Japanese occupation in Southeast Asia, the British-American occupation significantly weakened the French position as a colonial power in these territories. In 1943 in the Levant, the Free French felt compelled under British and US pressure, first, to approve the readmission of national governments and, then, even to grant independence. This was due in particular to the United States' anticolonialism, professed by Franklin D. Roosevelt. Even if the British made an effort at diluting this, with Winston Churchill declaring that he had "not become the King's First Minister to preside over the liquidation of the British Empire,"[57] the Atlantic Charter of August 21, 1941, affirmed rights of national self-determination (yet not of independence).

The Second World War acted as a catalyst for different developments from the interwar era. With great differences between the individual colonial territories, anticolonial movements and late-colonial policy gained momentum. In the territories occupied by Japan, armed national resistance movements emerged. In India, the conflict between the viceroy and the National Congress escalated, but the colonial state was strong enough to arrest the entire Congress leadership in

August 1942 and deactivate it politically until the end of the war. In Tunisia, Egypt, and Iraq, as well as in not-formally-colonized Iran, the Allied colonial powers had to intervene against the cautious attempts made by those countries' political and military elites to approach the Axis powers. Mandatory Palestine slipped increasingly out of control owing to increased Jewish immigration caused by National Socialist persecution of the European Jews. Violent protests against the bolstered presence of French troops erupted in Syria and Lebanon in 1943 and 1945. While Tunisian nationalism started to mobilize support on an international scale, nationalist positions caught on in the Algerian and Moroccan opposition movements.

With regard to the United States, Great Britain and France now sought a new and "modern" formula based on "partnership" for their claims to colonial rule. This became manifest in plans for political reforms, the second side of late-colonial development. The Free French under de Gaulle in particular felt put on the spot. In January 1944, they convened a conference in Central African Brazzaville on the postwar colonial order and undertook initial reforms for Algeria in 1943–44.

The Second World War ended with the collapse of the Italian, German, and Japanese war empires. Yet, even in the final months of the war, signs did not point toward worldwide decolonization. A large segment of the political class in Great Britain, France, and the Netherlands ruled out giving up the colonial empires. In most colonies, at any event, the intensification of authoritarian measures, especially those brought about by wartime emergency laws and forced labor, made themselves felt more strongly than any reform policy. In South Asia, North Africa, the Middle East, and southern Africa, the colonial powers remained masters of the situation in spite of many difficulties. The reoccupation of strategically important parts of Southeast Asia by British troops after the Japanese surrender laid the groundwork in the short run, not for independence, but for a return of the colonial powers. France recognized national governments in Lebanon and Syria in 1943–44, but in May 1945, it proceeded to the bloody repression of a major uprising in eastern Algeria (the Sétif and Guelma massacre) and to bombing as a response to nationalist unrest in Syria. Apart from Korea, Taiwan, and the Manchurian provinces of China, as well as the special cases of Lebanon and Syria, which were formally recognized but still partly under French control, and Ethiopia, which had already been liberated in 1941 from a short-lived Italian military rule and was recognized as an independent state in 1944, no colony became independent with the end of the war.

3
PATHS TO SOVEREIGNTY

THE INTENSIVE PHASE of actual decolonization began after 1945. Within a period of around three decades, most colonies in Asia, Africa, and the Caribbean were transformed into independent states. The overall picture reveals a more differentiated internal structure across time, but it does not call the fundamental coherence of this historical moment into question. Worldwide decolonization took place in several thrusts that occurred in distinct regional arenas but not entirely separated from each other. In South and Southeast Asia, the circumstances of the war set the course for decolonization. Here the situation was special inasmuch as, with the defeat of Japan in 1945, a regional imperial power was collapsing at the same time. Between 1946 (the Philippines) and 1949 (Indonesia), most of the region's colonies became independent. In 1954 and 1957, the highly embattled countries of Vietnam and Malaya followed.

Decolonization in North Africa and the Middle East is particularly difficult to pin down chronologically, in part because some early instances of independence (starting with Egypt in 1922) involved countries that were still constrained by informal types of rule. The Suez crisis of 1956 and the end of French Algeria in 1962 therefore delimit the intensive final phase of decolonization in this region. In southern Africa—which after 1945 was initially at the center of late-colonial modernization—two waves of decolonization may be distinguished (as was also the case in the Caribbean). A first wave between 1957 (Ghana) and 1965 (Gambia) replaced most of the British, French, Italian, and Belgian possessions with new nation-states. The collapse of the Portuguese colonies in 1974–75 marked the beginning of a second wave that extended through to the end of South African apartheid in 1994. To a lesser extent, we also find such instances of late decolonization from the 1970s through the 1990s in other parts of the world, especially in the Caribbean, as well as in the Pacific and Indian Oceans.

The series of decolonization conflicts and new state formations after 1945 has its own chronology, and so it can be told, with great leaps between the individual scenes, in chronological order. Earlier events created the preconditions for later developments, and domino effects cannot be easily dismissed, even if there was no unstoppable chain reaction across the continents.[1] Such interconnections were stronger in geographical propinquity than over great distances. Each of the individual empires also constituted an interactive field of forces: what happened in *one* part of an empire could not remain without consequences in its other parts. At the same time, the greater share of those political processes that resulted in independence was acted out within the borders of existing colonies, and the newly emerging state structures, as a rule, settled into the territorial molds of the colonial era.

SOUTH ASIA

There are four major turning points in the history of the twentieth-century British Empire: independence for the South African Union in 1910 as a state that could hardly be managed from London any longer; the founding of the Irish Free State in 1921, after Ireland had been part of Great Britain since 1804; independence for the most important African colonies in the period between around 1960 and 1963; and, prior to that, the end of British rule in India in 1947. With India, half the empire disappeared; overnight the British Crown lost 388 million subjects. After Ceylon and Burma also became independent in 1948, the empire no longer had a strategic presence in the gigantic space between Aden and Singapore. India with its large army could no longer serve as the base for projecting British power to Central Asia, East Africa, and the Far East. The empire had forfeited its geopolitical coherence. The United Kingdom was still the most important master of colonies, but it was no longer the unique Eurasian dual monarchy whose splendor it proudly cultivated ever since the proclamation of Queen Victoria as "Empress of India" in January 1877. In other words, Britain ceased to function as an autonomous Asian great power—a role it had been playing for the past one and a half centuries.

The end of empire in South Asia stands out by the vast amount of official documents, many of them published, that are available to its historians.[2] In recent years, a great number of unofficial sources have been unearthed, ranging from autobiographical materials and oral history testimonies to fictional and semi-fictional literature. This abundance of sources, however, has not led to an uncontested reconstruction of the emergence of India and Pakistan beyond a simple chronology of events. Even here, the multiplicity of places to be considered makes a unilinear narrative impossible to achieve. The various parts of British India were governed under several different systems of rule, and the several hundred semi-autonomous princely states with their limited stake in nationalist movements always have to be treated as a special case. The significance of chronology, too, is a controversial issue. When was a dynamic toward independence set in motion? Some historians opt for 1940; others prefer 1937. Yet another group takes a long view and traces the story back to the end of the First World War or even earlier.

While the unique richness of historiography on twentieth-century India reflects a general evolution of historical analysis—for instance, from the history of elites to a bottom-up history of subalterns—it is also deeply entangled with the divisiveness of the political scene. Even if a broadly acceptable story of the anticolonial struggle might be told for the time up to the late 1930s,[3] the partition of 1947 engendered dramatically different historiographies. What to some is a tragic disintegration of the common Indian heritage appears as a blessing to those who celebrate the birth of a Muslim state and one with Hindu majority rule. Praise and blame are apportioned differently in Pakistan and in the Republic of India, and statesmen like Mohandas K. Gandhi and Muhammad Ali Jinnah enjoy a vastly diverging reputation in the various parts of the subcontinent. Few other ex-colonies have produced grand national narratives of liberation on the scale of India's, but these narratives—liberal-nationalist, Hindu-nationalist, Pakistan-centered, Marxist, and so on—do not agree on essentials, and non-Indian scholars have only partly achieved overarching and politically "neutral" syntheses.

In light of India's immense importance, it is at first sight puzzling that, in comparison with other cases of decolonization, Great Britain did so little to fight for its position in India.[4] However, holding on to India in the face of a nationalist movement that counted itself among the winners of the recent World War and enjoyed much support in the international arena might have led to huge bloodbaths: something the British had always tried to avoid since the Jallianwala Bagh massacre of April 1919. The large-scale outbreaks of violence in 1947–48 that were associated with the subcontinent's division into India and Pakistan were not attributable to British repression or military action. If anything, the British were accused of passivity and neglect: too quick a retreat from a crisis-ridden situation and negligence apropos of a colonial power's responsibility to ensure a regulated transition respecting the need for balance among the participating interests.[5] It would be apt to say that the British had, by 1946 at the latest, turned from a driving force into a driven one; ultimately, they had lost any influence on events. There was no elegant transfer of power in India.

Nineteen forty-two became the fateful year.[6] In light of the large Indian contribution to the war effort and the Japanese advance up to the eastern border of Bengal, the British sought political participation from the Indian National Congress, whose members had resigned their offices at the beginning of the war. At the end of March, Great Britain held out the vague prospect of an elected national assembly that was to decide freely about the future of India immediately after the end of the war, though London did not concede the formation of an Indian national government while the war lasted (the so-called Cripps Offer). The National Congress, however, demanded the immediate transfer of power to an Indian cabinet. In further negotiations between the Congress and the British, the political problems between Hindus and Muslims emerged ever more clearly. In August, the militarization of the subcontinent owing to the war made it easier for the viceroy to answer the demand that they leave India immediately (the "Quit India!" campaign) by arresting the entire leadership of the Congress. A catastrophic famine in Bengal in 1943 was widely blamed on the colonial power and further damaged its prestige. In the same year, National Congress dissidents held as prisoners of war by the Japanese founded the Indian National Army (INA). Although these dissidents met with a certain amount of sympathy inside India, they never became a real danger to the British.[7] It is remarkable that the vast majority of the Indian political elite did *not* opt for being "liberated" by the Japanese. Ultimately, it was Indian soldiers who prevented a Japanese invasion.[8]

By 1945, even though India itself had not been a theater of war, it was a country deep in turmoil. The option of independence was on the agenda. Important structural preconditions for a transition were present, in contrast to most of Asia's other colonies. First and foremost, there was a liberation movement that had been successfully agitating for two decades with an experienced leadership and a broad mass base that extended to a prosperous peasantry. A process of building up an electorate and handing over government functions to Indian politicians as well as the Indianization of the state bureaucracy at senior levels were well under way by the end of the 1930s. When the war ended, there was already a pull in the direction of independence that got a renewed impulse when the Congress's leaders were released from prison. The large, if not always voluntary, contribution that India had made to the British war effort rendered additional concessions unavoidable. The Indian army had grown into an enormous cost factor. For that reason, among others, Great Britain was highly indebted to India.

An additional factor, finally, was that the character of British colonial rule facilitated its demise. For India was to a high degree a "statist" colony in which political power was concentrated in the viceroy and his staff. There was no settler population capable of independent political action, and even big business interests were less influential than in colonies where raw materials acquisition played a central role. In London, the Labour Party, in power since July 1945, was less prone to nostalgia for the empire than the Tories and their prime minister, Winston Churchill. The new government of Prime Minister Clement Attlee pursued three goals: (1) to evacuate India from a position of conciliatory strength; (2) to move the conflicting groups involved in Indian politics toward compromise; and (3) to keep a united India in the Commonwealth, prevent the emergence of a geopolitical power vacuum, and immunize the country against Soviet influence.[9] For the time being, however, London vacillated. A military mutiny early in 1946, though limited and unsuccessful, raised deep-seated fears of losing control over the chief instrument of British rule.

In February 1947, Attlee announced that the British would leave India for good in June 1948. After on-site exploratory talks that gave him the impression of British crumbling rapidly, the new viceroy, Lord Mountbatten, in office since April, decided to move the date up to August 1947. This was announced on June 3, 1947. In expectation of imminent independence, and accelerated by the promulgation of deadlines, political processes were sparked off that would be repeated in one case of decolonization after another: different parties, political orientations, and personalities jockeyed for the best possible positions in the newly emerging state. The speed of political events at the leadership level and the scale of local violence mounted as they reinforced each other. While the Attlee government sought to avoid a long drawn-out battle of retreat, it simultaneously intensified political conflicts in which, by the end, it neither would nor could intervene.

The nature of these conflicts resulted from the increasing "communalization" of Indian politics, the dissociation of communities from one another. It was a process that, promoted by the colonial power in its quest for a clear-cut categorization of the population, had already started earlier: the identification of political orientations with religious group identities. The gradual parliamentarization of Indian politics, connected to the organized representation of interests now taking shape, fortified this development. It gave rise to the burning problem of minority protection. The idea of a secular, pan-Indian nationalism, which Gandhi stood for in spite of his habitus as a holy man, was increasingly called into question. More and more Muslims did not see themselves adequately represented in the National Congress as the country's dominant party.

During the early 1940s, the Muslim League under the leadership of the lawyer Muhammad Ali Jinnah, by no means an Islamist demagogue, gained influence in national politics. The

League's demand that the large Muslim minority have a state of its own (i.e., Pakistan) became the explosive charge of Indian politics; it had a mirror image among National Congress leaders who now also aimed at a homogeneous and realigned territory as a framework for nation-building. After no negotiated solution for a united India could be found, after partition was agreed on in principle, and after a commission established a line of demarcation between India and the two parts of Pakistan (in the east and in the west), practical problems emerged of a kind similar to those experienced in Europe, following territorial reorganizations as a result of the two World Wars, and now simultaneously in Palestine: millions of people were not living where they were "theoretically" supposed to live.

The "population exchange" proceeded spontaneously and unregulated. From all parts of India, Muslims streamed behind the borders of Pakistan, while Hindus fled in the opposite direction. Away from the streams of refugees, too, the religious communities clashed. As early as August 1946, there were at least 4,000 deaths from communal rioting in Calcutta. In 1947, violence seized large parts of the subcontinent, especially in the North. Rumors were enough to trigger massacres; local power holders and gang leaders seized the opportunities provided by the breakdown of political order at the local level. Estimates of the number of victims fluctuate between 200,000 and two million; most historians accept one million as a realistic figure; women on both sides fell victim to extreme forms of sexual violence.[10] By mid-1948, relative peace had returned. The origins of the partition as political event and the causes of extreme violence are still hotly contested. Some historians see partition as an almost logical consequence of "divide-and-rule" policies on the part of the colonial power while others emphasize short-term and local developments and frame their analyses in terms of communal identity, gender, and memory.[11]

The decolonization of South Asia was an unparalleled fiasco, one of the greatest man-made disasters of the postwar period and a warning to colonial powers and liberation movements alike. With the persistent conflict between Pakistan and the Republic of India, it has bequeathed a dangerous legacy to the present. It is noteworthy that the political elite of India, in spite of bad experiences in the colonial era and during decolonization, did not turn away from British political culture and constitutional democracy in the aftermath of independence, in contrast to almost all of Asia's ex-colonies. India as well as Pakistan remained in the Commonwealth of Nations. Pakistan, however, did not find political stability under democratic auspices and drifted into military rule in the late 1950s. A constitutional detail marked an important difference from the outset: Whereas Jinnah immediately upon independence himself assumed the formerly colonial and autocratic office of governor-general of Pakistan, Nehru asked Mountbatten to stay on for almost a year as governor-general of India (i.e., a kind of proto-president) to supervise the establishment of a parliamentary democracy by the Indian politicians under Nehru's experienced leadership.

A striking contrast to chaos and violence on the Indian subcontinent is offered by Ceylon (Sri Lanka since 1972). As a Crown colony, it had always been administered separately from India and was also socially and culturally a very different kind of country, in some ways a bridge between South and Southeast Asia.[12] Its politicians did not want full and immediate independence from Great Britain, since this would have made them dependent on neighboring India, a prospect not cherished by the island's elite. In 1940s Ceylon, shaped by the Singhalese Buddhist majority, antagonisms between the religious communities were less pronounced than in India. The Tamil minority was integrated into the political process. No stratum of intellectuals critical of colonialism emerged from the Buddhist clergy as it did in Burma. A radical national movement remained weak and fragmented and was incapable of mobilizing the masses. The strongly export-oriented economy was doing well. In addition, Ceylon profited from its function as Allied headquarters in the war against Japan. For decades, the domestic politics of the colony had been dominated by culturally Anglicized large planters and landowners. They were an ideal "collaboration elite" to whom London willingly transferred sovereignty in 1948, especially since extensive British rights to military bases had been guaranteed. Henceforth, Ceylon was regarded in Whitehall as a model case of a successful transfer of power.

SOUTHEAST ASIA

In Southeast Asia, too, the Second World War created the preconditions for decolonization. On the eve of the war, the region was, with the exception of Thailand, seamlessly colonized. Without exception, these colonies were of considerable economic value to their respective metropoles. Only in the case of the port colony of Singapore was colonization primarily justified on strategic grounds. The colonial era brought about centrifugal effects. The various parts of a region that had never maintained strong bonds of cultural affinity drifted apart as they were incorporated into the maritime empires of the Netherlands, France, Britain, and the United States. Relations *between* the colonial empires were not particularly close. Only the Japanese occupation starting early in 1942 strengthened the region's internal cohesion, although entirely to the benefit of Japan. The old colonial orders were invariably destroyed under Japanese rule, except in Vietnam, where the Japanese left in place a pro-Vichy French administration until March 1945 while they exploited the country economically. By the end of the war, the nationalist movements that emerged almost everywhere, however divided, did agree on wanting to prevent a return of the old colonial masters. In the late summer of 1945, therefore, all signs pointed to conflict.

Only the Philippines broke this pattern, as the first colony east of Mesopotamia to become independent, on July 4, 1946.[13] Owing to the many peculiarities of the Philippine situation, this case was hardly suitable as a model for the Southeast Asian region. During the second half of the war, troops from the United States had reconquered the northern part of the archipelago. After years of brutal Japanese military rule, the former colonial power really did return as liberator and not—as in the case of the Dutch, French, or British—as what looked like the parasitic beneficiary of the Japanese collapse. Although the Philippine national movement was the oldest one in Southeast Asia, there was no militant resistance opposed to the colonial power, as in Vietnam or Indonesia. The Huk rebellion, a military movement initially directed against the Japanese occupation, later affiliated with the communists, would first gain in importance in 1950, and it was suppressed after two years with American assistance. The transfer of power could take place from a position of strength on the part of the colonial power, a prerequisite for an orderly transfer of any kind of authority.

It had already been agreed before the war that there would be such a transfer, for the United States had in principle promised the Philippines independence as early as 1916, and had set a ten-year deadline in 1935. The United States could do this without misgivings, since a local elite was there to provide political and social stability in the postcolonial phase (here there are striking parallels to Ceylon), an elite that had profited extensively from the colonial system (including privileged access to American markets) and had a stake in continuing good relations with the United States. The conditions of independence, moreover, envisioned that the United States would lease large military bases for ninety-nine years. This was sufficient to serve both American strategy in Asia and the securing of US business interests. The postcolonial regime in the Philippines became the southern anchor of the American base system in East Asia, supplementing the northern moorings that was the Japanese archipelago.

The losers were the simple peasant population. Although American colonial rule prided itself a great deal on its successes in modernization, it had not initiated any kind of land reform that would have diminished the extreme inequalities prevailing in the countryside. Here, among all the countries of Southeast Asia, decolonization was least tied in with a social revolution. It provides an interesting contrast to South Korea and Taiwan, where land reforms were carried out under American auspices after 1945. Over the long run, the Philippines did not escape from the poverty trap, while in Korea and Taiwan the power of the large landowning class was broken and an important prerequisite for economic advancement thereby created.[14]

In contrast to Ceylon and the Philippines, Burma (Myanmar since 1989) was regarded even by contemporaries as the cautionary example of a failed decolonization.[15] From a British perspective, the failure was indicated by the way that Burma turned its back on the former colonial power and on the Commonwealth after independence in 1948. Political conditions diverged more from the model of Westminster democracy than in any other British ex-colony in Asia; a tentative democratization was cut off in 1962 by the establishment of military rule that lasted for decades. This unusual development had historical roots: Since the annexation of the entire kingdom in the 1880s, Burma had been ruled directly from Britain and always with an iron hand. Unlike the situation in Malaya, the British did not fasten onto the traditions of premodern princely rule. There was never an easygoing relationship with the country's Buddhist monkhood. Since the key economic positions remained in British and Indian hands, there was little leeway for the development of a Burmese bourgeois elite. The 1930s were characterized by popular uprisings and a radical student movement. During the war, which in Burma caused an especially large amount of damage, these fiercely nationalist forces at first collaborated with the Japanese before turning away from them in disappointment. In contrast to Ceylon, it was militant nationalists that expedited Burma's decolonization after 1945. Their most able and charismatic leader, Aung San (1915–47), was assassinated in July 1947 by a rival. No one else replaced him as the Burmese Nehru or Sukarno. Burma entered into independence with extremely weak civil institutions, less than visionary leadership, and a militarized political scene.

While Burma was taken back into British possession immediately after the surrender of Japan, Dutch colonial rule in Indonesia and French control over the countries of Indochina had broken down so radically that their authority could not be rebuilt from within the region. The unexpectedly rapid surrender of Japan was handled by British or (in the north of Vietnam) Nationalist Chinese troops, not by the erstwhile colonial masters. In both cases, indigenous political forces had seized power. On August 17, 1945, in Jakarta, Sukarno announced the founding of the Republic of Indonesia, which covered Java and parts of Sumatra and thus included more than three quarters of the Indonesian population. Three weeks later, the leader of the Vietminh national liberation movement, which was supported by strong currents in Vietnamese society, proclaimed Vietnam's independence. Speaking in Hanoi in front of thousands of people, Ho Chi Minh confidently placed Vietnam's national revolution within the long history of struggles for freedom that began with the emblematic dates of 1776 in North America and 1789 in France.

The governments, parliaments, and military leaderships in The Hague and Paris needed to decide explicitly to reconquer territories that had been lost to all intents and purposes. Both for Indonesia and Vietnam, these highly controversial decisions should be explained primarily with reference to collective psychology in the metropoles. After the deep humiliation forced on the Netherlands and France by Germany in the Second World War, the expected easy victories against rebellious Asians would help improve those nations' prestige and strengthen their self-confidence. Furthermore, the French and the Dutch were clinging to the traditional mercantilist notion that colonies would be useful to a ruined home economy. They were also supposed to lend the imperial centers clout and reputation on the international scene. All this proved to be an illusion. In 1949–50, the Dutch military had to withdraw from Indonesia, and the French from Indochina in 1954.[16]

In the Indonesian archipelago, relatively stable structures emerged within a short period of time. This happened in spite of great regional differences, religious tensions, and spontaneous acts of revolutionary violence against old aristo-cratic and public service elites who were tied in to the colo-nial system. The power vacuum so eagerly coveted by colo-nial interventionists did not develop, and the Republic of Indonesia remained constantly accessible as an interlocutor to international diplomacy.[17] Quite early, the British, who were reluctant to serve the selfish interests of Dutch (and French) neo-imperialism, urged the Netherlands to compromise with Sukarno. The Hague, however, attempted to topple the re-public in two waves of invasions (euphemistically called "po-lice actions") in July–August 1947 and December 1948. In spite of resistance from guerrilla forces, these attacks were not militarily ineffective. But skilled diplomacy by the republic, including in the new forum of the United Nations, and the US government's comforting realization that Sukarno would resist communist temptations and was not really dangerous, as well as the declining willingness of the public at home to bear the growing costs of the war, ultimately brought the Netherlands to the negotiating table.

In Indonesia, a national identity was much less developed than in compact and culturally homogeneous countries such as Vietnam or Burma. Much like the idea of "Pakistan" that dated back to around 1930, a vision of "Indonesia" was anything but ancient and primordial, first taking shape during the 1940s.[18] It is therefore all the more remarkable that it was possible to create a relatively unitary state in the years from 1950 onward. Given the country's huge cultural diversity, a federal solution might have been a feasible alternative, but the most ambitious state builders prevailed. In contrast to South Asia, Korea, and Vietnam, Indonesia was not divided during the decolonization process. Internationally, this process led neither to isolation (as with Burma) nor to neocolonial dependency (as with the Philippines).

France intervened in Vietnam to a much greater extent than the Netherlands did in Indonesia.[19] With the attack on Hanoi and the port city of Haiphong in December 1946, this intervention turned into the (first) Indochina war, which lasted until 1954. The conflict escalated exactly at the moment when the Netherlands had to concede its defeat in Indonesia. It could only be conducted with support from the United States. France let opportunities for an orderly disengagement elapse, banking instead on military victory against an opponent that was increasingly viewed as part of an international communist conspiracy. In contrast to all other wars of decolonization, this one really was decided on the battlefield: in May 1954 at Dien Bien Phu when the French forces were decisively defeated by the Vietminh army fighting under brilliant leadership. After the French defeat, international diplomacy only managed to arrive at a precarious solution. At the 1954 Geneva conference, Vietnam was divided—according to the authors of this design only provisionally—exactly at its halfway mark, on the 17th Parallel. Only after a further military victory, this time over the United States, was this division rescinded in 1975. The reunification ended foreign rule in Vietnam long after the great age of Asian decolonization had passed. In Vietnam, there had been a multiple failure of empires (including Chinese, in the distant past), but never any transition to sovereignty in national unity facilitated even minimally by statecraft and compromise.

Another latecomer was Malaya.[20] This decentralized collection of British possessions had been governed, quite unlike Burma, lightly and indirectly, by way of established princes and aristocrats. For a long time, there were hardly any nationalistically motivated complaints about colonial oppression. Nonagricultural economic activity was largely in the hands of Chinese and Indians, who overall made up more than half of the population and were especially predominant in the cities. In no other colony of South and Southeast Asia were the relations between ethnically defined population groups of greater importance for the formation of economic and political structures. Nowhere else outside Vietnam was there also a comparably strong communist movement. It consisted almost entirely of Chinese, a segment of the population that had been treated with extreme brutality by the Japanese military occupiers and had become radical defending itself. When the Malayan Communist Party (MCP) switched over to armed struggle in 1947, the British reacted with a complete arsenal of anti-guerrilla and counterinsurgency techniques, including the resettlement of one million Chinese in secure "new villages."[21] This strategy of "emergency" (as it was officially called) was successful by the mid-1950s; the last fighters for the MCP disappeared into the jungle. Independence, long promised vaguely, came in 1957. It was preceded by negotiations, protracted although characterized by a general willingness to compromise, among the representatives of the three major ethnic groups. Independent Malaya (Malaysia since 1963, in an altered form) was constituted as a deliberately multiracial country, although retaining a certain Malayan priority. It maintained its Commonwealth tie.

There was rather much symbolic resonance to the fact that Singapore finally became sovereign in 1965 after a brief and unhappy period of merger with Malaya. The symbolism lies in the fact that the last major country in Southeast Asia to achieve full independence (not counting the latecomer Brunei, independent since 1984) was none other than the fortress city whose failure as a bastion against Japan a quarter-century earlier signaled the beginning of British decline in Asia. After independence, the city-state with its demographic majority of ethnic Chinese put into practice one of the world's most successful economic models and became Great Britain's most important trading partner in Southeast Asia.

THE MIDDLE EAST, NORTH AFRICA, AND THE MEDITERRANEAN

In comparison with Asia, relatively short spaces of time separated the establishment and the end of formal colonial rule in most parts of North Africa and the Middle East. Yet, since the nineteenth century, forms of informal penetration and control had played a central role in the region. In the twentieth century, a return to informal empire was also the response, particularly by Great Britain, to claims for national self-determination. In many cases, thus, decolonization proceeded in two stages: following the end of a phase of formal foreign control, the informal empire that lingered on was undermined, or it was replaced by the rising geopolitical influence of the United States in many parts of this economically crucial region.[22] Significantly, no country in the region (except for Malta and Cyprus) joined the Commonwealth.

A key role in these developments was played by Egypt. Occupied by Great Britain since 1882, the country was regarded as an indispensable geopolitical foundation for the empire in East Africa and the Middle East. The Suez Canal, opened in 1869, secured both military and civil shipping to East Africa, India, and the Far East. In addition, the Sudan, which fulfilled an important bridging function between North and East Africa, was governed jointly since 1898 as a British-Egyptian "condominium," a peculiar status in international law. What changed was the form that colonial influence and rule assumed: after Egypt had started to be governed as a "veiled protectorate" by British consul-generals as of 1883, it formally became an outright "protectorate" with the outbreak of the First World War. In light of persistent nationalist protests, the British government declared the country independent—in the form of a newly created monarchy—in February 1922.[23] The country's sovereignty, however, remained strongly restricted: the military, police, foreign policy, and key sectors of the economy remained subject to British control, as was Sudan. In 1936, an additional treaty terminated the military occupation and foreign privileges. The Suez Canal was exempted from these treaties and grew in the ensuing years into the world's largest military base, which by 1951 included about 40,000 soldiers. Toward Egyptian internal political affairs, too, Great Britain preserved an ultimate right of intervention, which became manifest in early 1942 when the king was compelled by force of arms to install a pro-British premier.

The end of formal colonial rule over Iraq (1932) and Transjordan/Jordan (1946) followed a similar model of collaboration with conservative elites and alliance treaties.[24] Henceforth, both nominally independent countries would be subject to Hashemite royal houses installed by Great Britain. The British-Iraqi independence treaty of 1930 was a textbook example in the informal safeguarding of imperial interests: it secured important petroleum interests for Great Britain and access to Iraqi infrastructure; in addition, there were two British military bases and a guarantee of support in case of war. In Syria and in Lebanon, the dissolution of the mandate proceeded with more conflict, which was due both to pressure from Syrian nationalists and to French resistance against incorporating any prospect for independence into the constitutions of both countries.[25] Treaties of independence, comparable to the British-Iraqi model and negotiated by the French Popular Front government in 1936, failed because of internal political opposition in France. Only under pressure from its wartime allies, particularly Great Britain, and local nationalists did the Free French reestablish national parliaments and governments, hold elections, and transfer administrative responsibilities to these governments in March 1944. Yet these countries continued to be occupied by French and British troops, which left open the option of a colonial restoration following the Southeast Asian model. Only after mass protests in Syria in 1945 did France and Great Britain accept a troop withdrawal, which ended by December 1946. Syria and Lebanon were the first colonies in the region to obtain sovereignty not restricted by treaty.

Palestine constituted a special case in many respects.[26] Here the commitment to Zionism placed clear limitations on the British policy of informally securing its rule by establishing conservative collaborationist regimes. The mandate collapsed in civil war. After numerous shifts in policy, Great Britain committed itself in 1939 to the region's independence within ten years and to restrictions on Jewish immigration and land-ownership. Rejected by Jews and Arabs alike, this policy also came in for international criticism in light of the Nazi exter-mination policy. For radical Zionists, above all, Great Britain now became the main obstacle to their project for a state; in 1944, militant Zionists resorted to acts of sabotage and terror against the mandatory power (supported in part by French intelligence). In light of a situation that could barely be con-trolled, Great Britain considered—earlier than in India—a partition of the territory. After negotiations about this had failed, and under increasing US pressure, London turned the Palestine question over to the United Nations at the begin-ning of 1947. At the end of November 1947, and in the midst of post-partition violence in South Asia, the United Nations presented a partition plan for Palestine; in December, Great Britain announced its withdrawal through mid-May 1948. With the announcement of the UN plan, violence between the population groups escalated, associated with the first ex-pulsions and refugee movements of Palestinian Arabs. On May 14, 1948, the State of Israel was proclaimed. The next day the invasion by Jordanian, Egyptian, Iraqi, Syrian, and Leba-nese forces marked the start of the first war between Israel and the surrounding Arab states, which ended in January 1949 with a victory for Israel.

The Israeli-Palestinian conflict and the war of 1948–49 were of decisive importance for the subsequent course of decoloni-zation in the Arab countries that had participated in the war. There, the end of formal colonial rule had not meant any rupture in the structures of political leadership. The Arab belligerents' unexpected defeat shattered the legitimacy of the regimes and allowed new actors to step forward, most prominently younger army cadres who were often recruited from the ranks of social climbers and were close to pan-Arab, nationalist, and socialist ideas. The military, above all in Iraq, had already been politically active, but it now became a revolutionary factor. In 1949, a coup ended the long-established political supremacy of urban notables in Syria. Even more consequential was the 1952 officers' coup in Egypt that ended the monarchy and prepared the way for the rise of Gamal Abdel Nasser, a head of state who set the political style for the region: emphatically nationalist, exhibiting pan-Arabic ambitions and an interest in socialism, aware of the role of global media, and ready to use the East-West conflict for his own agenda.

Even more so than it had at the time of the monarchy, Egypt under Nasser functioned as the sponsor and base of national movements in the Middle East, in the Maghreb, and in East Africa. Moreover, the remnants of colonial influence in Egypt came under pressure. Great Britain and Egypt did agree on letting Sudan become independent in 1956. In the case of the Suez Canal, however, the smoldering conflict escalated.[27] Since 1945, there had been repeated clashes between demonstrators, the local forces of order, and British troops stationed at the canal. In October 1954, both countries agreed on a troop withdrawal, which was completed by April 1956, but an option to return was held open. Against the background of conflicting British and Egyptian claims to hegemony and the formation of frontlines owing to the Cold War, the Suez conflict grew within months into a complex international crisis. Egypt reacted to the creation of an anticommunist alliance (the "Baghdad Pact") between Great Britain, Iran, Iraq,

Turkey, and Pakistan by making a weapons deal with socialist Czechoslovakia. When the United States thereupon held back funds for the planned Aswan Dam, Nasser on July 26, 1956, announced the nationalization of the Suez Canal Company, whose major shareholder was the British state.

The reaction of the Conservative British government under Anthony Eden provided the last step in escalating the conflict. After large parts of Middle Eastern decolonization had been marked by fierce Franco-British rivalry, the Suez crisis set the stage for "the most infamous case of joint imperial interventionism in the era of decolonization."[28] In secret plans with Israel and France, which saw in Egypt the main supporter of the Algerian independence struggle, the British prepared a military attack whose goal was less the restoration of the Suez Canal Company than the toppling of the Nasser regime. On October 29, Israeli troops pushed into Egyptian territory. Two days later, Great Britain and France, posing as "mediators," bombed Egyptian military airfields and began to occupy the Suez Canal Zone. Almost immediately, international protest stirred. In the United Nations, there were protests, which even Commonwealth member India joined. The United States, not informed in advance, made no doubt about its rejection of the secret action and hesitated to support the British pound, which had come under pressure. On November 7, France and Great Britain suspended combat, and a troop withdrawal began in early December.

Ever since, the Suez crisis has preoccupied the minds of political analysts and historians. It seems reasonable to interpret the ignominious withdrawal of Great Britain as definitive proof of its imperial decline. It makes more sense, however, to differentiate the impact of the Suez crisis according to different scales. *Regionally*, it strengthened Nasser's hegemonic position and gave a new impulse to the dynamic of decolonization. In 1958, a military coup deposed the monarchy in Iraq allied with Great Britain, and the Jordanian royal house was only able to assert itself by drawing closer to the United States which was about to become the new major foreign power in the region.[29] A latecomer to this revolutionary wave was Libya, which had been closely tied to Great Britain and the United States since a UN resolution gave it independence in 1951.[30] In 1969, a military coup under Muammar al-Gaddafi toppled the royal house. At the *international* level, the Suez crisis exposed the strongly reduced scope for action of the European colonial powers, who had been constrained by world public opinion and their dependence on the United States. These insights led at the *imperial* level to a reevaluation of the means available for asserting the interests of the ex-colonial European powers: from now on, a brute and uncoordinated imperialist line of action was regarded as unwise and counterproductive.

Yet the Suez crisis did not signal a point of no return for worldwide decolonization. First, even after 1956, France and Great Britain did not, as would be seen in Algeria and Kenya, desist in principle from the use of military force; Great Britain continued to expand its military role "East of Suez." Second, the impetus for decolonization in the years 1956–57 is not attributable to the Suez crisis. Independence for Tunisia, Morocco, Malaya, and Ghana had been decided beforehand. When it came to other territories, even after 1956 the colonial powers initially appeared hesitant. Third, the Suez crisis had rather more of the opposite short-term effect of increased colonial presence in Cyprus and South Arabian Aden. British military deployments there grew after 1956, and only violent nationalist resistance in 1960 and 1967, respectively, led to a hasty withdrawal and independence (yet not to a complete military retreat from Cyprus).[31] Fourth, there was no lasting damage done to relations between the United States and the two European countries that intervened in Suez.

Even if not entirely detached from the events in the Middle East, decolonization in western North Africa took a different course. The transformation of formal colonial rule into informal empire did not play a comparable role in French plans for the region. In retrospect, the decolonization of the Maghreb may appear to be dominated by the bloody end of French Algeria, looming so large that independence for Tunisia and Morocco all but disappear behind it. Such a view of things, however, ignores how tightly developments in the three countries were intertwined with each other. There were not only numerous ties among the national movements, but the decolonization processes also influenced each other reciprocally. Thus, crucially, the abolition of the two protectorates was accelerated by the outbreak of the Algerian war in November 1954. At the same time, since achieving independence in 1956, Tunisia and Morocco functioned as important areas of retreat for Algerian liberation forces and contributed greatly to that struggle's internationalization. It should also not be forgotten, in light of the large-scale war in Algeria, that the decolonization of Tunisia and Morocco also took place against the background of escalating violence. Even earlier than in Algeria, nationalist groups here went over to armed struggle and terrorism in the early 1950s; there were also phases of intensified repression. Moreover, the Europeans residing in Morocco and Tunisia also reacted to imminent decolonization with embittered resistance, which ranged from protest rallies to participation in terrorist organizations.

It was critical, however, that in both countries, independence ultimately came about by way of negotiations. Both cases show how differently politics could develop in a colonial state designed as a protectorate. In Morocco, Sultan Mohammed ben Youssef became the symbol of the independence movement.[32] After 1945, the sultan increasingly showed sympathy for the nationalists, yet at the same time he signaled a willingness to negotiate with France. While he succumbed to pressure from the colonial administration and took part in measures against the nationalists, Mohammed blocked plans to increase the power of the French settler population. The confrontation climaxed in the deposition and deportation of the sultan in August 1953. After a two-year wave of protests and unrest, the French government decided on the return of the sultan in November 1955 and on independence for the country (as a monarchy) in March 1956. One month later, Spain also withdrew from northern Morocco, which had been a Spanish protectorate since 1912.

With Habib Bourguiba, Tunisia saw the rise of a national leader whose support was not based on traditional legitimation but on a mass political party and the powerful national trade union center with which it was allied.[33] Bourguiba had mostly been in jail or in exile since 1938. By 1954, French authorities redefined him in the face of persistent and increasingly violent protests as a suitable negotiation partner, a strategy that would later be frequently repeated in southern Africa. After a brief phase of internal autonomy (starting in 1955), events in Morocco accelerated the timetable and cleared the way for the Republic of Tunisia to become independent in March 1956.

France's most dramatic colonial crisis unfolded in Algeria. With well over a million soldiers deployed, around 25,000 fallen French, and about 400,000 Algerians killed, the military action that took place between November 1, 1954, and the ceasefire of March 19, 1962, constituted the largest war of decolonization worldwide.[34] Only a combination of different factors can explain why French Algeria in particular came to such a violent end: First, the country conquered after 1830 was not only France's most important colony in the nineteenth and twentieth century; it was also unusually interwoven with the political structures of the metropole. Algeria was not officially regarded as a colony, but as an integral part of the French state's territory. This was also the foundation for France's dogged refusal to designate the "events," "operations," or "actions to maintain order" it undertook in Algeria as a war between two countries.

Second, along with South Africa, Algeria constituted the largest settler colony on African soil. The nearly one million Europeans who lived there in 1954 dominated Algerian political life and were represented in France by a vocal lobby that successfully blocked substantial political reforms. Third, the Algerian national movement exhibited a high degree of heterogeneity, arising from several important anticolonial currents (liberal anticolonialists, Islamic reformers, nationalists, and communists). While the massacre of May 8, 1945, did mark a decisive break between many Algerian anticolonialists and France, none of these movements achieved a hegemonic position comparable to what happened in Morocco with the sultan and in Tunisia with Bourguiba. The series of attacks with which the Front de Libération Nationale (FLN) made its appearance on November 1, 1954, was rather the act of desperation perpetrated by a small group of activists who saw armed struggle not only as the only way to oppose the colonial power but also as a way out of the national movement's internal blockades. The brutal and untargeted reactions of the French army to these attacks contributed decisively to facilitating the growth of the FLN base in the Algerian population.[35]

The war in Algeria gained its dynamic from an interplay between extreme forms of repression and late-colonial reform policy. Equipped with far-reaching powers via emergency laws, the army sought to bring the country under control by way of "anti-subversive" warfare. This included a systematic use of torture, and widespread internments and resettlements; by the end of the war, around two million Algerians, a good fourth of the overall population, was living in resettlement camps.[36] At the same time, comprehensive reform programs were meant to promote the country's political integration and socioeconomic modernization and win over the Algerians to the side of the colonial power.[37]

The conflict proceeded along different, complicated fronts: first, there was the guerrilla war, which played out above all in the countryside; second, there was the battle against the political-administrative organizations that the FLN built up as a sort of counteradministration; and third, there was the diplomatic war for international alliances and world public opinion, which the FLN targeted from the outset and which played out above all in the United Nations. While France, after a massive troop buildup in 1959, was able to decide the guerrilla war for itself, it failed on the two other fronts. It was growing international pressure that proved decisive for the resumption of ceasefire negotiations starting in 1960.[38]

The course of the war was also shaped, however, by numerous additional fronts that traversed both camps: the bloody conflict in which the FLN established its hegemonic claim against nationalist rivals and "collaborators"; the French opponents of the war and networks that supported the FLN; dissident army cadres and radicalized settlers who bitterly contested any kind of concession or peace negotiation, initially by staging mass demonstrations, but then later by attempting a coup, and ultimately by launching the terror campaign of the "Organisation armée secrète" (OAS).[39] The great extent to which the French metropole itself became a theater for Algeria's decolonization was demonstrated by the way the war accelerated the collapse of the Fourth Republic in 1958 and facilitated the creation of the Fifth Republic under Charles de Gaulle. Algeria became independent in July 1962.

SOUTHERN AFRICA

Between 1957 and 1965, most of the colonies south of the Sahara achieved independence, eighteen territories in 1960 alone. Only a few years earlier, such a development was hardly imaginable. After all, sub-Saharan Africa had been at the heart of late-colonial planning and European visions of a permanent colonial presence since the 1940s. Economically, too, the raw materials boom of the postwar years lent the African colonies a significance that they had never had before in peacetime. After 1945, sub-Saharan Africa became the last refuge for the imperial illusion of permanence.

It was critical that the horizon for what was politically imaginable in Africa changed fundamentally within a few years.[40] Symptomatic of this shift was a change in policy by Great Britain and France, who turned toward more active decolonization policies at the end of the 1950s. Both colonial powers wanted in this way to regain the initiative for a process that in the meantime had come to seem unavoidable to them, to shape the outcome of this process, and to secure—also with a view to the emerging frontlines of the Cold War—lasting influence in the new states. The too-readily invoked picture of a "managed" decolonization that was concerted, trouble-free, and controlled, however, is deceptive. First, decolonization in sub-Saharan Africa was strongly shaped by misjudgments, by the acceleration and then collapse of planned schedules, as well as by regional domino effects. British politicians in 1943, for example, regarded any self-government for the Gold Coast comparable to the one granted India in 1935 as something that would be possible only after several generations, and then in 1947 after twenty to thirty years; yet by 1957, the country had already become independent. Likewise, British officials in 1959 ruled out any self-government for Kenya before 1975; four years later, the country became independent. A unique mixture in each country of on-site political developments, international pressure, metropolitan debates, and regional feedbacks also saw to it that colonial planners and African politicians were overtaken by events. This was sometimes accompanied by radical role changes: once demonized nationalists turned almost overnight into "moderate" and acceptable partners at the negotiation table; and British prime minister Harold Macmillan, not long beforehand a committed imperialist, toured the south of the continent in 1960 as a friend of African nationalism.

Second, the political elites that sustained and advanced the process of decolonization here were only nascent, in contrast to Asia and North Africa. Many of them needed first to build up and stabilize their position as representatives and negotiators for their countries, and they saw themselves confronted with internal opposition and conflict about the degree of sovereignty and regional integration to be sought.

Third, violent confrontations played a subordinate role in many cases, to be sure, but Great Britain and France did resort to massive repression in some places. Concern about possible escalation and a turn to violence was a significant factor in more peaceful decolonization processes.

Fourth, African decolonization was, apart from its intensive phase around 1960, a long and drawn-out process. Until the mid-1970s, Portugal and Spain resisted withdrawal, and the settler regimes of Rhodesia and South Africa held out even longer. Between the introduction of general suffrage in the Gold Coast (1951) and in South Africa (1994), there was a stretch of over four decades.

In West Africa, there was a particularly intensive interaction between late-colonial policy and the decolonization process. Here, initial French and British approaches to the reform of colonial rule took on a dynamic of their own that could barely be controlled by colonial authorities. Trade unions, student and youth movements, and associations of veterans, farmers, and market women—as well as an emerging political class of educated elites—used the new institutions, platforms, and official ideological justifications to represent their interests. The growing cities became sites of political activity and social movement, of massive strikes and unrest. The fitful transition to forms of representative politics contributed considerably to the politicization of the postwar years. Between 1945 and 1948 alone, voters in the French colonial federations (French West Africa and French Equatorial Africa) went to the polls in six major elections, accompanied by the kinds of mobilization and formation of political camps that accompany electoral campaigns.

The political framework established by the colonial powers favored different paths to independence. In the British context, this pathway always presented itself as a specific constitutional process: first, reforms that were intended to strengthen local democratic participation and prepare the territories for self-government in a distant, otherwise unspecified future were quite soon overtaken by political developments on the ground; then came a series of constitutional reforms in rapid succession, ending with the country's independence.

Such a process could first be observed in the Gold Coast, a colony prospering thanks to cacao exports.[41] A constitutional reform in 1946 strengthened centralization and political participation there. The reform, however, did not satisfy the ambitions of urban educated elites in the coastal region, nor did it calm existing social conflicts. When riots broke out in Accra in 1948, Great Britain reacted with repressive measures and additional reforms. A new constitution in 1950 envisioned the expansion of the franchise and a dual sovereignty comparable to the dyarchy in India. Profiting from this arrangement was Kwame Nkrumah, who in 1947 had returned from his studies in the United States and England and sought to assemble a broad base of farmers, workers, and urban youth. In spite of repression and his incarceration, Nkrumah's party was able to win the elections in February 1951 with its demands for autonomy. Nkrumah emerged from prison as head of government and was then regarded in London as a more or less serious and reliable partner. At the same time, he used the available framework to expand his own clientele and keep up the tempo for the transfer of political sovereignty, especially as opposition took shape among the cocoa farmers and local chiefs in the interior country.[42] In March 1957, after two additional electoral victories, he led the country to independence under the new name Ghana. As in India in the 1930s, when a certain point of constitutional liberalization was reached, local politics acquired a dynamic that could barely be contained or channeled from outside.

Apart from regional variations and peculiarities, independence for Nigeria (1960), Sierra Leone (1961), Gambia (1965), and the two East African colonies not dominated by settlers—Tanganyika (1961) and Uganda (1962)—followed a comparable pattern. In the case of Nigeria, which was composed of three very different individual polities, this process proved especially intricate; in the 1950s, the federal political system here was already shot through with patronage based on ethnic identifications as well as with regional and ethnic interest conflicts. A few years after independence, this escalated into a war against the oil-rich breakaway eastern province of Biafra, which—fanned by Cold War alliances and a systematic propaganda war in international media—quickly grew into a major international crisis.[43]

The French colonies of West and Central Africa were integrated into a complicated structure made up of the French Union, regional federations, and individual territories. In light of France's late-colonial integration policy, political life here was initially oriented around demands for equality—for example, in education and labor relations. Metropolitan France was the frame of reference; Paris, the political center. The emerging class of politicians sharpened its image less by way of offices in the colonial state than by parliamentary representation of their regions and their ties with political parties and institutions in Paris. Some of them, like the Senegalese Léopold Senghor and the Ivorian Félix Houphouët-Boigny, held office in French governments—something unconceivable in the British Empire. Most of these politicians succeeded in establishing themselves as the dominant political force by party building. While the small Western-educated elite in French Equatorial Africa remained largely unchallenged, West African politicians came under pressure from more radical movements of workers, students, and youth groups.[44] At the same time, France saw itself confronting an ever-expanding spiral of demands for equality.

The reaction to this was the framework law (*loi-cadre*) of June 23, 1956. Like the Mandate of Togo (as of 1955), the individual territories obtained a higher degree of autonomy and came under the control of elected territorial governments. Their costly social welfare and development policy now became the responsibility of African politicians and their limited territorial budgets. There was no policy of decolonization behind this. Neither the law of 1956 nor the successor institution to the French Union created in 1958, the French Community, provided for the transfer of key departments like defense, foreign policy, and finance. Yet the *loi-cadre* marked a de facto departure from France's former integration policy. Two years later, this policy experienced a further setback when the territories voted on the constitution of the Fifth Republic and whether to remain in the Community. While almost all prominent leaders, some under massive French pressure, tried to win support for a "yes" vote, in Guinea the former trade unionist Sékou Touré successfully advocated rejection, a position for which rival nationalists and parts of his base were pushing him.[45] The other colonies came out in

favor of a continued French presence, some with clear majorities, and in Niger this even happened in opposition to campaigns by local politicians.[46] In order to prevent a possible
chain reaction, France reacted to the Guinean "no" with an
immediate cutoff in all bilateral cooperation. The disintegration of the colonial federations, however, could no longer be
stopped. With Guinea's departure and other West African
leaders' increasing skepticism of imperial federalism as a gen-
erator of equality and socioeconomic advancement, any kind
of independence within the framework of the two remaining federations associated with France, something Senghor
in particular promoted, became improbable. As early as September 1959, Senegal and French Sudan (later Mali) jointly
applied for independence, and the other territories soon followed suit. On the basis of individual negotiations, all the territories of French West Africa and French Equatorial Africa
became independent in the course of 1960, as did Madagascar
and mandatory Togo and Cameroon.

While France secured a (notorious) presence in West and
Central Africa even after independence, Belgian authorities
left the Congo hastily in 1960. As late as 1955, this colony that
had been managed with an iron hand was still regarded by
Brussels as particularly stable and quiet.[47] The mining sector,
with early rudiments of a welfare policy, developed a strong
dynamic after 1945; in 1949, partly in response to international
criticism, a ten-year modernization plan was issued. In January 1959, when social unrest broke out in Léopoldville (now
Kinshasa) under the impact of a latent economic crisis, an
abrupt process of decolonization set in. Early in 1960, a hastily summoned constitutional conference fixed the transfer of

power at the end of June; and in May, elections were held and a government formed. With independence, however, the institutions of the newly founded state disintegrated. Only a few days after, a rebellion against remaining Belgian officers broke out in the army, prompting the deployment of Belgian troops to protect Europeans and their property. Shortly afterward, two secessions occurred, first of the mining province Katanga, followed by the diamond region South Kasai. A military coup ensued in September, and Prime Minister Patrice Lumumba was arrested and assassinated shortly thereafter. Within a few weeks, the Congo became the biggest crisis spot in the region. A peacekeeping mission sent by the United Nations was able to restore national unity at the start of 1963 but did not bring about peace. From November 1965 onward, and after additional bloody conflicts, army chief Joseph-Désiré Mobutu (who later changed his name to Mobutu Sese Seko) built up a military dictatorship that would last almost thirty-two years.

Several conflicts converged in the "Congo crisis." First, there was the breakdown of a state that was barely prepared for independence and had only the rudiments of unified institutions. A strong primary education sector contrasted with the absence of higher education programs. Trade union and political organizations remained banned through the 1950s. Only then did a political life develop and were Congolese admitted to higher education. In 1960, there were fewer than twenty university graduates in the country. Independence for such a fragile state structure was regarded in Belgian government circles as a favorable condition for safeguarding economic and strategic interests. Even after the constitutional conference, colonial officials and influential mining companies worked toward destabilizing the country and actively promoted Katanga's secession.

Second, resistance took shape in the country in opposition to the central state that the constitution of 1960 envisioned and that Lumumba's party advocated. Most of the other parties, by contrast, were oriented toward regionally and ethnically defined loyalties. For its leaders, the Katanga secession was also a struggle to defend the interests of the Katangese "nation."[48] Decisive for the escalation of the crisis was a third factor: numerous regional and international interventions. Due to its large raw material deposits (including uranium), the Congo became a major Cold War battlefield. Lumumba's uncompromising conduct and his socialist rhetoric earned him the reputation of a radical and "communist" in the West. The United States above all aimed at his removal and also incorporated the UN mission into this objective. Katanga leader Moïse Tshombe and Mobutu found their most important promoters in the CIA and Belgian intelligence and army officers, who also provided support for Lumumba's removal and assassination.

The dramatic events in the Congo make it easy to forget that the British and French withdrawal from Africa also did not always proceed in an orderly and peaceful fashion. Both colonial powers had already acted violently against "radical" nationalists and disturbances in West Africa. It was in Central and East Africa, however, that the largest outbreaks of violence occurred. In mandatory Cameroon, in spite of UN observation, France suppressed the most important nationalist party that was demanding more autonomy and articulating this demand on the international stage in the early 1950s.[49] French authorities acted even more brutally in Madagascar, where a major (largely rural) uprising broke out in March 1947.[50] The repression, which lasted almost two years, took the lives of around 90,000 people and disrupted the colony's agricultural economy. In a political show process, French authorities also targeted the colony's political representatives in Paris. Madagascar's anticolonial movement, which had been fairly advanced in 1945, only regained momentum from the mid-1950s.

In the British colonies of Central and East Africa, especially in Kenya and Rhodesia, white settlers and Indian immigrants made a consistent constitutional liberalization difficult to achieve. Here, colonial politicians pursued a "multiracial solution," that is, a state structure that would slowly put the population groups on an equal footing and protect the rights of European and South Asian minorities. In Kenya, the situation escalated in the early 1950s in the so-called Mau Mau uprising of landless and unemployed Kikuyu men (the largest population group), who were most harshly affected by the land policy of the whites and the "development policy" of the postwar years.[51] Even more so than in Algeria, this was also a domestic, intra-Kenyan war: far more than settlers and colonial institutions, it was "collaborators" and the landowning Kikuyu establishment who were the targets of violence. Also under pressure from the settlers, Great Britain reacted with severity and declared a state of emergency in October 1952. The repression included massive force, torture, and resettlements, accompanied by land reforms. According to official figures, more than 11,000 insurgents died, and about a million people found themselves relocated to "new villages."

In contrast to the French war in Algeria, the British military action in Kenya encountered little international criticism.[52]

Great Britain succeeded in portraying the insurgents, who rejected modernizing interventions (such as the prohibition of clitoral circumcision) and deliberately perpetuated anti-modern male bonding rituals, as "barbarians" and holdouts against modernity. The state of emergency paralyzed political life that had been hitherto dominated by Kikuyu. Jomo Kenyatta, the leading nationalist, remained in jail through August 1961. By the end of the 1950s, however, the momentum of constitutional reforms revived, a momentum that led to the implementation of the majority principle and to the political rise of "radical" nationalists against British resistance. In December 1963, the country became independent under Kenyatta and an elite mainly drawn from "loyalist" Kikuyu.

Even more than in Kenya, the British colonial principles of trusteeship toward non-Europeans and of self-government for white settlers clashed with each other in central Africa. In 1953, the British government combined the settler colony of Southern Rhodesia, self-administered for thirty years, with the Crown colonies of Northern Rhodesia and Nyasaland into the new Central African Federation (CAF). The federation was a concession to the Southern Rhodesian settlers who were courted by the apartheid regime in neighboring South Africa. Presented as a paragon of "multiracialism," this federation turned out to be an instrument for cementing white supremacy and access to the Northern Rhodesian copper-mining sector. The founding of the CAF attracted a wave of settlers. In 1957, a constitutional reform reinforced their privileges; over the years, Southern Rhodesian governments grew increasingly hostile to "multiracialism."

African activists and labor leaders in Nyasaland and Northern Rhodesia mobilized for the dissolution of the CAF, which they viewed as a central obstacle to gaining more political rights. Early in 1959, states of emergency were imposed in all three territories. Only as of 1960—and following the international outcry over the brutal suppression of a demonstration in South African Sharpeville—did the British government gradually start backing away from the federation and opening up to the African protest movements. By the end of 1963, the CAF was officially dissolved, followed by independence for Nyasaland (as Malawi in 1964) and Northern Rhodesia (as Zambia in 1965). In Southern Rhodesia, a radical settler party took over the government in April 1964. After prior negotiations with Great Britain collapsed, the settler regime declared independence unilaterally in 1965. It was the first secession from the British Empire since 1776.

THE LATE DECOLONIZATIONS

Barely twenty years after the Philippines gained independence, large parts of the colonial world had achieved sovereign statehood. Colonial rule no longer seemed a model for the future, even in relation to sub-Saharan Africa, but an anachronism instead. Yet, in several regions, colonial regimes lingered on after 1965. In the decades to follow, these regimes disintegrated one by one until nothing remained of the modern era's extensive colonial empires but the confetti of isolated remnants.

In Africa, the settler regimes of South Africa and Rhodesia were initially successful in resisting the momentum of decolonization. There were also the colonies of the authoritarian regimes of Portugal and Spain, which defended their colonial possessions primarily for nationalistic reasons. A second wave of African decolonization in the 1970s marked the end for most of these colonies. More so than before, the individual processes of decolonization were also regional and international conflicts, for which there were several reasons. First, neighboring states with pronounced interests of their own increasingly emerged as actors in these conflicts; they acted either as areas of retreat for political and military liberation movements or (like South Africa) as supporters of colonial regimes or anticommunist movements. Second, both blocs in the Cold War were more closely involved, sometimes via diplomatic means, at other times by directly sponsoring parties to armed conflicts. The global bloc formation also helped cushion international pressure on Spain and Portugal as well as the apartheid regime in South Africa for a long time. Third, the international community was also trying harder to help shape the course of events via sanctions, mediation services, and court decisions. With the global delegitimization of colonialism, the justification for sustained racist rule changed. The Rhodesian and South African settler regimes no longer defended their political order in universal, civilizational, or imperial terms but in national terms.[53]

The end of Portuguese colonial rule in 1974–75 marked a critical moment in the subsequent course of Africa's decolonization.[54] Until the end, the "Estado Novo" created by Oliveira Salazar in Portugal held fast to its overseas "lusotropical community," so that decolonization here only became possible via the collapse of a metropolitan dictatorship exhausted by several colonial wars. After India seized Goa in 1961, the regime was determined to defend its African colonies, by force if need be. Angola and Mozambique, two countries rich in raw materials, had become a site for European settlement with the start of the twentieth century. After 1945, official settlement programs, increased development and investment plans (as of 1953), and the coffee and cotton booms set off the largest immigration drive in all of Africa, which raised the number of Europeans in the two colonies to over 500,000. Many of them moved into professions that had previously been practiced by Africans or Indian immigrants. Yet, the settlers here played a smaller role in the decolonization process than in other settler colonies. The Portuguese regime had no place either for white self-government following the Rhodesian model or for the formation of an influential lobby in the metropole as in the Algerian case.

Following initial protests under the leadership of educated elites, one guerrilla war after another erupted in Angola, Guinea-Bissau, and Mozambique at the beginning of the 1960s. As of 1964, Portugal was simultaneously waging three wars of decolonization, each taking a different course. While a unified and militarily successful movement was active in Guinea-Bissau, the Mozambique Liberation Front required a longer phase of consolidation. Most complicated of all was the situation in Angola, where three movements competed with each other. Another contributing factor was a particularly high level of international involvement in the Angolan war of independence. South Africa, Rhodesia, and Congo-Zaire, then later Zambia as well, supported different movements, as did the United States, the Soviet Union, China, and above all Cuba. In Angola, even before formal independence, the liberation struggle gave way to a bloody proxy war. Portugal reacted to the guerrilla movements with a mixture of moderate reforms, investment, modernization, and immigration programs, and military action, even extending to neighboring Guinea in 1970. In 1971–72, the country spent a good half of its public budget on the three wars. It was, however, neither the high costs nor international pressure that were the immediate causes of these wars' end. In April 1974, a group of war-weary young officers toppled the regime. In tandem with Portugal's transition to a republic, the colonies became independent in 1974–75. Metropolitan democratization and decolonization were closely intertwined in the Portuguese case.

The Portuguese colonies' rapidly acquired independence increased pressure on the remaining colonial regimes in Africa. At the end of 1975, shortly before the death of the dictator Franco, Spain withdrew from the Western Sahara, around which a bloody conflict flared between the local liberation movement and the neighboring countries of Mauretania and Morocco. The Rhodesian settler regime also came under intensified pressure. Ever since it seceded in 1965, Rhodesia found itself battling several guerrilla movements. International criticism and sanctions, including a UN embargo, were subverted with the help of the settler regimes in South Africa and (until 1974) Mozambique. Once Angola and Mozambique became independent, Rhodesia was not only deprived of important partners; there was also growing international pressure to seek a negotiated settlement. The United States, above all, feared an internationalization of the guerrilla war, comparable to what had happened in Angola, from which the Soviet Union might profit. Only at the end of 1979 did mediation by the Commonwealth result in a constitutional conference of all parties. Ironically, the path to decolonization led through a transitional period of direct British control.[55] After free elections in April 1980, the country saw its second declaration of independence as Zimbabwe.

The 1960s and 1970s were also critical for decolonization in the island worlds of the Pacific and Indian Oceans and the Caribbean, where some of the oldest colonial territories were located.[56] This crucial period was the time that decided in most cases whether these islands would become independent or remain tied to their metropoles as overseas territories. Once the heart of colonial plantation economy, the Caribbean had become little more than an imperial backwater by the beginning of the twentieth century. A wave of social unrest in the 1930s moved the region back into the focus of attention for European politicians and, in many places, produced the actors (political parties, trade unions) that would later pave the way to independence. The attempt to integrate the British Caribbean in a federal structure remained a short-lived experience. The West Indies Federation (1958–62) disintegrated rapidly after its most important member, Jamaica, left it in 1962. The federation's other major territories, Trinidad and Tobago, Barbados, and the nonmember-observer Guyana, where Great Britain had just taken military action against "communist" nationalists in 1953, became independent between 1962 and 1966; Mauritius in the Indian Ocean followed in 1968.

A second wave set in during the 1970s, when Great Britain and the Netherlands intensified their efforts to rid themselves of the remnants of their colonial possessions; now, even territories and enclaves that colonial planners, just some years before, had deemed too small and economically nonviable as separate states became independent. By the mid-1980s, only a few smaller islands or groups of islands were left. In some cases, the pressure coming from the metropoles was even greater than local aspirations to independence: in Suriname, for example, from which one-third of the entire population, especially from the important Hindustani population, emigrated to the Netherlands concurrent with independence in 1975; or Fiji, where the political elite, in light of the population's Indian majority, feared the loss of British protection following independence in 1970. Against this backdrop, the 1982 Argentinian-British war over the Falklands Islands remained an exception to the rule.

France acted differently, fighting—often in vain—against independence movements in some colonies (such as the New Hebrides and, most notoriously, in New Caledonia). Since 1946, it has tied (to different degrees and to some extent at high cost) most of its colonies in the Caribbean, in the Indian Ocean, and in Polynesia to the metropole and later also to the European Union, especially the "overseas departments" (Départements d'outre-mer, or DOM) Guadeloupe, Martinique, Guiana, and La Réunion (since 2011 also Mayotte).[57] Similarly, the United States did not conduct an active decolonization policy toward its Pacific and Caribbean "unincorporated" territories (most importantly, Puerto Rico and the Virgin Islands), not least with a view toward the revolution that broke US quasi-colonial control over Cuba in 1959. For both the United States and France, the remaining colonies played an important geostrategic role as military bases and nuclear testing zones. Apart from questions of gradual autonomy, it seems, any great push for complete independence seems to have occurred in only a few of the remaining overseas territories.[58] Quite a few among the existing British overseas territories found a particularly profitable economic model in offshore finance. Conflicts over potential national independence play out most virulently in French Pacific territories, even if the 2013 UN decision to reinstate French Polynesia on the list of territories "to be decolonized" has been a divisive issue in Polynesian politics.

The end of apartheid in South Africa at the beginning of the 1990s marked the conclusion of African decolonization.[59] Starting in the 1950s, the African National Congress (ANC) had become a mass movement against the system of racial segregation introduced in 1948. The massacre of black demonstrators in Sharpeville on March 21, 1960, with sixty-nine dead, rang in a phase of intensified repression, in spite of international outrage. Only in the late 1980s did a fundamental change set in. Starting in 1985, there were contacts and later negotiations between the ANC leader Nelson Mandela, imprisoned since 1962, and the Boer government. These led to the country's first free and equal elections in April 1994, from which the ANC and Mandela emerged as victors. In 1990, parallel to the end of apartheid, independence came to Namibia (the former Southwest Africa), which had initially been administered by South Africa as a mandate, then annexed in 1949 against opposition from the United Nations and managed as a South African subcolony.

The dissolution of apartheid happened neither by way of international negotiations (as did Namibia's independence) nor militarily but, rather, via a largely peaceful transition process. What made this possible was the erosion of a regime that can be explained by several factors. First, the mass protests, strikes, boycott and sabotage actions did not break off when the ANC was banned but were continued by trade unions; by women's, youth, and student movements; and by church groups. In the 1980s, the situation in some townships could barely be controlled by the regime. Second, South Africa in the 1980s was increasingly isolated both internationally and regionally. Contributing to this isolation were the ANC's international mobilization effort, the independence won by the remaining settler colonies of central and southern Africa, and South Africa's loss of strategic value with the end of the Cold War. Third, in the 1980s, the regime was weakened by an economic crisis connected to the fall of gold prices, but also to the systematic underdevelopment of the black majority.

The upheavals in South Africa were more far-reaching than the "handover"—as it was officially called—of the city-state of Hong Kong to the People's Republic of China in 1997, which completed a lease agreement concluded ninety-nine years earlier and an intergovernmental accord from 1984. Since the 1970s, the city had been co-governed by China according to British law; and long before that, it had been apparent that the territory could no longer be secured militarily by Great Britain. Enthusiasm among the ex-colony's Chinese majority for the annexation to the mainland was muted. Hong Kong was not released "into independence."

4
ECONOMY

EVEN WHEN THE COLONIAL STATE was unable or unwilling to intervene deeply into the economic life of the colonized, colonization had sweeping economic effects. It introduced new infrastructure, opened up new spaces of trade and migration, created new job and commercial opportunities, changed gender roles and work practices, frequently familiarized people with a modern monetary system, left its imprint on the environment, triggered both individual and collective migration, and redistributed wealth and poverty. Even if colonialism, especially in Asia, only gradually infiltrated existing economic structures, its cumulative impact by the end of the colonial era almost always amounted to an economic revolution.

There was hardly any national movement that aimed at reversing this revolution once the apparatus of colonial rule had been removed. It was sometimes the case, to be sure, that the level of economic and infrastructural development attained in the late-colonial period could not be sustained during the early phase of independence, that industries declined, mines fell into disrepair, and streetcars, streets, and ports decayed, while specialized export production shrank in favor of a subsistence economy. But these were never really the intended outcomes of anticolonial policy or of the will to get rid of the material vestiges of colonialism. The independent governments wanted to follow up on the colonial era's modernization gains. Their principal aim was to place the wealth-enhancing achievements of modern economic life under their own national management and prevent foreigners from profiting from these accomplishments. The elites of the new nation-states understood that only a prospering national economy could guarantee the strongest possible international standing for the fragile new state. In some ex-colonies, socialist programs were deliberately pursued: a high degree of state ownership in industrial plants and transportation services, collectivized or at least cooperative agriculture, and a rudimentary planned economy. These, too, were seen as manifestations of modernity, even as an especially progressive and promising one. The economy provided no occasion for precolonial nostalgia, for retrograde dreams of bucolic innocence.

PRIVATE INTERESTS

Colonialism created specific economic interests wherever it existed. Many members of the colonial powers lived off the empire and saw the dismantling of imperial structures as an attack on their vested rights and interests. Therefore, they attempted to influence the course of decolonization. Only rarely, in the nineteenth and twentieth century, did colonies arise *primarily* out of economic motives, such as "mercantilist" considerations to obtain direct access to raw materials, or to acquire protected and favored outlets for the products of the home economy. But once political control had been established, economic opportunities were exploited, and private businessmen commenced their activities in the protected colonial space. The colonial state was usually too weak to intervene in everyday business. It was not uncommon for the state to grant "concessions," thereby allowing gaps to open up in its sovereignty. Plantation or mine owners then ruled, de facto, without restriction over large enclaves. Especially when it came to the treatment of the local workforce, they did not tolerate any meddling. Sometimes—as when raw materials deemed important needed to be secured—the state could seize the initiative but would then have trouble generating the supplementary commitment it needed from the private sector. Conversely, we do not find many examples of governments acting under *direct* pressure from colonial private interests. In authoritarian systems, where the state placed great value on its autonomy, such responsiveness to direct pressure was as much of an exception as it was in parliamentary-democratic orders, where numerous lobbies competed against each other and the working of government was subject to the control of the legislature and public opinion.

In spite of all this, the significance of the economy in the history of the colonies should not be underestimated. There are several reasons why this is so. First, all colonial powers were interested in making sure that colonies—even ones that they had brought under their own control out of geostrategic considerations or on grounds of prestige—not become projects the state would have to subsidize over the long run. "Empire on the cheap" was an ideal almost universally shared among politicians and administrators. Colonialism therefore needed to be organized cost-effectively.

Second, it so happened that in various places and at different times, there would be a large-scale "drain of wealth" from the colonies to the metropoles. For example, just before the Second World War, the Dutch East Indies still aroused the envy of other colonial powers because that drain proved to be especially successful there, and the colony was a major prop of the Dutch budget.

Third, there were specialized colonial and imperial business interests everywhere. We may distinguish roughly among four kinds of interests: (1) import-export trade and transportation (especially shipping); (2) an indirect financial interest of investors in colonial capital assets, usually mediated by the international banking system centered on London; (3) direct investments and local business operations of foreign firms in the colonies: large farms and plantations, mines, manufacturing industries, infrastructure companies, and the like; and (4) similar activities in the hands of transnational corporations, in whose cross-border strategies a single colony constituted only one element among many. One way that firms of these four types were distinct from each other had to do with their opportunities for influencing policy. This influence was more limited in the case of local business interests confined to the colony than it was for big banks or corporations whose representatives had easier access to ministries, members of parliament, and the media.

Since the economic profiles of the individual colonies were extremely different, it is hard to make any general statements that go further. There can be no disputing the simple rule that even for those colonies that were of little relevance at a macroeconomic level—and some were not much more than a piece of desert or jungle—some private individuals always profited in terms of their particular microeconomics: there was always money to be made in the broad spectrum between the respectable big bank and the obscure gunrunner.

Settlers represented a special type of economic interest. Many colonies were nearly settler-free. In very few cases—most notably in Algeria—the settlers set the political and social tone; in some larger colonies—such as the Dutch East Indies—they did amount to a "critical mass" as a minority within the minority of expatriates. Settlers were not representatives of government agencies or agents dispatched by firms in the metropole; rather, their life was centered in the colony, and they tended to be self-employed entrepreneurs. They developed a local, homeland-like identification with the colony, and above all with its soil, which they viewed as their lawful and heritable property. The typical settler was a farmer; but the spectrum ranged from the aristocratic estate owner in British Kenya to the destitute small peasant settled by the state in Japanese-occupied Manchuria or Italian-held Libya. Private and official settlement, up to a point, followed different logics of political support and economic rentability.[1] Settlers offered the most tenacious resistance to the surrender of colonial positions. One reason was that a racist feeling of their own superiority and indispensability was more widespread than it was among other sections of the colonizing population. A transfer of power was outside the mental horizon of entrenched settler populations. In addition, there seemed to be no alternative to a settler's existence. The largely immobile property of settlers could only be liquidated and taken abroad with great difficulty.

The political influence of settlers was, as a rule, fragile and fleeting. Colonial officials usually saw them as inflexible and stubborn. Hence, there was rarely an alliance between settler interests and the colonial state that proved resilient in times of crisis. Only in the special case of Algeria was this tension weak, since here the settlers were highly autonomous. In the political life of the metropole, settlers were usually only able to gain a hearing in conservative circles that felt a social and racial solidarity with them and saw them as embattled outposts of "civilization." Exploiting this political linkage was easier for the French in Algeria than for settlers in the British Empire, because the former sent representatives to parliament in Paris. In the British case, contacts were predominantly maintained by way of lobbying. This influence was, however, rarely strong enough to commit conservative governments to a hard line in cases like Kenya and Rhodesia.[2] In Portugal, neither the Salazar regime nor its revolutionary successor let itself be used by settlers.[3] Settlers saw themselves as victims of decolonization, and frequently that is what they were.

Greater flexibility could be expected from economic interests less strongly tied to agriculture. In situations of informal empire, where the standard way for safeguarding foreign business interests was through claiming the privileged legal protection afforded by "unequal" treaties, large business corporations made themselves independent quite early. They frequently entered into direct negotiations with national governments in circumvention of the imperial umbrella. In colonies where there were not yet national governments of this kind, it was not only smaller interests in need of greater protection but also larger companies that were inclined to delay any transfer of power for as long as possible; only a few made an early effort to establish good relations with the independence movements. This stance was a logical product of their situation. First, "foreign capital" was an especially visible symbol of foreign rule and hence a frequent target of nationalist protest; at the height of decolonization, boycotts, strikes, and occupations of land or factories were the order of the day. Second, foreign firms did not know what to expect from the new regimes: would it be regimentation, discrimination, higher taxes, or even expropriation? In light of such uncertainty, they felt their situation to be more comfortable within the colonial framework. Pessimists cut back on their investments even before the end of colonial rule or held back information about newly discovered natural resources until a later moment.[4] Sometimes, third parties in a colonial triangle mostly made up of nonwhite commercial minorities with a background in immigration—such as the Chinese in Southeast Asia or Indians in South Africa—stood ready to fill the gaps left by the retreating Europeans.[5]

In the wars of colonial withdrawal, business interests could expect that the military would protect their property up to a certain point. Thus, in the first Dutch postwar military campaign in Indonesia in July and August 1947, the Dutch military looked after mines and plantations from the very outset.[6] This happened, among other reasons, because there was a particularly tight link between the business world and politics in the Netherlands, where colonial business found a strong hearing in a multiparty system dependent on maintaining coalitions. Business interests here vigorously supported those forces that wanted to hold on to the colony after the war.[7] In Great Britain, where the Tories governed from 1951 to 1964, the veto power of private business was much smaller. In France, politicians like Pierre Mendès-France and Charles de Gaulle, who made the seminal decisions on decolonization, hardly let themselves be influenced by the representatives of colonial interests. Generally speaking, the influence of colonial lobbies dwindled as they failed to represent their own interests as those of the nation.

Business interests thus never drove any individual decolonization forward, but they also were seldom able to hold it back in any appreciable way. They played a relatively major role above all in confusing situations that involved a great number of actors, as in the Congo in 1960–63 when secessionist regional politicians, with Belgian support, attempted to split off the copper-rich province of Katanga. During the brief phase of the Central African Federation, too, the copper industry gained considerable influence.[8] Otherwise, the role of private business in the individual transitions from colony to nation-state was a special one in each case. Seldom was the economic presence of foreigners extinguished completely along with the formal transfer of sovereignty. Sometimes new governments moved quickly to gain control of the most vital sectors of the economy. Burma (now Myanmar), for example, did not hesitate to expropriate foreign interests in teak forests and other natural resources. The Iranian parliament and Mohammad Mossadegh's government nationalized the country's oil production in 1951, which had been in British hands. An extreme instance was the People's Republic of China, since it understood its founding in October 1949 as a triumphant "liberation from imperialism" in the broadest possible Leninist sense and immediately proceeded to squeeze out all Western capitalist enterprises.[9] In other cases, such as Indonesia, an ambivalent attitude toward foreign capital hardened gradually over the decade after independence.[10] It often took some time to prepare and implement the necessary legal tools (e.g., laws regulating foreign investment) or to test and improve a country's standing in the international capital markets. Still, even radical economic nationalists—as the experience of Venezuela under President Hugo Chávez was to show in more recent times (1999–2013)—ignore public welfare at their own peril. Foreign business serves functions that are difficult to fulfill otherwise. Apart from aid and credit, both often hardly distinguishable from each other, foreign private investment, for example, was the main source of badly needed capital. The trick was to keep the foreigners in, yet under firm control.

TRANSITIONS

Even if this conflicted with the widely propagated spirit of nationalism: foreign capital and management know-how was, at least initially, needed in order to keep the modern sector of the economy running. The Dutch position in the East Indies collapsed so quickly that no *political* strategy of economic transition could be devised. Under the Japanese occupation between March 1942 and August 1945, Dutch firms were expropriated. Although the Netherlands gave up Indonesia from a position of international weakness, it was strong enough in 1949 to negotiate unusually favorable terms for continuing the economic presence that it renewed after 1945. Only in the years 1957–59 did it come to a de facto nationalization of Dutch firms and the legalization of these measures by the Indonesian parliament (compensation continued to be paid out to former owners until 2003).[11]

The follow-up costs of the colonial period might also include debts that had to be taken over by the independent states. This was a precondition for gaining recognition worldwide as subjects of international law. For most countries, a wholesale renunciation of debt like that following the 1917 Russian and 1949 Chinese revolutions was unthinkable in practical terms. The highest debt was assumed by Indonesia. In negotiations, the gigantic sum of 5.9 billion guilders that the colonial government owed the Dutch treasury was reduced to 3.5 billion guilders (US$1.13 billion). In 1956, when Indonesia's debt was unilaterally revoked, all of it had been repaid except for an amount equal to US$171 million.[12] It was different in the British-Indian case. In the course of the Second World War, India had moved from being a debtor to a creditor of Great Britain. Shortly before independence, the metropole implemented a moratorium that deferred the withdrawal of Indian reserves from the Bank of England.[13]

The French colonial economy in Indochina had a much worse recovery from the Second World War than did the Dutch economy in Indonesia. Above all, mining in the north of Vietnam was damaged physically by the war that was starting in 1946.[14] After the division of Vietnam along the 17th Parallel at the Geneva Indochina Conference of 1954 and the withdrawal of the French military, the state in the southern half of Vietnam remained in the Western orbit but aligned itself economically more and more toward the United States. As early as 1956, France had fallen to third place among South Vietnam's import trading partners, behind the United States and Japan, and in the years to follow it was even outstripped by additional satellite states of the United States like Taiwan and South Korea. In 1958, South Vietnam broke off its relations with the franc zone (founded in 1945). Only a few rubber plantations and business establishments remained French-owned.[15] Here, too, economic decolonization followed political decolonization after a few years' delay.

In agricultural Algeria, plans for industrialization during the Second World War and the war of independence were primarily motivated by political considerations.[16] A majority of French companies remained hesitant, in light of the possibility of independence, even if a few quite consciously invested in Algeria precisely with a view toward that outcome; the major raw material deposits of the Sahara were developed only later on. The war of independence with its massive resettlements and the departure of settlers, professional staff, technical-administrative managers, and private capital signified a major rupture. After an initial phase of large "self-managed" firms, there followed nationalizations and an industrial policy run by the state and financed out of natural gas and petroleum revenues.

In French West Africa, by contrast, precautionary measures were taken for a regulated transition, a precondition for the continued presence of French economic interests. Colonial trade revived after 1945, and colonial business dealings proved extremely profitable for individual firms. Even before independence, French firms and their chambers of commerce also learned how to seek direct contact with African partners instead of asserting their interests exclusively by way of the colonial state.[17] The late-colonial economic boom did happen at the expense of the French balance of payments—a clear example of a contradiction between the micro- and macroeconomic dimensions of colonialism.[18] Moreover, owing to the increased costs of late-colonial social welfare policy, influential consortiums shifted their business toward the European market.

Once again, the British Empire occupied a special position. Only here do we find anything like an imperial economic strategy after 1945, essentially supported by both parties in the

House of Commons. A two-track strategy was intended to cushion the economic consequences of decolonization. First, uniquely among the colonial powers, the United Kingdom could offer its current and former colonies (as well as everyone who wanted to join) a form of monetary integration in the shape of the "sterling area."[19] This zone was a legal construction originating as a makeshift during the Second World War and was retained after the war's end in a situation of great economic insecurity in order to stem the dominance of the US dollar. It served to facilitate trading opportunities for participants and offered a certain degree of protection against turbulence in the world economy. From the standpoint of the historian of empire John Darwin, with his long-term and comparative perspective, the sterling area, which was formally dissolved in 1972 but had already lost its impact before then, was "a closed economic bloc in a way the empire had never been at the height of British economic power."[20] This assessment has a lot to be said for it, especially through 1958, when the convertibility of the British pound, suspended in 1947, was restored.[21]

Second, one can argue that this was not an extension of the empire by other means, not a compulsory union, but instead a rather loose network from which no exploitative center was profiting at the expense of others.[22] The sterling zone was part of a successful policy in the 1950s to maintain a measure of British influence vis-à-vis countries like India, Pakistan, Ceylon, or Indonesia, a policy that also involved the provision of capital aid.[23] It became superfluous to the extent that the more important participants, led by the dominions, sought more than in the past to find trade contacts and capital outside the space of British influence. British policy, for its part, increasingly associated itself with US notions of an open, multilateral world economy. This world economy was never as homogeneous as general economic theories like to suggest. Along tortuous ways, imperial economic connections were slowly transformed into the landscape of interlocking region-alisms that characterize the current Asia-Pacific region—the only part of the globe where, apart from Belgium, all colonial powers of modern times were active at some time or the other.

On the other hand, the intensification of colonial efforts under the banner of development and modernization ini-tially served, above all in Africa, to postpone a constitutional separation, then later to reach a halfway position between maintaining and abdicating rule, and finally to create the pre-conditions for good economic relations with the ex-colonies. Private enterprise was roped into this strategy. This does not, however, mean an automatic identity between the goals of state and business. In the colony of Malaya, which prospered before the war by exporting rubber and tin and came under British control again in the autumn of 1945, an "army of tech-nocrats" attempted to streamline the economy. British firms offered resistance against this dirigisme, since it was accom-panied by a higher tax burden and, in the view of many Brit-ish businessmen, gave preferential treatment to Malayan and Malayan-Chinese producers.[24] However, British policy was less concerned with accommodating colonial business firms than with optimizing colonial economies that would earn precious dollars from their exports to third countries and in this way strengthen the metropole's weak currency base and balance of payments.[25]

It would be a mistake to believe that political and economic elites everywhere in Western Europe clung as long as possible to antiquated positions of imperial power. Especially in France, an increasingly influential current had been taking shape already from the 1930s in the higher levels of public administration and among the boards of large firms that saw the future not only politically but also economically, in an internationally competitive, modernized economy based in the French metropole. Followers of Cartierism (named after the journalist Raymond Cartier) regarded the colonial economy as backward or even parasitic and did not see why the French state was pouring so much money into the administrative maintenance and military defense of unproductive business practices in the colonies. According to this view, France would regain its position in the world not as the colonial guardian of monopolized resources but as a national economy modernized according to the newest standards and under the leadership of enlightened entrepreneurs and bureaucrats.[26] Repeatedly, the *complexe hollandais* was invoked: the economic boom that developed in the Netherlands immediately after the loss of Indonesia and was ascribed by influential commentators to liberation from the colonial burden, at the same time that the costly Indochina war was hindering the French economy's growth through 1953.[27] France's commitment to European supranational integration was entirely in line with such ideas.

Overall, European governments' major decisions about decolonization were made without any ultimately decisive influence from organized business interests. Still, such decisions were arrived at by taking into consideration the economic future of each individual country. In the British case, what mattered was maintaining the pound sterling as a currency with international standing for as long as possible and preserving the City of London's position as the world's financial center. Countries that had become independent were to be kept, both politically and economically, in the Western camp, that is, prevented from a socialist reorientation or even from embracing "neutralism." In the British case, there was the added factor that good relations with the United States were a high-ranking foreign policy objective to which, if need be, particular business interests had to be subordinated.

DEVELOPMENT AND BUSINESS STRATEGIES

Around the mid-1950s, it was no longer possible to overlook the fact that the United States, Western Europe, and a post-imperial Japan would be the future growth poles of the world economy. Trade would mainly be conducted between these regions and cause the old imperial contacts to recede. In the 1950s and 1960s, the countries in the global South that had already become independent or were in transition exhibited less economic growth than the industrial nations of the north. Within the world economy, therefore, they moved into a more marginal position than they had held during the colonial era. From the point of view of the metropoles, there were fewer and fewer economic reasons to maintain colonies or to court special relations with ex-colonies.

Since this period, economic development has been an overriding concern, not only for the new states. The ambiguous and protean concept of "development" became a powerful intellectual template that helped organize the postcolonial world into several groups or "worlds"—from the developed to the developing, less developed, or underdeveloped world. After European postwar reconstruction and in parallel to the unfolding Cold War, the two superpowers, industrialized countries (including the former colonial powers), and international agencies (such as the World Bank) turned toward international development as a new field of activity. Development aid—that is, different forms of financial and technical support for less developed countries—became an important element of bilateral and international cooperation, in which a growing number of national agencies, international organizations, NGOs, and think tanks engaged. Ever since the postcolonial states acquired more influence in the United Nations and its suborganizations, the criteria, goals, and means of international development, the terms of international trade, and the access to natural resources have been contentious issues in international politics and a main arena of the North-South conflict.

In many postcolonial states, this preoccupation with economic (and social) development was not entirely new. Attempts at modernizing agriculture by mechanization and land reform had been characteristic of the late-colonial phase; large and ambitious agro-industrial projects such as peanut plantations in British Tanganyika became famous for their failures involving heavy losses. There are numerous continuities with postcolonial development policy in terms of personnel, institutions, and concepts.[28] Each of the new states dealt with this kind of late-colonial legacy in its own way, with differences among them about whether, in what form, and for how long each state persisted in retaining and continuing economic *planification* (characteristically, a French term) and social welfare services. The ideal of the interventionist state, a bequest from the late-colonial period,[29] was fortified, from India to West Africa, by socialist models of varying strictness and design. Well into the 1970s, development under state guidance and technocratic-scientific planning remained a program on which nationalists of almost all shades could agree. While there was a great variety of strategies among the new states, quite a few among them saw state-run industrialization policy as the high road to development. Many postcolonial regimes and their international donors practiced modernization with a rigidity that was equal to what the late-colonial state had attempted to do. The social and ecological consequences were often no less devastating.

In numerous countries of Asia and Africa, the 1950s and 1960s were a period of moderate but stable economic growth that allowed a certain latitude about the state's expansion of the educational and health care system. In this period, however, financial obligations were incurred that, with the series of "oil shocks" starting in 1973, became an additional burden for many countries, particularly in sub-Saharan Africa. The ensuing period of development through imposed structural adjustment programs, with their tendency toward massive cuts in public expenditure and market liberalization, was experienced in many African (and Latin American) countries as the new dawn of exogenous rule.

What happened to foreign firms during the transition from colony to nation-state? We should bear in mind that transnational capital and cross-border manufacturing ties are not necessarily of a "colonial" nature but have been quite normal between developed economies since the nineteenth century. What mostly gave offense was *political* preference for expatriate business. The more it had relied on unequal privilege, the more vulnerable it became once the framework of protection was dismantled. A great deal of local business activity of those foreigners who remained soon had no place in the new national economic order. Trade, transportation, small businesses, and parts of manufacturing industries quickly moved into indigenous hands. Less dispensable in many cases were multinational corporations. In general, they had fared well under colonialism, which guaranteed an economic environment similar to the European order: calculable, with little corruption, and having extensive and reliable legal safeguards. The state's willingness and capability to suppress labor unrest was much greater than in Europe. As so often occurred during decolonization, uncertainty replaced the deceptive calm of the colonial period. Since most of the new states also made use of their sovereignty vis-à-vis large corporations, this familiar security and predictability became a thing of the past. On the other hand, the multinationals were welcome in principle as investors, taxpayers, employers, and perhaps sources of corruption for ruling oligarchs and the beneficiaries of "crony capitalism."[30] Their economic weight could assure them considerable negotiating power.

When companies stayed on, they could hardly afford to cultivate old imperial ties for merely sentimental reasons. Many of them salvaged or even strengthened their position in the economy of an ex-colony by inserting themselves into post-imperial networks of trade and capital. Thus, the potent British investment groups in Malaya (Malaysia since 1963) increasingly distanced themselves from the ailing British economy and developed new markets in Southeast Asia, the United States, and Europe.[31] As the competitive advantage of empire faded away, business adapted to changing circumstances. At the same time, foreign corporations frequently struck bargains with such governments in developing countries that were resistant to easy manipulation. Quite a few schemes of "Africanization" in the economic field were partly genuine and partly propaganda and camouflaged all sorts of compromise, though everywhere the moment of truth came when joint ventures had to function in real life on the basis of a genuine common interest. Foreign companies also had to keep in mind the general public of voters and consumers in the new order of majority rule. Staying on after the demise of colonial protection demanded projecting an image of attractiveness and benevolence and expressing sympathy with the dynamism and hopefulness of the young nation.[32]

Whereas political decolonization can be defined formally as the beginning of self-government and the exclusive validity of homemade laws, economic decolonization is a matter of degree. Only in a minority of cases has its concomitant ideology—economic nationalism—aimed at complete autarky and the expulsion of any "alien" factor from native economic life. Economic decolonization followed upon political decolonization with a certain time lag and was a part of strategies of transition pursued both by rulers of the new states and in company boardrooms (although for India, already in the 1930s the United States and Japan were becoming more important trade partners than Britain[33]). In many cases, the actors involved had a choice between alternative options.[34] Sometimes the economic side of liberation was extended beyond a simple confrontation between European business and indigenous political power. Then, commercial minorities such as Chinese in Southeast Asia, Greeks in Egypt, or Indians in Africa became target groups of a new economic nativism that justified the ethnic purification of the national economy through an explosive mixture of xenophobia and the paranoid obsessions of the Cold War era. Diaspora groups that could be construed as intruding agents of world market forces, and perhaps comprador elites under the colonial regime, were particularly vulnerable.

Consumption leads us finally to some important roots of economic decolonization. The primacy of political change in the sequence of decolonizing acts and measures should not obscure the fact that many of the most widely shared grievances against colonial rule had been of an economic nature: high taxes, bad treatment of workers, ruthless exploitation of natural resources, discrimination against indigenous business, and so on. These charges were often highly ambivalent: Were harsh labor relations in mines and plantations worse than having no jobs at all? Were native employers really always more benign than expatriate capitalists? Such ambivalence was especially marked when it came to the consumption of imported goods. While Western commodities from the cigarette to the watch and the motorcar were widely coveted and prized as symbols of prestige and tokens of modernity,[35] some of the most spectacular and effective outbursts of popular rage were directed at exactly such manifestations of imported progress. The broadly based consumer boycott or holdup, sometimes linked with strikes in foreign-run factories or public facilities, became a favorite weapon of economic nationalism across the colonial and semicolonial world. Peaceful "buy native" campaigns and violent attacks on European-owned property were two sides of the same coin.[36] Economic decolonization frequently was not just an elite project but a widely popular though deeply ambiguous concern inspired, not only for the ascetic Mohandas Gandhi, by a collective wish to get rid of a contamination through Western materialism and consumerism. This attitude carried over into the period of transition when boycotts accompanied many of the changes that were under way.

5
WORLD POLITICS

A distinction that emerged in the 1960s saw the international situation characterized by two "conflict formations" that complemented and intersected each other: the East-West conflict and the North-South conflict. This distinction is mainly an analytical device that helps to disentangle the dynamic complexities of an age when international relations could no longer be described merely in terms of war and peace between great powers and their empires. The two dimensions gave rise to different historiographies that are being brought together only recently.[1] The East-West conflict, often called the Cold War, was about the mutual threat posed to each other by the two superpowers, the United States and the Soviet Union.[2] Each of these superpowers gathered a camp of dependent and militarily protected states around itself, a camp that was also held together by ideological commonalities at the level of elite thinking. The liberal and capitalist West confronted an authoritarian and socialist East. While there had been *world* powers in the nineteenth and early twentieth century that pursued "world politics," the *super*powers that emerged during and after the Second World War went beyond all previous forms of large-scale politics. They had at their disposal nuclear weapons of mass destruction as well as land- and sea-based launching systems with an intercontinental range. The superpowers could use these arsenals, by the early 1960s at the latest, to reach every point on the globe. Both sides also had a second-strike capability, meaning that they retained enough nuclear material for a retaliatory strike in response to an atomic assault. Hence, there was—as it was called at the time—a "balance of terror" between the two camps.

Nuclear weapons were only usable for strategic deterrence, not for tactical warfare. They were not an extension of imperialist gunboat diplomacy, because they did not lend themselves to putting pressure on third states *outside* the two blocs. By no means did this make conventional war irrelevant in the "Atomic Age." On the contrary: arming even the smallest and poorest of the world's states became a business that attained unprecedented levels, and millions of soldiers and civilians met their deaths in wars during the second half of the twentieth century.[3]

The camp led by the Soviet Union comprised the states of the Warsaw Pact (founded 1955), Outer Mongolia, Cuba, and (less clearly) North Korea. The American camp included the members of the North Atlantic Treaty Organization (NATO, founded 1949) along with Japan, South Korea, Taiwan, Thailand, the Philippines, and other states in which the US military was stationed. Unlike the Soviet Union, the United States maintained a worldwide system of military bases that was no less important for the West than outright control over territories.

The picture of a simple East-West confrontation is complicated by the fact that many states belonged to neither of the
two camps, whether by treaty or by informal affinity. This
third group in world politics was quite heterogeneous and
had no overarching organization. A movement of the non-
committed had been initiated in a hopeful spirit in the 1950s,
above all at the 1955 Asian-African Conference in Bandung,
Indonesia, but thereafter it found it difficult to acquire more
than a modicum of influence on world politics, not least
owing to internal disagreements.[4] This third category of the
nonaligned included socialist states concerned about their independence, such as Yugoslavia and Romania, as well as such
countries as India, which avoided clear ideological bonds.

In addition, there was a whole series of cases that were sui
generis. This included the People's Republic of China, which
had freed itself from its role as the Soviet Union's junior partner at the beginning of the 1960s and even went to the brink
of war with its erstwhile "brother nation" in 1969. Another
special case was South Africa. This was a politically conservative, capitalist country that fulfilled all conditions for be-
longing to the West with the exception of its extremely racist
ideology and practice, which complicated any explicit membership in the "free world" (as the West called itself).[5] While
China abandoned the Eastern bloc and steered a course of
unaligned independence, Iran mutated with the Islamic revolution of 1978–79 from a zealous protégé of the United States
into a wildly anti-American power that was also hardly taken
with the atheistic Soviet Union, the successor to Iran's old
nemesis: the Russian Empire.

The East-West conflict was thus played out not only in
the North Atlantic and along the "Iron Curtain" (as Winston

Churchill called it) in Central Europe. The superpowers contended for influence all over the world, including in regions where they could not station troops directly. There they used economic assistance or dispatched military advisers as instruments for securing loyalty indirectly. China, now acting autonomously, also tried to win clients for itself in Africa during the early 1970s using similar strategies of material aid and symbolic recognition. The global character of the Cold War was manifested in the way that the conflict between the United States and Soviet Union shaped the foreign policy of every state. Even those that wished to remain neutral needed to keep redefining and permanently negotiating this neutrality within the inescapable framework of tension created by the superpowers. Calling the Cold War a special type of world order may overemphasize its stable and static dimension. Beneath the nuclear stalemate at the strategic level, the Cold War was an ever-shifting field of power relations where actors were under continuous pressure to define and defend their interests, bargain about loyalties, and test their room for maneuver.

It is harder to understand what "North-South" conflict might mean.[6] This designation arose from the long and rich history of anticolonial resistance and struggles to improve one's position within empires or even to escape from them. In contrast to East-West conflict, this term is not about military power, nuclear deterrence, or territorial spheres of interest. Rather, it is about a revolt by poor countries—above all, in the tropical and subtropical regions of the planet—against unfair relations of dependence on the powerful and affluent countries of the northern hemisphere. The North-South conflict was carried as much with weapons as with words, mainly at the forum of the United Nations in New York. It was and still is a battle for gaining a hearing in world public opinion. Its goal was not—as in the East-West conflict—to weaken the adversary militarily and economically, and to discredit it ideologically, but to champion new principles of international justice and global governance. Since this was about changing balances in the world economy, the critique made by countries from the "Third World"—a term that became popular with the decolonization wave of the 1960s—was directed less against the "Second World," meaning the Soviet bloc, than against the US-dominated West (the "First World"), which set the conditions for international trade and capital flows.

To the extent that the conflict between the South and North assumed militant forms, the actors could sometimes be, for example, governments that might nationalize foreign assets, or armed liberation movements that attacked client regimes of the West. A special case was the monopolistic pricing policy of the Organization of Petroleum Exporting Countries (OPEC) from 1973 onward, the group in which the oil-producing countries had joined forces. This led to the most radical and successful reversal of the South's economic dependence, without being motivated by any ideological reservations the oil producers might have had against the "neo-imperialist" North. At the same time, rising world market prices for natural resources only favored their producers while they caused trouble for fuel-importers in the South. The biggest war that a very rich and a very poor nation conducted against each other, the Vietnam war, was also atypical: it was not a case of a world-revolutionary uprising, but a classic defensive action by a nation-state in the making against outside aggression.

Decolonization can be situated at the intersection of the East-West conflict and the North-South antagonism; it was always embedded in a two-dimensional matrix. The Cold War was not triggered by decolonization. But, at least in East and Southeast Asia, the colonial powers had already become acquainted with communist parties and movements since the 1920s and, in this way, also with the Comintern, which tried to control these forces from out of Moscow during the interwar period. Immediately after the war, Stalin did not explicitly pursue a strategy of world revolution, but any communist party in the colonial and semicolonial world was likely to aim at national liberation and to enjoy some kind of support from the Soviet Union. That the communist factor only played a marginal role in the independence of India contributed to the general approval this signal event met with on the international stage. Both the United States and the Soviet Union welcomed the demise of British India, and the departing imperial power resigned, amid chaos and local violence, to its long-expected fate while hoping to keep South Asia in its Commonwealth orbit. The rupture between the United States and the Soviet Union that occurred in 1947–48 over European issues (Greece, Czechoslovakia, Berlin), was not causally related to the colonial empires' beginning dissolution—a process that was, during those years, by no means generally anticipated as an unstoppable sea change in world history. But both superpowers understood that Asia and the Middle East would not revert to colonial languor of a prewar type. Europe would no longer be the only arena of great power antagonism.

The roots of decolonization and the antagonism between the Soviet Union and the Western powers can both be traced back to those seminal years after the end of the First World

War, when hopes were raised of worldwide self-determination while the young Bolshevik state was treated as a pariah among nations. In the aftermath of the Second World War, the specious Wilsonian moment of 1919–20 reappeared as a much more promising and less charismatic "San Francisco moment" of 1945. The United Nations Charter promised "equal rights" to "nations large and small" (preamble), and the new world organization was established with active participation of delegates from China, India, and South Africa in a spirit of inclusiveness, if only with the built-in contradiction between the revitalized idea of trusteeship and demands for genuine equality. In contrast to 1919, when emissaries and private individuals from many quarters of the globe had been lobbying the three dominant statesmen in Paris, the founding of the United Nations encouraged better organized initiatives of anticolonial activism.[7] This was a moment of supreme openness: Would the United Nations preserve the colonial status quo, or would it inaugurate a post-imperial world order? And would the alliance of the victorious powers shape the future international scene as it did at the Potsdam conference?

A few weeks after the signing of the Charter, however, the atomic bombs on Hiroshima and Nagasaki indicated that the price of peace was the rise of a new kind of warfare. The true novelty of 1945 was not the prospect of a world of equal nations and nation-states but the new inequality in an age of superpowers. The unprecedented order of nuclear bipolarity took some time to gain shape. It reached the maturity of a stable equilibrium at the very moment when African decolonization was sped up, China became an independent player, and the United States began to get militarily involved in Vietnam and the Middle East. By that time, a reciprocal interaction had developed between the Cold War and decolonization. No single North-South conflict was free from an East-West dimension after Fidel Castro's shadow fell over Latin America from 1959. Concurrently, the clash of East and West extended to Third World theaters once, after the Cuban missile crisis of 1962, détente had lowered the temperature of confrontation in Europe and the Atlantic.

COLD WAR: FROM KOREA TO ANGOLA

In spite of cross-border "pan-"movements and numerous contacts between anticolonial activists in different countries, until the Second World War every move in the direction of independence was, in a way, an internal matter for each individual empire. The World War weakened the position of the Europeans in Asia irreversibly. With the fall of Singapore in 1942, the big strategic clamp broke that had held the British Empire together from Suez to New Zealand. Unlike what happened after the First World War, the United States did not withdraw from the former war zone but instead assumed the role of leading power in the Pacific. Since 1945, every kind of European colonial policy in Asia was subject to tacit or explicit US approval.

The central element of the new American strategy in Asia was building Japan into the greatest of all "unsinkable aircraft carriers" (a designation from the Second World War for naval bases on islands) for the United States. This was facilitated by the way that the surprise dropping of atomic bombs in August 1945 thwarted any participation of the Soviet Union in the occupation of Japan. The Philippines became the second anchor of American power, and Thailand quite soon turned into another reliable ally. Initially, the United States came to terms only reluctantly with the "loss" of China, much bemoaned by conservative hardliners. It did not use ground troops to support the anticommunist Guomindang in the Chinese civil war (1946–49), nor did it even try pressing its protégé Chiang Kai-shek toward accepting a north-south division of China, to which Stalin might have consented though perhaps not the Chinese communists. The People's Republic, founded in October 1949, signed with the Soviet Union a "treaty of friendship, alliance and mutual assistance" in 1950. Thus arose, from the Western perspective, a "red" continental bloc extending from the Elbe to the Yellow Sea.

President Franklin D. Roosevelt was convinced that old-style colonialism had become obsolete; he left no doubt about this in discussions with his European partners. His successor, Harry S. Truman, in office as of April 1945, expressed himself more cautiously, although initially he did not fundamentally depart from Roosevelt's anticolonial line. The United States expected that the Europeans would reestablish themselves relatively smoothly in Southeast Asia (Africa did not play a role in these considerations). But then US diplomats strongly recommended that the Europeans take the rapid and soft decolonization of the Philippines—creating strong postcolonial ties to the former colonial power—as a model.[8] For the United States, no less than for the Europeans, it was surprising how profoundly the Japanese occupation and the war had interfered with the societies of Asia affected by the occupation and how strong the liberation movements had become everywhere. Nowhere was it possible to speak of a peaceful transition on the Philippine model. Since the turn of the century, the larger region had been almost permanently in a state of war. This great war for Asia continued after 1945—in marked contrast to the pacification of Europe. It would go on until the withdrawal of the last US troops from Vietnam in 1975.[9]

Until 1949, the United States was primarily striving for stability in Asia, in order, among other reasons, to facilitate the rehabilitation of foreign markets for its own exporters and for what had now become its most important partner in the Asia-Pacific: Japan. Hence, Indonesian independence in 1949 still met with American approval; it was even accelerated by US pressure on the Netherlands. Only North Korea's unexpected invasion of the southern peninsula below the 38th Parallel in June 1950 and the entry of the People's Republic of China into the war in October, which turned the conflict into a de facto Chinese-American war, altered the situation. It nourished the impression that a monolithic communism was even more aggressively on the march in Asia than in Europe and called into question the new hegemony of the United States.[10] The Cold War had come to Asia. From now on, the United States supported every action that would curb and "contain" communism. Truman and his successor, Dwight D. Eisenhower, did recoil, however, from a more aggressive rollback of communism. They reined in those military officers who recommended using nuclear weapons against the Chinese and Vietnamese communists.

Even after 1950, the United States had no intention of restoring prewar European colonialism. The old European colonialism served America merely as a means to the end of containing communism. From an American perspective, there was a visible or invisible front stretching across the entire globe. The states and regimes along this front needed to be strengthened, whether or not they were colonies. European powers could count on American support if they managed to convince the United States that they were indispensable in the battle against communism. The French in particular proved successful taking this approach in Indochina, where after 1950, the United States assumed a constantly growing share of the war's costs, around 40 percent by the end of the French engagement.[11] From the American perspective, Vietnam was worth this effort above all because Ho Chi Minh was receiving extensive military help from Communist China. From this point on, likewise, it became a goal of American policy to prevent the victory of communist forces in Laos and Cambodia. The withdrawal of the French from Indochina in 1954 was nevertheless bearable for American policy because a durable north-south division of Vietnam following the Korean model began to take shape. That such hopes for a pro-Western and simultaneously domestically stable southern state came to naught, mainly for local reasons, was the root cause of the United States' subsequent military intervention. The British Empire also received an array of American support. Thus, as of around 1950, the empire's character changed so that it became "more than British and less than an imperium."[12]

Experiences in Asia from the early 1950s, reinforced in 1959 by the revolution in Cuba, nourished a way of thinking in US policy that can be characterized as aggressive defensiveness or even paranoia: everywhere in the world, anti-Western machinations of a communism controlled from Moscow were a threat and had to be fought preventively. This communism was said to operate covertly, to camouflage itself, and to abuse naive centrist forces as allies, "useful idiots," and "crypto-communists." This danger was held to be especially great in Asia and Africa, because these parts of the world were regarded as lacking a capacity for self-government.[13] A country "infested" with communism would "infect" its neighbors. This diagnosis dictated a strategy of lending economic support to European empires, above all in places where they were fighting against radical insurgency movements (as with the British in Malaya). In the unavoidable process of independence and during the period immediately following, "moderate" politicians ("reformers") had to be located and provided with resources. In no case should there arise a "power vacuum" into which communism might advance—as the Eisenhower administration feared in the Middle East following the Suez crisis.[14] Members of NATO were expected to participate worldwide in the anticommunist struggle. During the 1960s, the British government in particular found itself caught in a dilemma between an empire-weary public at home and the American expectation that it should make its presence felt at distant fronts of the Cold War.[15]

The more rigid the nuclear balance of terror became, the more opportunities for nationalist movements opened up in arenas throughout the Third World. Nasser's victory during the Suez crisis was a much admired model that was not always easy to copy. National liberation within the strategic triangle of the colonial power, the United States, and the Soviet Union had its heroes but also its martyrs (e.g., Patrice Lumumba). When the great African decolonization wave took place around 1960, there was still little direct interference from the United States and Soviet Union.[16] As a rule, the superpowers were wary of meddling with individual transfers of power. Rather, they became interested in the new states once independence had been proclaimed. The first and principal exception was the Belgian Congo—the cockpit of the Cold War in 1960s Africa. The Congo crisis was the first instance when

African politics became polarized along pro-Western vs. anti-imperialist lines.[17] Thereafter, the attention of the Cold Warriors in both camps was drawn to the continent on a broad basis. At that time, conflict focused on the remaining Portuguese colonies and on the white supremacy states in southern Africa. For settler regimes, increasingly ostracized internationally because of their racism, anticommunism became their most important rationale for legitimation and even an incentive to destabilize the postcolonial states in their neighborhood. For their part, liberation movements and secessionist groups gladly accepted military and economic assistance from the Soviet Union and its satellites. The charms of socialism for newly independent states should not be underestimated. African elites were genuinely attracted to a strong state's self-imposed task of keeping political order and to visions of transformation that emphasized a "scientific" approach to social planning. In many multiethnic states, a socialist political language had the enormous advantage of being ethnically neutral. To some extent, a Marxist rhetoric without any relationship to actual revolutionary practice was gladly adopted by many of the new governments. Military regimes were showing a special fondness for filling an ideological void with verbal radicalism.[18] Just like the West, the Eastern bloc also offered civilian assistance in the spheres of health and education. The Soviet Union provided some military hardware ever since the onset of the Cold War but became a large-scale arms dealer only after decolonization: in the 1980s, the Soviet Union exported three times as many weapons to the Third World than did the United States.[19]

The most intensive overlap between decolonization and the Cold War occurred in the 1970s in connection with the battles for independence in the Portuguese colonies and the struggles for their postcolonial future. For the first time, Marxist regimes came into being south of the Sahara. In Angola during the mid-1970s, whether directly or by way of native proxies, the Soviet Union, Cuba (at times with as many as 50,000 soldiers), China, the United States, and South Africa were all involved in military action.[20] After the sudden withdrawal of the Portuguese, these wars of liberation morphed into internationalized civil wars that sometimes lasted until the East-West confrontation was over.[21] From 1961 to 1991 (and with offshoots lasting through 2002), Angola experienced its very own Thirty Years' War with hundreds of thousands dead.[22]

ELEMENTS OF A NEW ORDER

Decolonization did not by itself create a new international order. The East-West confrontation lasted until 1990 as the overarching pattern of world politics. The enormous increase in the number of sovereign states and statelets was absorbed into the existing configurations of power and easily accommodated by the United Nations and its agencies. None of the new nation-states created since the independence of South Korea, India, and Indonesia rose to become even a great power or a beacon of stability and prosperity within its own region. The postcolonial (mainly economic) success stories since the 1960s—Trinidad, Singapore, Brunei, or the former British protectorates on the Persian Gulf—are highly specific cases and exceptions to a general rule.

Western support for postcolonial dictatorships like Mobutu Sese Seko's rule in Congo/Zaire (now the Democratic Republic of the Congo) and the interventions carried out by a vari-

ety of external forces in Africa in the 1970s caused immeasur-
able damage, but they did not contribute in a major way to
weakening the Soviet Union and thus to ending the Cold
War. Only the Soviet invasion of Afghanistan, a country
never successfully colonized heretofore, which began in December 1979 and would soon turn out to be incredibly costly,
spelled the beginning of the end for the Soviet Union. Ironically, the erstwhile champion of worldwide anti-imperialism
was fatally enfeebled by a colonial occupation undertaken in
the immediate aftermath of the disappearance of the Western
empires.[23]

Where decolonization did have a lasting impact on world
politics was in changing the conceptual underpinnings of the
international order. It put to the test its normative foundations and made many things that had been taken for granted
during the age of empire unthinkable or at least unspeakable.
Even if there were more than just anti-imperialist impulses at
work in its emergence, the United Nations and some of its
suborganizations (such as UNCTAD, UNDP, and UNESCO)
did become, during and after the decolonization process,
arenas for articulating "Southern" views and interests.[24] The
United Nations contributed greatly to the process that gradually made the principle of national state sovereignty absolute
and uncontestable. Only the governments of nation-states
were acceptable actors on the world stage in New York, apart
from a few special cases such as the Palestine Liberation Organization (PLO), which was granted "observer status" by the
United Nations General Assembly in 1974.[25] Since around 1960,
the struggle for legitimacy and recognition came to be conducted everywhere with an eye to the General Assembly, and
to international public opinion with its broad range of media.

That was also the year when the United Nations proclaimed "the necessity of bringing to a speedy and unconditional end colonialism in all its forms and manifestations."[26] However, world opinion was influenced with varying skill and success: if Great Britain was still able to present the Mau Mau uprising internationally as a civilizing battle against antimodern "barbarians," and thus retain its control over how that uprising was interpreted, the FLN later succeeded in mobilizing international pressure against France's warfare in Algeria.[27] Unlike the partition of India or the Chinese civil war of the late 1940s, which were only flimsily covered by the international media and of which very few images of violence and misery are being recalled by posterity, real wars since then have been duplicated as wars of headlines and images.

"Racism"—often understood so broadly as to encompass numerous forms of ethnic and cultural discrimination—came to be internationally ostracized as a result of decolonization.[28] At the same time, "colonialism" changed from a more or less neutral label for a particular historical condition into a weapon of international opprobrium, whether directed against the United States (in Iraq), Indonesia (in East Timor and Western New Guinea), China (in Tibet), or Israel (in the West Bank). That human rights became a yardstick for evaluating political systems and a major topic of international law and political philosophy after the Second World War is widely due to the critique of late colonialism, and especially to outrage over practices used to suppress liberation movements.[29] Western Europeans had, on the one hand, promoted the ideas of unconditionally valid individual rights and constitutional procedures (the rule of law) as some of their civilization's greatest achievements. In practice, on the other hand, they repeatedly retracted these principles during the numerous military and police actions of the late-colonial era.[30] To be sure, diplomats and jurists from the Third World, in addition to any stress they laid on the rights of the individual, emphasized at least as much a *collective*—or "Wilsonian"—right to national self-determination as the prerequisite for the guarantee for individual human rights.[31]

The imprint decolonization left on the normative foundations of the international order quickly developed a life on its own. While human rights discourse had served anticolonial movements to uncover European hypocrisy during the late-colonial period, many postcolonial regimes were later confronted with their own poor human rights records. And even after colonialism as a system of alien rule has largely disappeared, self-determination has proven an indomitable principle that both former colonial powers and postcolonial states have grappled with.

6
IDEAS AND PROGRAMS

DECOLONIZATION WAS NOT just something that happened in the realm of politics and economics; it also took place in the world of ideas and discourses. This is true even if one's explanation for the end of the colonial empires is not primarily based on the emergence of emancipatory ideologies. The transitions between political and intellectual activity in Asian, African, and Caribbean liberation movements were often fluid: many intellectuals were not just following events from the position of a remote observer but were active participants. After 1945, for example, pan-African thinkers Aimé Césaire, Leopold Senghor, and Jomo Kenyatta were also establishing themselves as leading politicians in their home countries of Martinique, Senegal, and Kenya. And even those who in practice saw themselves primarily as freedom fighters (such as Gandhi or Sukarno) frequently reflected on their actions and embedded their approach in elaborate systems of thought and historical references; Gandhi's *Collected Works*, published by the Government of India, fill ninety-seven volumes of densely printed text.[1] Decolonization thus constituted "as much a verbal contest as it was a set of physical confrontations."[2]

While it is possible to identify a few common and constantly reiterated motifs in colonialist thought and ideology across the empires,[3] the thinking of the decolonization era reaches a level of polyphony that makes the reduction to a few standard tropes nearly impossible. The most plausible candidates for some widely shared ideas may be discerned in some—ambiguous and emphatic—keywords from the various programs of emancipation: "freedom," "self-determination," and "development." These concepts had an aura that was already fading when they became (as they remain, to some extent, even today) the mantra of authoritarian postcolonial regimes. Yet behind these concepts there is thinking that is rich and differentiated. This thinking does not simply boil down to a fierce indictment of the excesses of colonial rule or to utopian visions of total self-government. Instead, what evolved was a broad spectrum of analyses and future scenarios, each of which needs to be seen in its respective (biographical, social, and political) context and sphere of activity: from hard-hitting journalistic reportage on the realities of colonial rule and poetic reflection on the human consequences of colonization to the historiographic or ethnological upgrading of non-European civilizations, from religious reform movements to economic development programs, from specific forms of political liberalism to the theory of people's war. Decolonization bequeathed to contemporary thought a dazzling legacy that questioned many old certainties—and continues to do so.

THEMES AND POSITIONS

An intellectual history of decolonization could be written as a long series of anticolonial thinkers (from Sun Yat-sen[4] and Marcus Garvey through Senghor and Nehru to Ho Chi Minh and Frantz Fanon), their liberation ideologies, programs, and analyses, as well as their mutual influence on each other.[5] An undertaking like this tends toward the formation of canons. And it raises many questions which can be answered in very different ways: Should such an intellectual history only comprise ideas of thinkers from the global South, some of which are only partly connected in any direct way with post-1945 decolonization (such as the Islamic modernism of Jamal al-Din al-Afghani, who had died already in 1897)? Or are we dealing with thinking *about* decolonization that was also shaped by writers and political activists from ex-metropoles or from uninvolved countries? Should only "revolutionary" and charismatic leaders have a say, or political pragmatists and sober-minded scholars as well; only "modern" urban intellectuals with command of influential media, or also "peasant intellectuals" and local journalists?

Another possibility is to start looking for key areas in the history of ideas, for the intellectual challenges that fostered the end of colonial empires and that, in turn, were raised by decolonization.[6] This allows us to capture voices both in the formerly colonized world and in the ex-metropoles, as well as to do justice to the overlap between intellectual and practical-political questions. At least four such challenges may be discerned: the "discovery" of decolonization as a normal historical path; the different ways of thinking about postcolonial sovereignty; the interpretation of colonialism as a historically finite situation; finally, the "invention" of the Third World as a new concept for world order.

(*1*) *Naturalizing decolonization.* In spite of what people knew about the decline and fall of previous empires, modern colonial empires lived well into the twentieth century with a belief in their own permanence. This illusion of permanence also withstood the early attacks from Asian and African thinkers who, since the late nineteenth century, started to imagine their world free from imperial—mostly European—rule.[7] The "discovery" of decolonization—in other words, the transformation of decolonization from something anomalous into an irreversible, and unavoidable historical fact—is therefore one of the most remarkable events in twentieth-century history of political ideas. Like decolonization itself, its intellectual naturalization was a process that took place at different times in different regions, though overall it caught on with astonishing speed. The Algerian war of independence played a key role here—and not only for France.[8] Like no other decolonization conflict, this war was accompanied by fundamental intellectual controversies: many intellectuals and scholars were even involved in one way or another in the war. The debates surrounding Algeria in the late 1950s and early 1960s therefore make it especially fascinating to observe how thinking about civilization in terms of universal norms and values and the widespread belief in the desirability and feasibility of a complete "assimilation" of non-European societies to generally valid civilizational standards were replaced by the notion that these societies and their members were irreducibly different. The long-cherished idea of making Algeria and its inhabitants into an integral part of France ultimately came to be regarded as an illusion. The regulations of citizenship that followed the war mirrored this intellectual turnaround in political and legal practice.

From this moment, at the latest, "decolonization" was no longer only a technical term for the transfer of power; it designated the overall sweep of history. This idea also caught on around 1960 in the political discourse of the metropoles. Above all, the naturalization of decolonization showed up in the way that administrative documents, political speeches, and contemporary public diagnoses increasingly characterized it as something analogous to a force of nature. An especially frequent metaphoric usage was to talk about a "storm," "the tide of history," or "the current of history."[9] Certainly the catchiest formula, repeated over and over again, is the "wind of change" that British prime minister Harold Macmillan saw blowing through Africa at the beginning of 1960.[10]

(2) *Varieties of sovereignty.* It did not follow inevitably from the alleged naturalness of decolonization what goal this historical process might have. Another aspect of Asian-African decolonization was the contest of ideas about what should replace authoritarian colonial relations of subjugation. The 1940s and 1950s were a phase of intense political imagination about postcolonial forms of sovereignty. Although it had already been embraced by the Atlantic Charter and the nascent United Nations, the completely "sovereign" nation-state did not constitute the only intellectual point of reference. Anti-imperialist thinkers as different as Rabindranath Tagore and Frantz Fanon provided powerful critiques of nationalism as the presumed one and only alternative to colonialism. Pan-Arab, pan-Maghreb, and pan-African solidarity as well as a new emphasis on religious affiliations suggested frames of ref-

erence for political vision and practice that transcended territorial borders.

Federative thinking had a secure place in late-colonial planning as well as in African and Arab anticolonialism. Even if it has attracted new interest in a time more skeptical of the emancipatory potential of nation-states, it is not clear if supranational federalism would have provided a lasting framework for a post-imperial, post-racist, and more egalitarian age. Late-colonial and early postcolonial federalism was no less multifaceted and ambiguous than nationalist thinking. It ranged from plans for sustained colonial or neocolonial rule to designs for a more egalitarian post-imperial order. Building on larger imperial traditions, schemes for federal units popped up in various parts of the disintegrating British, French, and Dutch empires—in places such as Indonesia, Malaysia, South Arabia, French West Africa, the French-controlled parts of the Sahara, the British West Indies, or the Dutch Antilles. Among these, the federal experiments between France and its empire, particularly West Africa, stood out for the dynamics they unleashed and the utopian visions of a "Eurafrican" union they generated. While specific forces were at play in the various regions, colonial planners resorted to federations as a "panacea" to cope with the uncertainties of imperial disintegration.[11] They regarded federal association as a means to stabilize territories that were considered too small to be self-sufficient, but also as a way to play aspiring nationalist leaders off against each other. Federative ideas also proliferated in African and Arab anticolonialist thinking. To the last, for example, the founder of Negritude, Léopold Senghor, mobilized against what he feared as the "Balkanization" of Africa. Various African and

Arab states made steps toward supranational integration in the immediate post-independence years. Similar to their colonial precursors, even the most ambitious of these postcolonial federal experiments, such as those between Senegal and Mali, Syria and Egypt, or Ghana, Guinea, and Mali, remained small-scale and short-lived. And the longest lasting of them, the UN-sanctioned federation between Ethiopia and Eritrea, eventually served as a springboard for Ethiopian secondary colonialism. In Asia, by contrast, any kind of "pan"-ideas were largely discredited by the Japanese war empire and its guiding ideology of Asian "co-prosperity" under Japanese leadership.

Only by the 1960s did such alternatives to nationalism disappear and the nation-state—in most cases in its unitary and centralized version—finally emerge as the "generalized form of sovereignty."[12] The naturalization of decolonization found its counterpart in the globalization of the nation-state model. This was the case even for such national leaders as Nkrumah and Nasser, who championed the pan-African and pan-Arab causes. Pan-Africanism, for example, now stood for a united Africa made up of nation-states. In 1963, the inviolability of inherited borders was enshrined as a principle in the founding charter of the Organization for African Unity.[13] This meant that nations and their states finally moved into the focus of intellectual activities: they got their own historiography and ethnology, were called by names that were partly historical or "authentic" such as Ghana, Mali, or Zaire. In Asia, this happened only later when Ceylon became Sri Lanka, and Burma reemerged as Myanmar.

These anticolonial nationalisms were neither a mere copy of the European model nor a simple reversion to ostensibly authentic organizational forms and local traditions; they were "neither traditional nor modern, neither Western nor anti-Western, but a kind of bricolage and an ongoing effort to negotiate what is 'traditional' and what is 'modern', what is 'indigenous' and what is 'foreign', and what is 'right' and what is 'wrong'."[14] Numerous other aspects of the ex-colonial countries' newly acquired sovereignty—such as the degree and form of economic sovereignty and the chances and perils of integration into the world market—became the subject of intellectual as well as of political debates in the new states. The enshrinement of sovereignty as an absolute value took place, interestingly enough, during a time in which the military security of the conventional nation-state was attenuated owing to the potential omnipresence of missile threats and governmental authority was undermined by newly emerging international actors.

(3) *Colonialism as a historical situation.* To the extent that decolonization came to represent the mainstream of history, colonialism became tangible as a finite and changeable, that is to say, a historical phenomenon. It is symptomatic that one of the most influential concepts for the academic study of colonialism—the concept of the "colonial situation" coined by the French sociologist and ethnologist Georges Balandier—emerged in 1951 in late-colonial Africa against the background of unfolding decolonization in Asia and emerging anticolonial activism in sub-Saharan Africa.[15] Intellectuals had previously reflected on the peculiarity of "plural" colonial societies, but Balandier's concept radicalized several aspects: he emphasized the totality of this situation by bundling all the features of the colonized and colonizing society into one overarching power relationship; he also pointed out the centrality of the colonial experience for presumably untouched population

groups and cultures; and, finally, he underscored the historic-ity of colonialism, which appeared as a specific, unstable, and malleable *situation*.

The concept of the "colonial situation" was the most strik-ing product of a broad intellectual trend. Sometimes linked with Balandier's reflections, but usually independent of these, colonialism as a social and psychological totality became the subject of many different critical analyses. In this perspective, racism and violence no longer appeared as the misdemeanor acts of some individuals (as metropolitan politicians persis-tently claimed) but instead articulated an inherent feature of colonialism as a system of rule. Many anticolonial writings of the time no longer focused on the injured dignity of the subjugated and the injustice of their colonial masters but in-stead analyzed the specific *relationship* between the two. Col-onizer and colonized now appeared as interdependent roles that could only be understood in interaction with each other. Thinkers like Césaire and the Tunisian Albert Memmi were interested, above all, in the incompleteness and even dehu-manized vacuity of these roles. In the 1950s, their writings and analyses amounted to a comprehensive pathology of the colo-nial situation. Where Césaire saw primarily a "de-civilization" and "brutalization" of both colonizer and colonized, and an-ticolonialism as a means to the "salvation of Europe" as well as of its colonies,[16] Memmi (in critical reference to the writ-ings of the French psychoanalyst Octave Mannoni) empha-sized the psychopathological sides of this relationship.[17] In this sort of psychologizing perspective, decolonization mani-fests itself at the level of the individual as a kind of therapy.

The psychopathology of colonialism and political practice meshed most powerfully in the writings of Frantz Fanon, certainly the most influential anticolonial thinker of his time. Fanon combined clinical studies, psychoanalysis, Marxism, existentialism, and a severe critique both of the antiracism inherent in Negritude's search for black identity and of anti-colonial bourgeois nationalisms, into a complex and pene-trating theory of the anticolonial struggle. Even before he worked as a psychiatrist in Algeria and joined the FLN there, he had identified the colonial system as a source of psycholog-ical disorders among blacks in his homeland of Martinique.[18] In his eyes, colonialism created the figure of the inferior col-onized person who was inclined to self-hatred as a result of internalizing white, colonialist stereotypes. In the context of the Algerian war, revolutionary struggle became for Fanon the only way out of psychological deformation: the violent oblit-eration of the colonial system and of the colonial masters not only served to achieve political freedom; for the individual, it also had the function of physical and mental self-liberation.[19]

(4) *The Third World.* In the context of decolonization, the "Three Worlds," with special attention to the "Third World" (*tiers monde*), emerged as a model of world order that was influential for roughly three decades in mapping the uneven distribution of power and prosperity on the globe.[20] This concept's connection to the process of decolonization is obvi-ous; the term referred empirically to the new states of Asia and Africa, and then later also to the economically stagnant countries of Latin America, where a long history of postco-lonial statehood had failed to overcome structural disadvan-tages within the world system. The same group of countries is nowadays often referred to as the global South—a category that owes its prominence to unexpected difficulties of emerg-ing countries such as India, Brazil, or South Africa in catch-up

with the erstwhile First World. As a concept, the "Third World" was the focal point of intellectual, scholarly, and political reflections about the postcolonial world order.

It was the term's very ambiguity that explains the astounding success of the Third World concept. It included at least two very different meanings.[21] The "Third World" was, first of all, a social science concept, and it turned into a distinct research discipline (Third World Studies) with its own methods and institutions. At its core lay questions about underdevelopment and how to overcome it, about explaining and possibly rectifying the global wealth and development gap. After an initial period when scholars of the developing world breathed in the heady optimism about rapid modernization prevalent in the 1960s, a more pessimistic variant of the Third World emerged in the 1970s based on "dependency theory" and the idea of a sustained and systematic economic and financial dependence of Third World countries on the developed countries. Second, the "Third World" designated a revolutionary-utopian design, an intellectual and political project to cure the ills of the existing world order.[22] As a political movement, Third Worldism stood for a shared space of political solidarity between the new (or old) states of the South, but also between political and social movements in the three "Worlds." It expressed the self-awareness of the new states that were setting themselves as a "revolutionary Third World symbolizing the future" in opposition to an "imperialistic, exploitative, and decrepit West."[23] The intellectual project of the revolutionary "Third World" always harbored a utopian moment, too, extending to designs for a "new humanity." Also reflected in the revolutionary-utopian version of the Third World was the fundamental critique that anticolonial thinkers had been leveling against Europeans' ideas about the superiority of their own civilization. This antiracist and non-Eurocentric "new discourse of civilization"[24] may be regarded as an intellectual legacy of decolonization, a bequest to our political thinking that has outlasted disenchantment with the Third World as a utopia in easy reach of fulfillment.

THINKING FOR A POSTCOLONIAL AGE?

Ever since the colonial powers began to remove their flags, Asian, African, and Caribbean writers, artists, and filmmakers have addressed the intellectual and cultural consequences of decolonization: How were colonial elements in elite and popular cultures identifiable? What would be a suitable way of emancipating oneself from the colonizer's cultural legacy? And what does sovereignty in the cultural and intellectual sphere look like at all? Under slogans such as "decolonizing the mind" or "decolonizing history," many have called for liberation from colonial categories of thought.[25] These slogans could entail different programs of intellectual emancipation: from the appropriation of European languages to the return to vernacular languages; from cosmopolitan opening toward the world to the quest for authenticity and cultural centrisms other than Eurocentrism. During the past two decades or so, however, postcolonial studies has been regarded as the main agent of decolonization as an intellectual project.

Following the publication of Edward Said's highly influential book *Orientalism* in 1978, postcolonial studies emerged as an independent academic field in the 1980s and 1990.[26] In the meantime, postcolonialism has acquired a dominant status as a kind of trustee for the anticolonial critique of Eurocentrism, a status that has sometimes relegated other critical traditions and alternative theoretical offerings (such as the historiography of the African diaspora, some strands of Marxist historiography, subaltern studies, the historiography of popular imperialism, or the works of independent African or Asian scholars) to the fringes.[27] A prominent postcolonial theorist considers it even the primary advocate of all the oppressed and marginalized in the world.[28]

In its broadest sense, postcolonial studies today stands for a renewed and critical interest in colonialism and its intellectual legacies. The range and diversity of postcolonial theory—in the stricter sense of the term—already become apparent in the major differences separating its three founding theoreticians—Edward Said, Homi K. Bhabha, and Gayatri Chakravorty Spivak—from each other. Over the years, postcolonial studies has further diversified and differentiated into several branches (such as an Anglo-Saxon branch and an increasingly important Latin American branch, not to speak of the multiple appropriations in various parts of the world). One leitmotif to which postcolonial thinking has adhered is a critical interest in colonial forms of representation and knowledge as well as in "identities" and "subjectivities" that developed both among the carriers and the victims of colonial rule (and their successors).

Many postcolonial theorists share the critical stance on colonialism characteristic of earlier anticolonial thinkers, and they draw explicitly on some of them (especially Frantz Fanon). Yet it is only with difficulty that one can establish an unbroken tradition between the anticolonial literature of the decolonization period and postcolonial studies. The emergence of postcolonialism owes a great deal to other factors, especially to the reception of post-structuralist literary criticism and discourse analysis, and also in part to a Gramscian critique of ideology and feminist theory in US academia in the 1980s and 1990s. Put bluntly, postcolonialism did not emerge out of a colonial or postcolonial situation shaped by decolonization, nor has it altered the worldwide hegemony of US- and European-based institutions in the production and dissemination of knowledge.

In terms of content, too, making an overly tight interconnection between postcolonial theory and the thought of the decolonization era does not do justice to either way of thinking.[29] First, postcolonial thinkers' main interest in colonialism's cultural and epistemological dimensions is different from the thematic breadth of thinking at the time of decolonization, which extended to all aspects (political, economic, social, psychological, etc.) of colonial rule. Second, postcolonial theory inclines toward an abstract and homogenizing conception of colonialism that on occasion is completely detached from the physical colonial situation. Although the thinkers of the decolonization era also reflected on colonialism in general categories, they never questioned the distinctive character and experience of actual colonial rule. Third, and notwithstanding nativist tendencies among some of its proponents, the postcolonial critique of essentialisms and universalisms is ultimately also directed against some of the entities and categories (of national and cultural identity, of the Third World, modernity, etc.) to which anticolonial thinking was generally committed. Likewise, postcolonial thinkers have started to look more critically into certain normative assumptions and biases (e.g., in terms of gender norms) in earlier anticolonial writings. Fourth, in contrast to the thinking of the decolonization era, postcolonialism has essentially remained an academic phenomenon; only recently do we find political grassroots movements actually founded on postcolonial ideas.

The contributions of postcolonial theory to the study of colonialism have been widely praised or lamented.[30] In conjunction with other intellectual trends, postcolonialism (in a broad sense) has contributed to a greater awareness of the resilience of colonialist stereotypes and of colonialism's legacies not only in formerly colonized societies. Its emphasis on how "centers" have been shaped by their colonial "peripheries" has contributed to a more complex picture of the interactions between colonies and metropoles, and some postcolonial thinkers have revisited anticolonial nationalism and its pitfalls.

But how does postcolonialism relate to our understanding of decolonization? A central point of departure for the postcolonial critique is the observation that colonial patterns of thinking lingered in the mental inventory of ex-colonies and ex-metropoles, that there was no decolonization of knowledge and thought following up on political (and economic) decolonization. In a way, postcolonial studies provides an epistemological counterpart to the neocolonialism debates centered on economic factors. In contrast to these earlier debates, postcolonialism does not provide an explanation for the demise of colonial rule. Apart from the observation that decolonization is incomplete or that it did not even happen, an elaborate postcolonial theory of decolonization is yet to come.

7
LEGACIES AND MEMORIES

ON AUGUST 15, 2015, a new time zone was born: Pyongyang Time. On that day, the North Korean government set its clocks thirty minutes behind those of South Korea and Japan and 8.5 hours ahead of Coordinated Universal Time (UTC –08.30). The new time zone was to undo, in the words of an official statement, one of the "unpardonable crimes" committed by "the wicked Japanese imperialists."[1] The gesture accordingly marked the seventieth anniversary of Japan's surrender in the Second World War, a date also celebrated as independence day in both Koreas.

The emergence of Pyongyang Time—as odd as it may appear at first sight—leads straight into the thorny question of decolonization and its legacies. Looked at from the present, it appears as yet another example of how the colonial past and official anti-imperialism are subject to political uses, particularly in the political language of an authoritarian state that is both an ex-colony and still deeply entrenched in Cold War rhetoric. Even setting the clock back can turn into a symbolic act of anti-imperialist self-assertion. Yet, the story may also be told differently if we approach it from the beginning of the twentieth century. Recent research reminds us that the European- and US-led process of unification of global time since the end of the nineteenth century unfolded in a highly hierarchical and uneven world.[2] At the turn of the century, Korea had already set its clock for some years according to what is now called Pyongyang Time before Japan annexed the country in 1910 and included it in the Japanese time zone in 1912. Against this backdrop, the more-than-one-hundred-years-old Korean time zone *can* be considered as a colonial legacy and its undoing as a move toward decolonization.

The contemporary world is still full of such remnants of colonialism. In most cases, contemporaries do not consider their removal as a necessary ingredient of decolonization or rank them high in their list of priorities. These remnants epitomize the analytical difficulties of drawing a clear line between ongoing decolonization efforts and decolonization's becoming part of national and transnational memories or, in other words, of determining when decolonization has definitively passed into history. This problem is, in large part, due to the historical process itself. Decolonization amounted to more than its most obvious outcome—the serial production of sovereignty for one nation-state after another. The transfer of power and the international recognition of political sovereignty occupied center stage in the decolonization struggles, yet they need to be seen in conjunction with more protracted processes of transformation in different spheres, such as international or local politics, the economy, education, and culture. These processes followed different temporalities; some of them only materialized at a slow pace, gradually, or after intervals and intermissions. From this broader angle, decolonization turns into a "historically loose-ended" subject, as historian Raymond Betts has termed it.[3] The continuous debate on what, how fast, and how thorough decolonization should be, and whether it should be considered a closed chapter or go on, was thus inherent to the decolonization process itself.

These processes of separation varied highly from one case to another. Just as importantly, they affected not only the formerly colonized territories but the ex-metropoles in the making as well. Just as decolonization was gaining momentum, late-colonial policies intensified exchanges between the metropoles and their colonies. In some cases (especially France, but also Portugal), colonies had never been so strongly integrated into the political structures of their metropoles as they were after 1945. This integration frequently included a relatively broad freedom of mobility for citizens inside a shared imperial space. But in other cases, too, where late-colonial policy did not put a premium on integration (as in Great Britain and the Netherlands), the period after the Second World War brought about a lowering of imperial barriers to geographic mobility. The British Nationality Act of 1948, for example, gave all inhabitants of the empire the right to settle in the British Isles and enjoy citizenship rights after a one-year stay.[4] The end of the colonial empires did not disrupt these spaces of intra-imperial mobility abruptly, but they did set off their step-by-step curtailment.

Decolonization thus also marked a crucial phase in West European nation-building—a particular kind of nation-building by way of contraction. After decades or (especially in the British case) centuries with a prevailing imperial orientation toward the outside world, the metropoles found themselves trimmed back to a status as "ordinary" European nation-states. The abandoned centers became more European than ever, not just in their political and economic orientations but also according to their self-image. At the same time, owing to migration, their societies at home achieved a degree of pluralism which they had previously only encountered in remote colonial contexts.

LEGACIES

Decolonization dramatically changed the contemporary world. It had tremendous effects on the lives of a large portion of the world population and altered the ways in which international power can be legitimately exercised. It seems reasonable that many people try to understand the structures and problems of today's world by looking back on this historical juncture. The legacies decolonization bequeathed are no less complex, ambiguous, and multifaceted than the process itself.

A widespread way of assessing these legacies is not to approach them directly but to define them negatively: with regard to what decolonization—by intention or by default—did *not* change. It is hard to ignore the long-lasting marks the colonial past has left on formerly colonized countries, on the ex-metropoles as well as on the international system. Colonial legacies are so diverse, their specific occurrence and composition so varied, and their interpretation so contested that it is difficult to make general statements. A full inventory would range from the Queen as head of state, the Commonwealth, and the African and Pacific Franc zones to territorial borders, legal systems, or constitutional patterns; from religious cultures, consumption, and sports preferences to official languages, educational systems, and infrastructures (or lack thereof); from the destruction or preservation of ecosystems to migration patterns and strong armies. Some of them (e.g., urban landscapes) are tangible and obvious, others, often the more tenacious among them, intangible (e.g., the ideological outlook of administrative and political elites). Some (e.g., agricultural monocultures, business networks, or weak governmental structures) proved to be more burdensome for the new states than others (e.g., industrial plants, cricket, or a different time zone). To make things even more complicated, these colonial legacies rarely appear in a pure form, and they have been subject to debate and to change over time. It was easier a few years after independence to identify certain international inequalities, social or ethnic conflicts, public institutions, or political practices as aftereffects of alien rule than it was after several decades. And it is hard to imagine that many people still identify English as a world language with the British Empire that was the prime vehicle for spreading English across the planet.

The topic of colonial legacies can be of purely anecdotic interest. It strips off this antiquarian character when it is considered against the backdrop of economic distress and underdevelopment; of military coups, political instability, and authoritarianism; of civil wars and ethnic violence that engulfed many countries of the former colonial world within one or two decades after independence. The search for colonial legacies is inextricably linked to the question of whether, and to what extent, they help to explain posterior developments or even the current situation of postcolonial countries. This analytical question also has a political counterpart: the debate about the former colonial powers' lasting responsibility for the fate of their ex-territories.

There is no simple and general answer to this question. The highly diverse nature and intensity of colonial rule, the manifold paths to independence, and the different trajectories afterward (not all of them ending in failure) show a muddled picture. While quite a few postcolonial ethnic or religious conflicts clearly have roots in the colonial period, there is no general correlation between a country having a colonial past and that country experiencing outbursts of large-scale violence in the second half of the twentieth century.[5] And while different colonial regimes left distinct marks on structurally similar regions, a specific form of colonial rule does not determine a particular political regime in the present.[6] Hence, the fact that the colonial past still puts its imprint on the contemporary world does not mean that it has determined it thoroughly. To fully understand how the colonial past shapes the present, we need to go beyond mono-causal models and abstract categories. A more diachronic approach is necessary that looks into *how*, in each single case, these colonial legacies were transmitted and incorporated into the postcolonial order and how they changed their meaning over time.[7]

This approach may even help to revisit the question of decolonization's specific legacies. Defining these legacies only in negative terms tends to obscure decolonization as an actual historical process. In each single case, this process produced a specific mixture of rupture, change, and continuities. In some areas—such as with regard to the developmental impetus—

continuities prevailed and locked together the late-colonial period and the early postcolonial years in a broader transformational period. The ways in which this transformational process played out, and the deals, decisions, and arrangements made over its course, left deep marks on the postcolonial world up to the present. For sure, there was no historical path-dependence from the critical moment of independence. The long-term outcome was never independent of the course of events unique to each specific decolonization, but it was also always related to further developments within the postcolonial state and its international environment.[8]

Decolonization's most generalizable legacy is certainly the primacy of political nationhood as opposed to other forms of constitutional, economic, or cultural emancipation. With only a few exceptions—partition in India and Palestine, unification in Somalia and Cameroon—decolonization did not create new territorial entities. Most borders—and the conflicts they entail or generate—were not the product of decolonization. Decolonization's momentous legacy consists in having translated borders between colonial states into international borders between nation-states. The result is that almost 40 percent of the length of all international borders today have been originally drawn by Great Britain and France.[9] Decolonization clearly took a different course than the imperial collapse in the wake of the First World War. Whereas the 1919–20 Paris peace provisions sought to provide international stability through the creation of ethnically homogeneous nation-states, the midcentury arrangements aimed at a stable postcolonial order based on the sanctity of the already existing territorial organization. Except for very few cases (Bangladesh and recently South Sudan), attempts at secession from post-colonial states have failed—not least due to the lack of international recognition.[10]

This does not mean that the postcolonial international order has been a success story. Coupled with the promise of self-determination, the colonial-turned-into-national borders have proven an explosive legacy. Particularly in the first decades after independence, violent border disputes and expansionist ambitions of some states (e.g., Indonesia, Morocco, Ethiopia, Somalia, Jordan) have challenged the postcolonial order. From the inside, new national borders have been no less fiercely contested by groups spread over several states (e.g., the Kurds, West African Hausa, and Saharan Tuareg) and by conflicts between different population groups over political and economic dominance in the independent states. Several conflicts, of which quite a few had already emerged or even been stirred up under colonial rule, culminated in mass killings, secessionist movements, and waves of what one might call "decolonization migration": emigration and refugee movements that were directly triggered by the decolonization process and its aftermath.[11] And yet, the multiethnic and multireligious outlook of many states at the moment of independence alone cannot account for the widespread instability of postcolonial states. The only early attempts at creating more homogeneous national units through partition, in British India and Palestine, have resulted in two of the longest-lasting postcolonial conflicts. One of the most disastrous state disintegrations in the past couple decades occurred in Somalia, one of the ethnically most homogeneous states in Africa. Finally, the fact that quite a few political compromises tailored during the decolonization era (such as in Lebanon or in Nigeria) became a catalyst of sectarianism should not obscure the recognition that others (e.g., in Mauritius) turned into rather successful systems of balancing interests in plural societies.

Potential conflicts arising from colonial borders and multi-ethnicity were not the only or, in many cases, the foremost challenges the newly independent states had to face. Some countries achieved political independence under circumstances of political, social, and economic disruption, chaos, and mass violence. But also those new states that were more fortunate had to grapple with the particular structures and weaknesses of their late-colonial predecessors. Full political sovereignty—not to speak of economic or cultural self-determination—did not materialize with the hoisting of a new flag and the election of a new government. All postcolonial states remained dependent on outside economic and military support and foreign investment. The dependence was rarely as obvious as in the neocolonial arrangements in Iraq in 1932 and the Philippines in 1946, or in "Françafrique," which has become the common term for the amalgam of political and business networks and military support linking France and authoritarian leaders and elites of many postcolonial states in Francophone southern Africa.[12] But also in most other cases, longstanding economic and political networks and patterns did not disappear with independence, or they reemerged in the form of foreign technical experts and political advisers.

With only a few exceptions and despite their diverse paths to independence, the political and economic development of most Asian, African, and Caribbean states fell short of the high-flying hopes and promises, of the optimism and enthusiasm so characteristic of the moment of decolonization. The new age of universal emancipation, prosperity, and progress did not materialize. In a way, the era of decolonization thus ended as it had slowly emerged at the end of the First World War: with a surge in expectations and their dramatic disappointment. While it is hard to ascertain to what extent this was avoidable and who was to blame, this widespread disillusionment had a tremendous impact on the way decolonization is being retold and remembered. It has disrupted certain guiding ideas, such as the belief in the manageability of development or the conviction that a thorough political and economic independence would necessarily lead to more equality or higher living standards. Alternative paths abandoned in the course of the historical process (such as federal or supranational schemes) now appear to some observers as missed chances. And still, the hopes and promises, decolonization's utopian "surplus," are also among its lasting legacies that would endure authoritarian turns and economic hardship. The struggles against colonial rule provided inspiration for movements all over the world fighting against discrimination, for equal rights, or for self-determination, however defined.

REPERCUSSIONS

Recently, it has been asked with increasing frequency: in what manner and to what extent did the possession of colonies affect the different metropoles? The positions taken on this matter are highly divergent: they range from the theory of a minimal impact, which regards colonial expansion as a matter pursued by a few interest groups and otherwise ignored by an indifferent majority, to the conception of maximal impact, which views empires and colonial rule as constitutive for the nations of Europe.[13] A simple and uncontested answer to this question is not possible. The degree and form of colonial repercussions varied according to the field of activity under consideration (e.g., politics, society, economy, culture), the historical moment in time, the colony, and the metropole.

This also applies to the consequences of decolonization for the metropoles. It stands to reason that the loss of extremely important colonies (e.g., Indonesia, Algeria, Belgian Congo, Korea) also affected the metropoles to a great extent. *How* such impacts turned out exactly, however, can only be established by adopting a perspective that is thematically, socially, and historically differentiated and that does not neglect interactions with other macro-processes like European integration or the Cold War.[14] As with the former colonies, each single metropole experienced decolonization with a specific mixture of continuity, change, and rupture.

There were great variations in the political consequences of decolonization. In some countries, such as Great Britain, the process of decolonization was supported by a relatively broad consensus among the political elites.[15] In every instance where decolonization was accompanied by major domestic conflicts, this led to a restructuring of the political landscape. This was most obviously the case in France and Portugal, where the end of colonial rule also manifested itself as a crisis of the metropolitan state. Starting in 1958, and in the wake of the Algerian war, a rapid restructuring of France's governing institutions toward a strengthened presidential democracy took place. In Portugal, democratization and decolonization were inextricably linked to each other in the program of the

1974 "Carnation Revolution." A different kind of common problem was the integration of political-administrative elites and soldiers from the colonies. There were striking continuities of personnel in the field of postcolonial development policy; in France, there was a high concentration of former colonial officials in the newly created Ministry of Culture.[16]

Economically, the metropoles emerged from decolonization unscathed. This was also related to a general shift of emphasis in foreign economic relations. In the case of Japan, this meant a stronger orientation toward the United States; in Europe, orientation toward the European single market, a shift that had begun *prior to* the great wave of decolonization and that afterward more than compensated for declining foreign trade with the ex-colonies. If this meant that the West European boom promoted decolonization in the *long run*, in the *short run* it could also have the opposite effect: the economic boom placed tiny Portugal in a financial position where it was able to brace itself for a long time against independence for its African colonies. The reorientation was clearer in the case of the European Economic Community (EEC) founded in 1957, which since the 1960s acquired ever greater importance for its member states; the buildup of the Common Agricultural Policy in particular also contributed to the weakening of post-imperial economic relations.[17] There was symbolic meaning to the first British EEC application, which took shape after the 1956 Suez debacle and occurred in 1961 at the high point of African decolonization. While Britain's efforts at joining the Common Market (which eventually succeeded in 1973) were never uncontroversial, and while they did not completely call into question the United Kingdom's strong economic (and political) orientation toward the Commonwealth since 1945, they did permanently attenuate that orientation.[18]

When it comes to its social repercussions, a question that needs to be addressed is how decolonization relates to the migration movements that turned Western Europe after 1945 from a net source of emigration into a continent with a positive migration balance.[19] The precise role and importance of decolonization varied from country to country. The connection is most obvious with regard to decolonization migration, or the involuntary migration movements triggered by decolonization. The majority of these movements were not in the direction of Europe: they either followed territorial partitions (as in India and Palestine) or else were movements into neighboring countries, to Israel (as with many North African Jews), or countries farther away in the South; many British settlers from Kenya and Central Africa ended up heading to South and Southwest Africa. Yet the metropoles also became an important destination for decolonization migrants.[20] For Western Europe, their number is estimated at five to eight million. As a rule, these were settlers who had frequently lived overseas for several generations, to some extent also indigenous "collaborators" or military auxiliaries and other minority immigrant groups (e.g., South Asians in East Africa) who were fleeing political repression, dispossession, or violence after independence. Japan's imperial breakdown triggered similar population transfers. Until the end of 1946, about five million Japanese soldiers and civilians were repatriated to Japan under US guidance.[21] With the "repatriated" European (and Japanese), there emerged a new, often neglected type of migrant, usually also a unique legal status.

The metropoles were affected by decolonization migration in different ways. Decolonization migration was particularly dramatic in cases where it coincided with military demobilization: in Japan and Italy in 1945, France in 1962, and Portugal in 1974–75. The largest wave of civilian migration went to France, where the French from Algeria (later often referred to as *pieds-noirs*) constituted the dominant group. Also important were the *retornados* who left Angola and Mozambique for Portugal, as well as the migrants from Indonesia and the Dutch Caribbean who headed to the Netherlands. Even if they arrived in Europe under what were often chaotic circumstances, their socioeconomic integration went by and large smoothly—at least with regard to those who were considered of European descent. Contributing to this fairly easy adjustment were the postwar economic boom and government programs for integration as well as a kind of "postcolonial bonus": many of the migrants were already equipped with the metropole's citizenship and cultural capital (such as language and education).[22] Some of the decolonization migrants, above all the *pieds-noirs*, developed specific group identities and established themselves as sociopolitical actors to be reckoned with.

While the labor migration to Western Europe that intensified after 1945 ran parallel to decolonization, it was not triggered by it. If we measure its "colonial" dimension according to how large the share of labor migrants from colonial territories was in each case, major differences come to light: in France and Great Britain, the share was relatively large; in Belgium and Japan, it was quite small. Parallels show up in the legal regulations surrounding "colonial" labor migration and their growing severity. In many metropoles, colonial immigrants after 1945 enjoyed certain advantages, such as visa waivers and easier access to citizenship. In a mixture of imperial traditions and bilateral relations with the new states, these kinds of regulations often outlasted decolonization, yet they were gradually revoked. In a series of laws starting in 1962, Great Britain began restricting nonwhite immigration from the Commonwealth; and in 1964, France implemented a quota on migration from Algeria.[23] In cases where labor immigration had been closely linked to the colonial empires, decolonization "registered as a broadly social process" that had an impact on the classification of population groups and on the reconfiguration of social relationships in the emerging postwar welfare states.[24]

It seems reasonable to suggest that we view migration movements and the conflicts associated with them as a symbol of Europe's more general post-imperial contraction. Yet, this symbolic meaning should not be overdone. While the "reflux" of settler populations was indeed seen by contemporaries as a demographic withdrawal, it was offset by new forms of emigration in the context of international cooperation and development policy. In the 1970s, for example, there were more French officials posted to the former French West Africa, in addition to French private individuals, than ever before.[25] The conflicts experienced by European immigration societies are only in some cases related to migration from ex-colonies, most notably in today's France. In general, such conflicts tend to represent a broader experience, in that the integration problems of "plural" societies are not (or rather no longer) restricted to the colonial situation.

The cultural repercussions of decolonization have become a central topic in recent debates. Historians have started to trace the possible impact the end of empire had on areas as diverse as literature, popular culture, museum collections and exhibitions, art production and consumption, and schoolbooks.[26] The background to this is the hard-to-answer question of how strong an impact colonial possessions had on the mentalities and mindsets of the metropoles. With respect to decolonization, this translates into the no less difficult question about how and when these mental ties between metropole and former colony dissolved. Usually it is the inertial force of colonial cultures and mindsets that is the focus of attention. Thus, for example, well into the 1950s and to some extent even beyond, a vague reference to empire continued to shape British popular culture.[27] At the center of the debate are the increase of racist and xenophobic reactions against non-European immigrants since the 1960s. In the light of the colonial past, these responses are sometimes interpreted as a persistence of colonial mental patterns, and sometimes as a collective psychological reaction to the "trauma" of decolonization.[28] As important as it is that colonialism not be absent from a history of racism, theories of this kind pose problems about how to specify the exact mechanism of action at work: colonialism was not the only context in which racism was practiced, and forms of racism and xenophobia marked European societies long before decolonization. The arguments about the colonial dimensions of xenophobia are also part of the fierce debates over public memory that have taken hold of many European countries over the last several years.

MEMORIES

Decolonization bequeathed shared and divided memories. On the one hand, these often relate to a past that most of the countries of Asia, Africa, and Western Europe have in common, that they share in an inclusive sense. On the other hand, decolonization marks the starting point at which these memories came to be cultivated and hence divided (up) mainly within a framework exclusive to each individual nation-state. Occasionally, this kind of segmentation happened in very concrete ways because of how archives, monuments, and other repositories of memory were redistributed in the course of the decolonization process. Yet, these memories were split up not only between different states but also between groups inside the countries themselves. In many postcolonial states, this compartmentalization has been a source of conflicts over memory.

In both former colonies and former metropoles, each country's particular decolonization process as well as subsequent developments contributed to shaping memories. In almost all the new states, remembering the colonial period and decolonization was strongly influenced at first by postcolonial nation-building. With different and shifting emphases, the path to independence constituted an important element in the emerging symbolism of the state and the official politics of remembrance.[29] Almost everywhere, independence day became the most important official holiday, if the anticolonial liberation struggle did not actually determine the entire (secular) holiday calendar. Parallel to this, in many places, a canon of national heroes emerged that found expression in schoolbooks, monuments, street names, and other media. The identity of these heroes did, however, vary greatly: from the flesh-and-blood "father of the nation" to the anonymous liberation army.

Even in the most dramatic cases of decolonization, constructing a postcolonial politics of remembrance was a lengthy, often gradual procedure. In India, up to the present day, many symbolic remnants of the British Raj have remained untouched and only barely been complemented with memorials to Indian victimhood under colonial rule.[30] In Congo-Zaire, it took years following independence before people got around to toppling Belgian monuments and searching for "authentic" names, symbols, and points of reference. Even in Algeria, the scene of a genuine revolutionary war of liberation, colonial monuments and patterns of French commemoration frequently lingered on and were later absorbed in an emerging cult of national martyrs.[31] These slow transformations were also related to the way that conflicts and processes of marginalization that had started during the struggle for nationhood continued after independence in disputes about which conception of the national past should become hegemonic. In these processes, memories of violence—such as of forced migration or violence between rival nationalist movements— took considerably longer to emerge than official heroic memories. Nation-building was in fact often linked to attempts at concealing memories of the violence that accompanied it. Many societies are still grappling with finding appropriate framings for these disturbing memories, an often painful process in stark contrast to other recent tendencies toward rather depoliticized, commodified versions of the colonial past, consumed by tourists and local aspiring middle classes.[32]

Apart from these kinds of commonalities, there is strong variation in the concrete relationship between the colonial past and the politics of remembrance. First, the significance that this past is accorded in symbols of the state turns out to be extremely different from case to case. During the fiftieth-anniversary celebrations of independence in Africa, for example, the relationship of some Francophone countries to the former colonial power was articulated more clearly than was the case in former British colonies.[33] Never does the colonial past constitute the only resource for a given country's politics (and policy) of national history and identity. Second, the image of the colonial period varies greatly between individual cases. Even when one system of colonial rule has a strong structural resemblance to another, as with the Japanese in various parts of East Asia, each experience is "remembered" and assessed quite differently in retrospect: as deplorable "colonialism" in South Korea, as helpful "modernization" in Taiwan.[34] Third, it is impossible to extrapolate from a concrete instance of decolonization to the way that this is later remembered. While the Algerian war of independence, for example, has functioned since 1962 as the symbolic center of gravity for the FLN state, the Mau Mau rebellion remained a marginal topic in official Kenyan memory for several decades after independence.

The greatest differences show up with regard to the former metropoles. While political decolonization was happening, government agencies in the metropoles were keen to maintain their prerogative to control how the events should be interpreted and to shape the formulas that would later be used to remember them.[35] In general, part of the metropoles' post-imperial nation-building included renunciation of a past that quite often had come to be regarded as disturbing. In Japan, the US occupation and the Cold War facilitated a fade-out of the imperial record.[36] In general, an active policy of "repressing" the past was unnecessary to turn public attention away from colonial history. Usually it was enough that government agencies and private lobbies abandoned their efforts at popularizing the colonies among the metropolitan population. In addition, in several countries, grappling with sensitive topics other than the colonial past (e.g., the dictatorships in

Spain and Portugal or the Vichy regime in France) seemed or still seem more pressing for many.

There has been a considerable upsurge in debates and government initiatives surrounding the colonial past in several European countries and Japan since the 1990s.[37] The focus of many debates, particularly those that receive great media attention, are moments of colonial violence: the Mau Mau uprising, the Algerian war, the assassination of Lumumba, Italy's use of poison gas in Ethiopia, the Japanese massacre in Nanjing, the German-Herero war in Namibia. Since the turn of the millennium, the governments of Great Britain, France, and the Netherlands have recognized with great symbolic gestures their countries' responsibility for slavery. These kinds of developments are inadequately described by the frequently invoked formula about a "return" of a collectively "repressed" past. Rather, what underlay these changes was a set of complex and, in part, extremely contested social processes in which the states are just one participant among many. Governments frequently confront a variety of historical actors (repatriated settlers, veterans, etc.) who mobilize in order to influence official commemoration, to be recognized as victims, and partly also to obtain material compensation. In many countries, the debates about memory have also been tied in with questions of discrimination, xenophobia, and the problems of integration faced by immigration societies. In France, an outright "memory war" has erupted in which present-day conflicts are framed with reference to the colonial past.[38]

The international arena has also proven a driving force in this recent memory boom. Over the past few years, some countries have engaged in a diplomacy of remembrance about their historical entanglements, a dialogue in which govern-

ments and civil societies relate to each other. This is particularly obvious in Japan, where the upsurge in colonial memories was associated with the reinsertion of the country in the
East Asian regional context after the end of the Cold War.[39]
Since then, people in Seoul and Beijing keep a meticulous
watch on how Japanese war atrocities in Asia are commemo-
rated in Tokyo. Yet, also in other contexts, demands for repa-
rations or symbolic gestures of apology arise every now and
then, making the memory of colonialism and decolonization
an element of soft diplomacy across the North-South divide.
The division of roles between ex-metropole and ex-colony,
however, is not always clear: demands for an accurate reap-
praisal of war crimes during the decolonization of Indonesia
have recently found little favor among either the conservative
Dutch or the Indonesian government.

Showing up in these struggles around the past is an even
more general tendency toward a "duty to remember" the negative aspects of a nation's history, a trend that since the 1980s
has been closely linked with the internationalization of Holo-
caust commemoration.[40] This also helps explain why debates
about colonial pasts are often full of talk about "crimes
against humanity" or "genocide." South Africa, with its Truth
and Reconciliation Commission from the 1990s, became a
frequently copied model, even in postconflict settings that are
not colonial. The growing international remembrance of colonialism, however, has not led to transnational forms of
commemoration comparable to the World Wars or the Holo-
caust. Most debates between former colonizing and colonized
countries remain in a bilateral framework. At last, the profound delegitimization of colonial rule has arrived in the realms
of public memory: "colonialism" today has sometimes become

an abstract code word for any kind of "alien" meddling and for all kinds of conflict between those who are cultural strangers to each other—be they inhabitants of different continents or only of one single country.

NOTES

1. DECOLONIZATION AS MOMENT AND PROCESS

1. That "foreignness" is a construct that changes with mentalities and linguistic usage is shown (for the period before 1945) by Christian Koller, *Fremdherrschaft: Ein politischer Kampfbegriff im Zeitalter des Nationalismus* (Frankfurt: Campus, 2005).

2. Prasenjit Duara, "Introduction: The Decolonization of Asia and Africa in the Twentieth Century," in Prasenjit Duara (ed.), *Decolonization: Perspectives from Now and Then*, 2nd ed. (London: Routledge, 2004), 1–18, quote at 2.

3. On the history and career of the word, see Charles-Robert Ageron, *La décolonisation française*, 2nd ed. (Paris: A. Colin, 1994), 5; Todd Shepard, *Voices of Decolonization: A Brief History with Documents* (Boston: Bedford/ St. Martin's, 2014), 8–10. The most extensive discussion of Bonn's use of the term is Stuart Ward, "The European Provenance of Decolonization," *Past and Present* 230 (2016): 227–60, esp. 233–46.

4. See Frederick Cooper, *Decolonization and African Society: The Labor Question in French and British Africa* (Cambridge: Cambridge University Press, 1996), 6.

5. This has only recently become fully apparent. See Remco Raben, "On Genocide and Mass Violence in Colonial Indonesia," *Journal of Genocide Research* 14 (2012): 485–502.

6. Caroline Elkins, "Looking beyond Mau Mau: Archiving Violence in the Era of Decolonization," *American Historical Review* 120 (2015): 852–68.

7. A careful appraisal is provided by Huw Bennett, *Fighting the Mau Mau: The British Army and Counter-Insurgency in the Kenya Emergency* (Cambridge: Cambridge University Press, 2013).

8. Anthony Clayton, *The Wars of French Decolonization* (London: Longman, 1994), 79–87.

9. For the numbers mentioned here, see Bouda Etemad, *Possessing the World: Taking the Measurements of Colonisation from the 18th to the 20th Century* (New York: Berghahn, 2007), 200; "The United Nations and Decolonization," UN.org, accessed February 25, 2016. http://www.un.org/en/decolonization.html.

10. Dietmar Rothermund, *The Routledge Companion to Decolonization* (London: Routledge, 2006), 1.

11. Sebastian Conrad, "Dekolonisierung in den Metropolen," *Geschichte und Gesellschaft* 37 (2011): 135–56, quote at 145.

12. For an introduction to modern colonial history, see Jürgen Osterhammel and Jan C. Jansen, *Kolonialismus: Geschichte, Formen, Folgen* (Munich: C. H. Beck, 2012), 28–45; an earlier version of this book is Osterhammel, *Colonialism: A Theoretical Overview*, 2nd ed. (Princeton, NJ: Markus Wiener, 2005). See also Wolfgang Reinhard, *A Short History of Colonialism* (Manchester: Manchester University Press, 2011); and the same author's massive *Die Unterwerfung der Welt: Globalgeschichte der europäischen Expansion, 1415–2015* (Munich: C. H. Beck, 2016). An overview of current research on empires and imperialism is provided by Stephen Howe (ed.), *The New Imperial Histories Reader* (London: Routledge, 2010).

13. W. David McIntyre, *The Britannic Vision: Historians and the Making of the British Commonwealth of Nations, 1907–48* (Basingstoke: Palgrave Macmillan, 2009), 76–79.

14. John Darwin, *The Empire Project: The Rise and Fall of the British World-System 1830–1970* (Cambridge: Cambridge University Press, 2009), esp. xi–xii.

15. Libya was, it should be added, occupied as an administered trusteeship by Great Britain and France between 1943 and 1949.

16. On the dimensions and complexities of US imperial history, see Paul A. Kramer, "Power and Connection: Imperial Histories of the United States in the World," *American Historical Review* 116 (2011): 1348–91.

17. According to Etemad, *Possessing the World*, 104 (table 6.1). In individual cases, labeling a certain territory as a "colony" might be open to dispute.

18. But see the reservations expressed by Antony G. Hopkins, "Rethinking Decolonization," *Past and Present* 200 (2008): 211–47.

19. For a chronology showing the growth of the community of states, see "Growth in the United Nations Membership, 1945–Present," UN.org, accessed February 29, 2016. http://www.un.org/en/members/growth.shtml.

20. For a more precise definition, see Osterhammel and Jansen, *Kolonialismus*, 16.

21. "Declaration on the Granting of Independence to Colonial Countries and Peoples," UN.org, accessed February 29, 2016. http://www.un.org/en/decolonization/declaration.shtml.

22. For a comparative analysis of such celebrations, see "Freedoms at Midnight," special issue of *Round Table: The Commonwealth Journal of International Affairs* 97 (2008), also published as Robert Holland et al. (eds.), *The Iconography of Independence: "Freedoms at Midnight"* (London: Routledge, 2010).

23. This metaphor is inspired by Frederick Cooper, *Colonialism in Question: Theory, Knowledge, History* (Berkeley: University of California Press, 2005), 19.

24. For a model study of these kinds of processes, see Marc Frey, "Drei Wege zur Unabhängigkeit: Die Dekolonisierung in Indochina, Indonesien und Malaya nach 1945," *Vierteljahreshefte für Zeitgeschichte* 50 (2002): 399–433.

25. See John Darwin, *After Tamerlane: The Global History of Empire* (London: Allen Lane, 2007); Jane Burbank and Frederick Cooper, *Empires in World History: Power and the Politics of Difference* (Princeton, NJ: Princeton University Press, 2010).

26. See chapter 5 of this book.

27. On this, see William G. Beasley, *Japanese Imperialism 1894–1945* (Oxford: Clarendon Press, 1987).

28. David Armitage, *The Declaration of Independence: A Global History* (Cambridge, MA: Harvard University Press, 2007).

29. Jörg Fisch, *Das Selbstbestimmungsrecht der Völker: Die Domestizierung einer Illusion* (Munich: C. H. Beck, 2010), 88–93.

30. On the historiography of the "human dimension" of the partition, see Ian Talbot and Gurharpal Singh, *The Partition of India* (Cambridge: Cambridge University Press, 2009), 17–19.

31. Elizabeth Buettner, *Empire Families: Britons and Late Imperial India* (Oxford: Oxford University Press, 2004); Sarah E. Stockwell, "Ends of Empire," in Stockwell (ed.), *The British Empire: Themes and Perspectives* (Oxford: Blackwell, 2008), 282–87. With a comparative perspective: Andrea L. Smith (ed.), *Europe's Invisible Migrants* (Amsterdam: Amsterdam University Press, 2003).

32. The following draws on Jürgen Osterhammel, "Die Auflösung der modernen Imperien: Tendenzen und Interpretationen," *Praxis Geschichte* 17, 2 (March 2004): 6–12.

33. For other compilations of analytical tools, see John Darwin, *The End of the British Empire: The Historical Debate* (Oxford: Blackwell, 1991); Raymond F. Betts, "Decolonization: A Brief History of the Word," in Els Bogaerts and Remco Raben (eds.), *Beyond Empire and Nation: The Decolonization of African and Asian Societies, 1930s–1960s* (Leiden: KITLV Press, 2012), 23–37.

34. A nice example of this is the analysis of the 1968 British withdrawal "East of Suez" in David French, *Army, Empire, and Cold War: The British Army and Military Policy, 1945–1971* (Oxford: Oxford University Press, 2012), 268 et seq.

35. Wolfgang J. Mommsen, *Theories of Imperialism* (Chicago: University of Chicago Press, 1982).

36. At the time, there did emerge a few clear-sighted analyses, such as in two German-language books published simultaneously in 1966 and later translated into English: Rudolf von Albertini, *Decolonization: The Administration and Future of the Colonies, 1919–1960* (Garden City, NY: Doubleday, 1971); Franz Ansprenger, *Dissolution of the Colonial Empires* (London: Routledge, 1989).

37. See, e.g., the data from the IMF: "World Economic Outlook Database," IMF.org, accessed February 29, 2016. http://www.imf.org/external/pubs /ft/weo/2015/02/weodata/index.aspx.

2. NATIONALISM, LATE COLONIALISM, WORLD WARS

1. John H. Morrow, Jr., "The Imperial Framework," in Jay Winter (ed.), *The Cambridge History of the First World War*, vol. 1 (Cambridge: Cambridge University Press, 2014), 405–32.

2. David Motadel, *Islam and Nazi Germany's War* (Cambridge, MA: Harvard University Press, 2014), 18–27.

3. See Christian Koller, *"Von Wilden aller Rassen niedergemetzelt": Die Diskussion um die Verwendung von Kolonialtruppen in Europa zwischen Rassismus, Kolonial- und Militärpolitik (1914–1930)* (Stuttgart: Steiner, 2001), esp. part 2.

4. Robert Gerwarth and Erez Manela, "The Great War as a Global War: Imperial Conflict and the Reconfiguration of World Order, 1911–1923," *Diplomatic History* 38 (2014): 786–800; Robert Gerwarth and Erez Manela (eds.), *Empires at War, 1911–1923* (Oxford: Oxford University Press, 2014).

5. Versailles Treaty, June 28, 1919, Part I, The Covenant of the League of Nations, Art. 22.

6. With reference above all to literary testimonies, see Michael Adas, "Contested Hegemony: The Great War and the Afro-Asian Assault on the Civilizing Mission Ideology," *Journal of World History* 15 (2004): 31–63. A less clear picture, based on soldiers' letters, is David Omissi, "Europe through Indian Eyes: Indian Soldiers Encounter England and France, 1914–1918," *English Historical Review* 122 (2007): 371–96. On non-European experiences of the war, see Heike Liebau et al. (eds.), *The World in World Wars: Experiences, Perceptions and Perspectives from Africa and Asia* (Leiden: Brill, 2010); Santau Das (ed.), *Race, Empire and First World War Writing* (Cambridge: Cambridge University Press, 2011).

7. On the impact of the Russo-Japanese war, see Cemil Aydin, *The Politics of Anti-Westernism in Asia: Visions of World Order in Pan-Islamic and Pan-Asian Thought* (New York: Columbia University Press, 2007), 71–92.

8. See Erez Manela, *The Wilsonian Moment: Self-Determination and the International Origins of Anticolonial Nationalism* (Oxford: Oxford University Press, 2007).

9. John Gallagher, "Nationalism and the Crisis of Empire 1919–1922," *Modern Asian Studies* 15 (1981): 355–68.

10. Woodrow Wilson, "Address to Congress, February 11, 1918," in *The Papers of Woodrow Wilson*, vol. 46 (Princeton, NJ: Princeton University Press: 1966–1994), 318–24, quote at 321; V. I. Lenin, "The Socialist Revolution and the Rights of Nations to Self-Determination [April 1916]," in Lenin, *Collected Works*, vol. 22 (Moscow: Progress Publishers, 1964), 143–45.

11. Manela, *Wilsonian Moment*.

12. Susan Pedersen, *The Guardians: The League of Nations and the Crisis of Empire* (Oxford: Oxford University Press, 2015), 5.

13. On West Africa, for example, see Gregory Mann, *Native Sons: West African Veterans and France in the Twentieth Century* (Durham, NC: Duke University Press, 2006).

14. On Pan-Africanism and Negritude, Imanuel Geiss, *The Pan-African Movement* (London: Methuen, 1974); J. Ayodele Langley, *Pan-Africanism and Nationalism in West Africa 1900–1945: A Study in Ideology and Social Classes* (Oxford: Clarendon Press, 1973); Gary Wilder, *The French Imperial Nation-State: Negritude and Colonial Humanism between the Two World Wars* (Chicago: University of Chicago Press, 2005), esp. chaps. 6–8.

15. On the movements mentioned, see James McDougall, *History and the Culture of Nationalism in Algeria* (Cambridge: Cambridge University Press, 2006); Adrian Vickers, *A History of Modern Indonesia*, 2nd ed. (Cambridge: Cambridge University Press, 2013), 74–86.

16. See also the regional chapters 11–16 in John Breuilly (ed.), *The Oxford Handbook of the History of Nationalism* (Oxford: Oxford University Press, 2013).

17. David G. Marr, *Vietnamese Anticolonialism, 1885–1925* (Berkeley: University of California Press, 1971), 166–67.

18. See Adria K. Lawrence, *Imperial Rule and the Politics of Nationalism: Anti-Colonial Protest in the French Empire* (Cambridge: Cambridge University Press, 2013), esp. 50–131.

19. See, e.g., Frederick Cooper, " 'Our Strike': Equality, Anticolonial Politics and the 1947–48 Railway Strike in French West Africa," *Journal of African History* 37 (1996): 81–118.

20. Dietmar Rothermund, *Gandhi und Nehru: Zwei Gesichter Indiens* (Stuttgart: Kohlhammer, 2010), 210–11.

21. James L. Gelvin, *Divided Loyalties: Nationalism and Mass Politics in Syria at the Close of Empire* (Berkeley: University of California Press, 1998).

22. For example, Anshuman Mondal, "The Emblematics of Gender and Sexuality in Indian Nationalist Discourse," *Modern Asian Studies* 36 (2002): 913–36.

23. See, e.g., Neil MacMaster, *Burning the Veil: The Algerian War and the "Emancipation" of Muslim Women, 1954–62* (Manchester: Manchester University Press, 2012). For a broader argument with regard to India, Algeria, and Kenya, see Philippa Levine, "Gendering Decolonisation," *Histoire@Politique: Histoire, Politique, Société* 11 (2010): 1–15.

24. These non-Western, colonial migrant communities in the imperial centers have become a focus in recent scholarship. See, e.g., Marc Matera, *Black London: The Imperial Metropolis and Decolonization in the Twentieth Century* (Berkeley: University of California Press, 2015).

25. Benedikt Stuchtey, *Die europäische Expansion und ihre Feinde. Kolonialismuskritik vom 18. bis in das 20. Jahrhundert* (Munich: Oldenbourg, 2010); Claude Liauzu, *Histoire de l'anticolonialisme en France, du XVIe siècle à nos jours* (Paris: A. Colin, 2007); Stephen Howe, *Anticolonialism in British Politics: The Left and the End of Empire, 1918–1964* (Oxford: Clarendon Press, 1993).

26. See, e.g., the development of trade statistics as discussed in Bouda Etemad, *De l'utilité des empires: colonisation et prosperité de l'Europe (XVIe–XXe siècle)* (Paris: A. Colin, 2005), 177, 211, 239, 267, 288.

27. David K. Fieldhouse, "The Metropolitan Economics of Empire," in Wm. Roger Louis (ed.), *The Oxford History of the British Empire*, vol. 4 (Oxford: Oxford University Press, 1999), 88–113; Martin Thomas, *The French Empire between the Wars* (Manchester: Manchester University Press, 2005), 93–124.

28. See, e.g., John M. MacKenzie, *Propaganda and Empire: The Manipulation of British Public Opinion, 1880–1960* (Manchester: Manchester University Press, 1986); Raoul Girardet, *L'idée coloniale en France* (Paris: La Table Ronde, 1972), 175–99.

29. On the concepts "late colonialism" and "late-colonial state," see Jürgen Osterhammel, "Spätkolonialismus und Dekolonisation," *Neue Politische Literatur* 37 (1992): 413–18; Martin Shipway, *Decolonization and Its Impact: A Comparative Approach to the End of the Colonial Empires* (Malden, MA: Blackwell, 2008), 12–14.

30. A.D.A. de Kat Angelino, *Colonial Policy*, 2 vols. (The Hague: M. Nijhoff, 1931); Albert Sarraut, *La mise en valeur des colonies* (Paris: Payot, 1923);

Albert Sarraut, *Grandeur et servitude coloniales* (Paris: Editions du sagittaire, 1931); John S. Furnivall, *Colonial Policy and Practice: A Comparative Study of Burma and Netherlands India* (Cambridge: Cambridge University Press, 1948).

31. Tony Chafer and Amanda Sackur (eds.), *French Colonial Empire and the Popular Front: Hope and Disillusion* (Basingstoke: Palgrave Macmillan, 1999).

32. For an overview of the late-colonial policy debates, it is still useful to consult Albertini, *Decolonization*.

33. Osterhammel and Jansen, *Kolonialismus*, 115–17.

34. On Algeria, see Patrick Weil, *How to Be French: Nationality in the Making since 1789* (Durham, NC: Duke University Press, 2008), 207–25.

35. Leo T. S. Ching, *Becoming "Japanese": Colonial Taiwan and the Politics of Identity Formation* (Berkeley: University of California Press, 2001).

36. A detailed account is François Borella, *L'évolution politique et juridique de l'Union française depuis 1946* (Paris: Librairie générale de droit et de jurisprudence, 1958); for a broader imperial context, see Frederick Cooper, *Citizenship between Empire and Nation: Remaking France and French Africa, 1945–1960* (Princeton, NJ: Princeton University Press, 2014).

37. Miguel Bandeira Jerónimo and António Costa Pinto, "A Modernizing Empire? Politics, Culture, and Economy in Portuguese Late Colonialism," in Jerónimo and Pinto (eds.), *The Ends of European Colonial Empires: Cases and Comparisons* (Basingstoke: Palgrave Macmillan, 2015), 51–80.

38. Darwin, *End of the British Empire*, 116.

39. Tony Chafer, *The End of Empire in French West Africa: France's Successful Decolonization?* (Oxford: Berg, 2002), 83–141; Shipway, *Decolonization*, 237.

40. On development policy in a broader context, Gilbert Rist, *The History of Development: From Western Origins to Global Faith*, 4th ed. (New York: Zed Books, 2014), 47–92; on the period after 1940, Andreas Eckert, " 'We Are All Planners Now': Planung und Dekolonisation in Afrika," *Geschichte und Gesellschaft* 34 (2008): 375–97.

41. Frederick Cooper, "Writing the History of Development," *Journal of Modern European History* 8 (2010): 5–23, quote at 8.

42. Louise Young, *Japan's Total Empire: Manchuria and the Culture of Wartime Imperialism* (Berkeley: University of California Press, 1998).

43. See, e.g., Alice Conklin, *A Mission to Civilize: The Republican Idea of Empire in France and West Africa, 1895–1930* (Stanford: Stanford University Press, 1997), esp. chaps. 6–7.

44. See Andreas Eckert, "Exportschlager Wohlfahrtsstaat? Europäische Sozialstaatlichkeit und Kolonialismus in Afrika nach dem Zweiten Weltkrieg," *Geschichte und Gesellschaft* 32 (2006): 467–88.

45. On the late-colonial state in comparative perspective, see "The Late Colonial State," special issue of *Itinerario* 23 (1999).

46. The term was used for the first time in D. A. Low and John M. Lonsdale, "Introduction: Towards the New Order 1945–1963," in Low and Alison Smith (eds.), *History of East Africa*, vol. 3 (Oxford: Oxford University Press, 1976), 1–64, at 12–13.

47. See, e.g., Achim von Oppen, "Matuta: Landkonflikte, Ökologie und Entwicklung in der Geschichte Tanzanias," in Ulrich van der Heyden and Achim von Oppen (eds.), *Tanzania: Koloniale Vergangenheit und neuer Aufbruch* (Münster: Lit, 1996), 47–84, esp. 64–67.

48. Martin Thomas, *Empires of Intelligence: Security Services and Colonial Disorder after 1914* (Berkeley: University of California Press, 2008), 7. On late-colonial repression, see also Martin Thomas, *Violence and Colonial Order: Police, Workers and Protest in the European Colonial Empires, 1918–1940* (Cambridge: Cambridge University Press, 2012).

49. Nicola Labanca, *Oltremare. Storia dell'espansione coloniale italiana* (Bologna: Il mulino, 2002), 320–24.

50. See esp. Mark Mazower, *Hitler's Empire: How the Nazis Ruled Europe* (New York: Penguin, 2008).

51. See Patrick Bernhard, "Die 'Kolonialachse': Der NS-Staat und Italienisch-Afrika 1935 bis 1943," in Thomas Schlemmer et al. (eds.), *Die Achse im Krieg: Politik, Ideologie und Kriegführung 1939 bis 1945* (Paderborn: Schöningh, 2010), 147–75.

52. Beasley, *Japanese Imperialism*; Yoshihisa Tak Matsusaka, "The Japanese Empire," in William M. Tsutsui (ed.), *A Companion to Japanese History*, 2nd ed. (Malden, MA: Blackwell, 2008), 224–40.

53. See Sven Saaler and Christopher W. A. Szpilman (ed.), *Pan-Asianism: A Documentary History*, 2 vols. (Lanham, MD: Rowman and Littlefield, 2011).

54. David Williams, *Defending Japan's Pacific War: The Kyoto School Philosophers and Post-White Power* (London: RoutledgeCurzon, 2004), 31.

55. On the British Empire in the Second World War, see Ashley Jackson (ed.), *The British Empire and the Second World War* (London: Hambledon Continuum, 2006).

56. See Eric Jennings, *Vichy in the Tropics: Pétain's National Revolution in Madagascar, Guadeloupe, and Indochina, 1940–1944* (Stanford: Stanford University Press, 2001); Jacques Cantier, *L'Algérie sous le régime de Vichy* (Paris: Jacob, 2002); Eric Jennings, *Free French Africa in World War II* (Cambridge: Cambridge University Press, 2015).

57. Winston Churchill, "Speech at the Lord Mayor's luncheon, Mansion House, London, November 10, 1942," in *The Collected Works of Sir Winston Churchill*, vol. 20 (London: Library of Imperial History, 1975), 342–45, quote at 344.

3. PATHS TO SOVEREIGNTY

1. Still important: D. A. Low, "The Asian Mirror to Tropical Africa's Independence," in Prosser Gifford and Wm. Roger Louis (eds.), *The Transfer of Power in Africa: Decolonization, 1940–1960*, 2nd ed. (New Haven: Yale University Press, 1982), 1–29.

2. The most important series, reflecting different historiographical stances, are Nicholas Mansergh and Penderel Moon (eds.), *The Transfer of Power 1942–1947: Constitutional Relations between Britain and India*, 12 vols. (London: HMSO, 1970–83); and Sabyasachi Bhattacharya (gen. ed.), *Towards Freedom: Documents on the Movement for Independence in India* (New Delhi: Indian Council for Historical Research, 1997–2013).

3. The classic text is Jawaharlal Nehru's *Autobiography* (London: Bodley Head, 1936, many reprints).

4. The history of Indian independence has frequently been told. For the period after 1942, see, e.g., Claude Markovits, "The End of the British Empire in India," in Markovits (ed.), *A History of Modern India, 1480–1950* (London: Anthem, 2002), 469–91.

5. Thus, most recently, Stanley A. Wolpert, *Shameful Flight: The Last Years of the British Empire in India* (Oxford: Oxford University Press, 2006).

6. On the domestic situation in India during the war years, see Yasmin Khan, *The Raj at War: A People's History of India's Second World War* (London: Bodley Head, 2015).

7. Sugata Bose, *His Majesty's Opponent: Subhas Chandra Bose and India's Struggle against Empire* (Cambridge, MA: Belknap Press, 2011).

8. Christopher Bayly and Tim Harper, *Forgotten Armies: Britain's Asian Empire and the War with Japan* (London: Allen Lane, 2004), 463.

9. On the Labour government and India, see Ronald Hyam, *Britain's Declining Empire: The Road to Decolonisation, 1918–1968* (Cambridge: Cambridge University Press, 2006), 105–16.

10. On violence during the partition, see Talbot and Singh, *Partition of India*, 60–89; see also Gyanendra Pandey, *Remembering Partition: Violence, Nationalism, and History in India* (Cambridge: Cambridge University Press, 2001); Yasmin Khan, *The Great Partition: The Making of India and Pakistan* (New Haven: Yale University Press, 2007).

11. Panhuree R. Dube, "Partition Historiography," *Historian* 77 (2015): 55–79. On the need to integrate elite politics and cultural approaches from below in accounting for the partition in India see Mushirul Hasan, "Partition Narratives," *Social Scientist* 30 (2002): 24–53.

12. Eric Meyer, "Sri Lanka: Specificities and Similarities," in Markovits, *History of Modern India*, 520–38; Patrick Peebles, *The History of Sri Lanka* (Westport, CT: Greenwood Press, 2006), chaps. 5–8.

13. Still a good introduction: Alfred W. McCoy, "The Philippines: Independence without Decolonisation," in Robin Jeffrey (ed.), *Asia: The Winning of Independence* (London: Macmillan, 1981), 23–65.

14. Wonik Kim, "Rethinking Colonialism and the Origins of the Developmental State in East Asia," *Journal of Contemporary Asia* 39 (2009): 382–99.

15. Michael W. Charney, *A History of Modern Burma* (Cambridge: Cambridge University Press, 2009), 46–71; Norman G. Owen et al., *The Emergence of Modern Southeast Asia: A New History* (Honolulu: University of Hawai'i Press, 2005), 322–34; a great deal of material in Christopher A. Bayly and Timothy Harper, *Forgotten Wars: Freedom and Revolution in Southeast Asia* (Cambridge, MA: Belknap Press, 2007).

16. In the following discussion, for the sake of brevity, we focus on Vietnam and ignore Cambodia and Laos, which also belonged to French Indochina.

17. Good general surveys are Bob Moore, "Dutch Decolonization," in Martin Thomas, Bob Moore, and Larry J. Butler, *Crises of Empire: Decolonization and Europe's Imperial States, 1918–1975*, 2nd ed. (London:

Bloomsbury Academic Publishing, 2015), 223–303, esp. 244–78; Marc Frey, "The Indonesian Revolution and the Fall of the Dutch Empire," in Frey, Ronald W. Pruessen, and Tai Yong Tan (eds.), *The Transformation of Southeast Asia: International Perspectives on Decolonization* (Armonk, NY: M. E. Sharpe, 2003), 83–104; M. C. Ricklefs, *A History of Modern Indonesia since c. 1200*, 4th ed. (Basingstoke: Palgrave Macmillan, 2008), 233–70.

18. A standard work is R. E. Elson, *The Idea of Indonesia: A History* (Cambridge: Cambridge University Press, 2008).

19. K. W. Taylor, *A History of the Vietnamese* (Cambridge: Cambridge University Press, 2013), 532–60; Jacques Dalloz, *La guerre d'Indochine 1945–1954* (Paris: Editions du Seuil, 1987).

20. Barbara Watson Andaya and Leonard Y. Andaya, *A History of Malaysia*, 2nd ed. (Basingstoke: Palgrave Macmillan, 2001); Richard Stubbs, *Hearts and Minds in Guerrilla Warfare: The Malayan Emergency* (Singapore: Oxford University Press, 1989).

21. A great deal of material on this subject is covered in David French, *The British Way in Counter-Insurgency, 1945–1967* (Oxford: Oxford University Press, 2011).

22. On British Near Eastern policy after 1945, see Wm. Roger Louis, *The British Empire in the Middle East, 1945–1951: Arab Nationalism, the United States and Postwar Imperialism* (Oxford: Clarendon Press, 1984).

23. See M. W. Daly (ed.), *The Cambridge History of Egypt*, vol. 2: *Modern Egypt, from 1517 to the End of the Twentieth Century* (Cambridge: Cambridge University Press, 1998), chaps. 10–11.

24. On Iraqi "independence," see Charles Tripp, *A History of Iraq*, 3rd ed. (Cambridge: Cambridge University Press, 2007), 65; Peter Sluglett, *Britain in Iraq: Contriving King and Country*, 2nd ed. (London: I. B. Tauris, 2007); on Jordan, see Mary C. Wilson, *King Abdullah, Britain, and the Making of Jordan* (Cambridge: Cambridge University Press, 1987).

25. A standard work is Philip S. Khoury, *Syria and the French Mandate: The Politics of Arab Nationalism, 1920–1945* (London: I. B. Tauris, 1987).

26. From an extensive literature: Wm. Roger Louis and Robert W. Stookey (eds.), *The End of the Palestine Mandate* (London: I. B. Tauris, 1986); Gudrun Krämer, *A History of Palestine: From the Ottoman Conquest to*

the Founding of the State of Israel (Princeton, NJ: Princeton University Press, 2008), chap. 13.

27. On the Suez crisis in all its complexity, see Wm. Roger Louis and Roger Owen (eds.), *Suez 1956: The Crisis and Its Consequences* (Oxford: Clarendon Press, 1989).

28. Martin Thomas, *Fight or Flight: Britain, France, and Their Roads from Empire* (Oxford: Oxford University Press, 2014), 188.

29. Wm. Roger Louis and Roger Owen (eds.), *A Revolutionary Year: The Middle East in 1958* (London: I. B. Tauris, 2002).

30. On Libyan decolonization and the post-independence period, see Adrian Pelt, *Libyan Independence and the United Nations: A Case of Planned Decolonization* (New Haven: Yale University Press, 1970); Dirk J. Vandewalle, *A History of Modern Libya*, 2nd ed. (Cambridge: Cambridge University Press, 2012).

31. See Robert Holland, *Britain and the Revolt in Cyprus, 1954–1959* (Oxford: Clarendon Press, 1998); Spencer Mawby, *British Policy in Aden and the Protectorates, 1955–1967: Last Outpost of a Middle East Empire* (London: Routledge, 2005).

32. See C. R. Pennell, *Morocco since 1830: A History* (New York: New York University Press, 2000), 268–96.

33. Kenneth J. Perkins, *A History of Modern Tunisia*, 2nd ed. (Cambridge: Cambridge University Press, 2013), 115–34.

34. The best surveys to date are Sylvie Thénault, *Histoire de la guerre d'indépendance algérienne* (Paris: Flammarion, 2005); and Martin Evans, *Algeria: France's Undeclared War* (Oxford: Oxford University Press, 2012). An English-language classic, which came out in 1977, is Alistair Horne, *A Savage War of Peace: Algeria, 1954–1962* (New York: New York Review Books, 2006).

35. On the complex interior history of the FLN, see Gilbert Meynier, *Histoire intérieure du FLN: 1954–1962* (Paris: Fayard, 2002).

36. On the systematic use of torture during the war, see Raphaëlle Branche, *La torture et l'armée pendant la guerre d'Algérie, 1954–1962* (Paris: Gallimard, 2001).

37. A classic on this (originally published in German in 1974) is Hartmut Elsenhans, *La guerre d'Algérie, 1954–1962: La transition d'une France à une autre* (Paris: Publisud, 1999); more recently, also, Moritz Feichtinger

and Stephan Malinowski, " 'Eine Million Algerier lernen im 20. Jahrhundert zu leben': Umsiedlungslager und Zwangsmodernisierung im Algerienkrieg 1954–1962," *Journal of Modern European History* 8 (2010): 107–35.

38. On these different fronts, see Matthew Connelly, "Rethinking the Cold War and Decolonization: The Grand Strategy of the Algerian War for Independence," *International Journal of Middle East Studies* 33 (2001): 221–45; Sylvie Thénault, *Violence ordinaire dans l'Algérie coloniale: Camps, internements, assignations à domicile* (Paris: Jacob, 2012), 293–94. On FLN's important south-south diplomacy, see Jeffrey James Byrne, *Mecca of the Revolution: Algeria, Decolonization, and the Third World Order* (Oxford: Oxford University Press, 2016).

39. See, inter alia, Raphaëlle Branche (ed.), *La guerre d'indépendance des Algériens (1954–1962)* (Paris: Perrin, 2009); Raphaëlle Branche and Sylvie Thénault (eds.), *La France en guerre 1954–1962: Expériences métropolitaines de la guerre d'indépendance algérienne* (Paris: Autrement, 2008).

40. Frederick Cooper, *Africa since 1940: The Past to the Present* (Cambridge: Cambridge University Press, 2002), 64–65, 83.

41. Dennis Austin, *Politics in Ghana, 1946–1960*, 2nd ed. (London: Oxford University Press, 1970).

42. On Nkrumah's and his Convention People's Party's rise to power within the Gold Coast and local resistance, see Richard Rathbone, *Nkrumah and the Chiefs: The Politics of Chieftancy in Ghana, 1951–60* (Oxford: James Curry, 2000); Jean Allman, *The Quills of the Porcupine: Asante Nationalism in an Emergent Ghana* (Madison: University of Wisconsin Press, 1993).

43. Lasse Heerten and A. Dirk Moses, "The Nigeria-Biafra War: Postcolonial Conflict and the Question of Genocide," *Journal of Genocide Research* 16 (2014): 169–203; Morris Davis, *Interpreters for Nigeria: The Third World and International Public Relations* (Urbana: University of Illinois Press, 1977).

44. On the much less studied case of AEF, see Florence Bernault, *Démocraties ambiguës en Afrique centrale: Congo-Brazzaville, Gabon, 1940–1965* (Paris: Karthala, 1996).

45. Elizabeth Schmidt, *Cold War and Decolonization in Guinea, 1946–1958* (Athens, OH: Ohio University Press, 2007), 158–68.

46. Finn Fuglestad, "Djibo Bakary, the French, and the Referendum of 1958 in Niger," *Journal of African History* 14 (1973): 313–30.

47. Guy Vanthemsche, *Belgium and the Congo, 1885–1980* (Cambridge: Cambridge University Press, 2012), 31. An early detailed account of the Congo crisis is Crawford Young, *Politics in the Congo: Decolonization and Independence* (Princeton, NJ: Princeton University Press, 1965); on the international dimensions, see John Kent, *America, the UN and Decolonisation: Cold War Conflict in the Congo* (London: Routledge, 2010). For Belgian popular perceptions of the Congo, see Matthew G. Stanard, *Selling the Congo: A History of European Pro-Empire Propaganda and the Making of Belgian Imperialism* (Lincoln: University of Nebraska Press, 2012).

48. Miles Larmer and Erik Kennes, "Rethinking the Katangese Secession," *Journal of Imperial and Commonwealth History* 42 (2014): 741–61.

49. See Richard A. Joseph, *Radical Nationalism in Cameroun: Social Origins of the UPC Rebellion* (Oxford: Clarendon Press, 1977).

50. Still fundamental is the work by Jacques Tronchon, *L'insurrection malgache de 1947: Essai d'interprétation historique* (Paris: F. Maspero, 1974).

51. David Anderson, *Histories of the Hanged: The Dirty War in Kenya and the End of Empire* (New York: W. W. Norton, 2005); Caroline Elkins, *Britain's Gulag: The Brutal End of Empire in Kenya* (London: Cape, 2005); Daniel Branch, *Defeating Mau Mau, Creating Kenya: Counterinsurgency, Civil War and Decolonization* (Cambridge: Cambridge University Press, 2009).

52. Fabian Klose, *Human Rights in the Shadow of Colonial Violence: The Wars of Independence in Kenya and Algeria* (Philadelphia: University of Pennsylvania Press, 2013), 192–219.

53. Burbank and Cooper, *Empires in World History*, 427–28.

54. See Norrie MacQueen, *The Decolonization of Portuguese Africa: Metropolitan Revolution and the Dissolution of Empire* (London: Longman, 1997); António Costa Pinto, *O fim do império português: A cena internacional, a guerra colonial, e a descolonização, 1961–1975* (Lisbon: Livros Horizonte, 2001). On the international context in Portuguese decolonization, see Miguel Bandeira Jerónimo and António Costa Pinto (eds.), *Portugal e o fim do colonialismo: Dimensões internacionais* (Lisbon: Edições 70, 2014); Luís Nuno Rodrigues, "The International Dimensions of

Portuguese Colonial Crisis," in Jerónimo and Pinto, *European Colonial Empires*, 243–67.

55. Luise White, *Unpopular Sovereignty: Rhodesian Independence and African Decolonization* (Chicago: University of Chicago Press, 2015), 265–67.

56. With numerous comparisons, see Gert Oostindie and Inge Klinkers, *Decolonising the Caribbean: Dutch Policies in a Comparative Perspective* (Amsterdam: Amsterdam University Press, 2003).

57. See the overview in Robert Aldrich and John Connell, *France's Overseas Frontier: Départements et territoires d'outre-mer* (Cambridge: Cambridge University Press, 2006).

58. Other European countries (Denmark, Spain, and Portugal) and former British dominions (Australia, New Zealand) have also retained smaller overseas territories. A good, if slightly outdated, overview is provided by Robert Aldrich and John Connell, *The Last Colonies* (Cambridge: Cambridge University Press, 1998).

59. Christoph Marx, *Südafrika: Geschichte und Gegenwart* (Stuttgart: Kohlhammer, 2012), 254–90.

4. ECONOMY

1. Caroline Elkins and Susan Pedersen, "Settler Colonialism: A Concept and Its Uses," in Elkins and Pedersen (eds.), *Settler Colonialism in the Twentieth Century: Projects, Practices, Legacies* (New York: Routledge, 2005), 1–20.

2. On the influence of settlers on metropolitan policy, see Miles Kahler, *Decolonization in Britain and France: The Domestic Consequences of International Relations* (Princeton, NJ: Princeton University Press 1984), 316–53.

3. Malyn Newitt, "The Late Colonial State in Portuguese Africa," *Itinerario* 23 (1999): 110–22, quote at 119; Malyn Newitt, *Portugal in European and World History* (London: Reaktion, 2009), 210–11.

4. See, e.g., the American and Dutch owned New Guinean oil company withholding information about important oil fields for roughly 25 years; see Moore, "Dutch Decolonization," 284.

5. Robert L. Tignor, *Capitalism and Nationalism at the End of the Empire: State and Business in Decolonizing Egypt, Nigeria, and Kenya, 1945–1963* (Princeton, NJ: Princeton University Press, 1998), 381–82.

6. J. Thomas Lindblad, *Bridges to New Business: The Economic Decolonization of Indonesia* (Leiden: KITLV Press, 2008), 65–66.

7. Hendrik Spruyt, *Ending Empire: Contested Sovereignty and Territorial Partition* (Ithaca, NY: Cornell University Press, 2005), 161–64.

8. Larry J. Butler, *Copper Empire: Mining and the Colonial State in Northern Rhodesia, c. 1930–1964* (Basingstoke: Palgrave Macmillan, 2007), 194–232.

9. See Beverley Hooper, *China Stands Up: Ending the Western Presence, 1948–1950* (Sydney: Allen and Unwin, 1986); Jonathan J. Howlett, "'The British Boss Is Gone and Will Never Return': Communist Takeovers of British Companies in Shanghai (1949–1954)," *Modern Asian Studies* 47 (2013): 1941–76.

10. J. Thomas Lindblad, "British Business and the Uncertainties of Early Independence in Indonesia," *Itinerario* 37 (2013): 147–64, quote at 154.

11. J. Thomas Lindblad, "Economic Growth and Decolonisation in Indonesia," *Itinerario* 34 (2010): 97–112, at 103–105; see also Nicholas J. White, "Surviving Sukarno: British Business in Post-Colonial Indonesia, 1950–1967," *Modern Asian Studies* 46 (2012): 1277–315.

12. Jan Luiten van Zanden and Daan Marks, *An Economic History of Indonesia, 1800–2010* (London: Routledge, 2012), 138.

13. Rothermund, *Routledge Companion to Decolonization*, 66–67.

14. Hugues Tertrais, "Le patronat français et la guerre d'Indochine," in Hubert Bonin et al. (eds.), *L'esprit économique impériale (1830–1970): Groupes de pression et réseaux du patronat colonial en France et dans l'empire* (Paris: Publications de la Société française d'histoire d'outre-mer, 2008), 185–92.

15. Pierre Brocheux, *Une histoire économique du Viet Nam 1850–2007: La palanche et le camion* (Paris: Indes savantes, 2009), 175.

16. On these plans, see Daniel Lefeuvre, *Chère Algérie: Comptes et mécomptes de la tutelle coloniale, 1930–1962* (Saint-Denis: Publications de la Société française d'histoire d'outre-mer, 1997).

17. Roger Pasquier, "Les milieux d'affaires face à la décolonisation (1956–1960)," in Charles-Robert Ageron and Marc Michel (eds.), *L'Afrique noire française: L'heure des indépendances*, 2nd ed. (Paris: CNRS Éditions, 2010), 331–60, at 352.

18. Jean-Pierre Dormois and François Crouzet, "The Significance of the French Colonial Empire for French Economic Development (1815–1960)," *Revista de Historia Economica* 15 (1998): 323–49.

19. Not to be confused with the more loosely organized sterling bloc of the interwar period.

20. Darwin, *End of the British Empire*, 46

21. Gerold Krozewski, *Money and the End of Empire: British International Economic Policy and the Colonies, 1947–58* (Basingstoke: Palgrave Macmillan, 2001).

22. Catherine R. Schenk, *The Decline of Sterling: Managing the Retreat of an International Currency, 1945–1992* (Cambridge: Cambridge University Press, 2010), 88–89.

23. Shigeru Akita, Gerold Krozewski, and Shoichi Watanabe (eds.), *The Transformation of the International Order of Asia: Decolonization, the Cold War, and the Colombo Plan* (London: Routledge, 2015).

24. Nicholas J. White, "The Frustrations of Development: British Business and the Late Colonial State in Malaya, 1945–57," *Journal of Southeast Asian Studies* 28 (1997): 103–19, quote at 105; Sarah Stockwell, "Trade, Empire, and the Fiscal Context of Imperial Business during Decolonization," *Economic History Review* 57 (2004): 142–60, esp. 145 et seq.

25. Nicholas J. White, "The Business and the Politics of Decolonization: The British Experience in the Twentieth Century," *Economic History Review* 53 (2000): 544–64, quote at 550.

26. Jacques Marseille, *Empire colonial et capitalisme français: Histoire d'un divorce*, 2nd ed. (Paris: A. Michel, 2005), 478–98, 579–92.

27. Ageron, *Décolonisation française*, 120–21; Hugues Tertrais, "Conjoncture française et guerre d'Indochine: Le temps des périls (1945–1954)," *Relations Internationales* 82 (1995): 197–211, quote at 210.

28. On continuities, even across different ideological camps, see Michael Mahoney, "*Estado Novo, Homem Novo* (New State, New Man): Colonial and Anti-Colonial Development Ideologies in Mozambique, 1930–1977," in David C. Engerman et al. (eds.), *Staging Growth: Modernization, Development, and the Global Cold War* (Amherst: University of Massachusetts Press, 2003), 165–97; Joseph M. Hodge, *Triumph of the Expert: Agrarian Doctrines of Development and the Legacies of British Colonialism* (Athens, OH: Ohio University Press, 2007).

29. As summarized in Nicholas J. White, "Reconstructing Europe through Rejuvenating Empire: The British, French, and Dutch Experiences Compared," in Mark Mazower, Jessica Reinisch, and David Feldman (eds.), *Post-war Reconstruction in Europe: International Perspec-*

tives, 1945–1949 (Oxford: Oxford University Press, 2011), 211–236, esp. 220–228.

30. This ambivalence is presented in detail in David K. Fieldhouse, *Unilever Overseas: The Anatomy of a Multinational, 1895–1965* (London: Croom Helm, 1978); also see Fieldhouse, *Merchant Capital and Economic Decolonization: The United Africa Company, 1929–1987* (Oxford: Clarendon Press, 1994).

31. Nicholas J. White, *British Business in Post-Colonial Malaysia, 1957–70: "Neo-Colonialism" or "Disengagement"?* (London: RoutledgeCurzon, 2004), 8–9.

32. See, as a case study, Stephanie Decker, "Corporate Legitimacy and Advertising: British Companies and the Rhetoric of Development in West Africa, 1950–1970," *Business History Review* 81 (2007): 59–86.

33. Thirthankar Roy, *India in the World Economy: From Antiquity to the Present* (Cambridge: Cambridge University Press, 2012), 220.

34. A striking example for this is James R. Brennan, "The Cold War Battle over Global News in East Africa: Decolonization, the Free Flow of Information, and the Media Business, 1960–1980," *Journal of Global History* 10 (2015): 333–56.

35. Jeremy Prestholdt, *Domesticating the World: African Consumerism and the Genealogies of Globalization* (Berkeley: University of California Press, 2006).

36. Karl Gerth, *China Made: Consumer Culture and the Creation of the Nation* (Cambridge, MA: Harvard University Press, 2003); Nancy T. Reynolds, *A City Consumed: Urban Commerce, the Cairo Fire, and the Politics of Decolonization in Egypt* (Stanford: Stanford University Press, 2012).

5. WORLD POLITICS

1. See Michael E. Latham, "The Cold War in the Third World," in Melvyn P. Leffler and Odd Arne Westad (eds.), *The Cambridge History of the Cold War*, vol. 2 (Cambridge: Cambridge University Press, 2010), 258–80; Ryan M. Irwin, "Decolonization and the Cold War," in Artemy M. Kalinovsky and Craig Daigle (eds.), *The Routledge Handbook of the Cold War* (London: Routledge, 2014), 91–104.

2. By way of introduction, see Michael H. Hunt, *The World Transformed: 1945 to the Present*, 2nd ed. (New York: Oxford University Press, 2015);

Michael H. Hunt, *The World Transformed: 1945 to the Present; A Documentary Reader*, 2nd ed. (New York: Oxford University Press, 2015); Jussi M. Hanhimäki and Odd Arne Westad, *The Cold War: A History in Documents and Eyewitness Accounts*, 2nd ed. (Oxford: Oxford University Press, 2004); Edward H. Judge, *The Cold War: A Global History with Documents* (Boston: Prentice Hall, 2011); with special attention to Asia, Robert J. McMahon, *The Cold War: A Very Short Introduction* (Oxford: Oxford University Press, 2003); comprehensively, Melvyn P. Leffler and Westad (eds.), *The Cambridge History of the Cold War*, 3 vols. (Cambridge: Cambridge University Press, 2010); Richard H. Immerman and Petra Goedde (eds.), *The Oxford Handbook of the Cold War* (Oxford: Oxford University Press, 2013); Kalinovsky and Daigle, *Routledge Handbook of the Cold War*.

3. There are many estimates. Relatively well acknowledged are those provided by Milton Leitenberg (including figures on decolonization conflicts) in "Deaths in Wars and Conflicts in the 20th Century," cf.edliostatic.com, accessed March 3, 2016. http://cf.edliostatic.com/rj VDXUiI3oTJZUqoSFdfkdTxVPfGcZJb.pdf. (Print version: Ithaca, NY: Cornell University Press, 2006).

4. See Seng Tan and Amitav Acharya (eds.), *Bandung Revisited: The Legacy of the 1955 Asian-African Conference for International Order* (Singapore: NUS Press, 2008); Christopher J. Lee (ed.), *Making a World after Empire: The Bandung Moment and Its Political Afterlives* (Athens, OH: Ohio University Press, 2010); Naoko Shimazu, "Diplomacy as Theatre: Staging the Bandung Conference of 1955," *Modern Asian Studies* 48 (2014): 225–52; Jürgen Dinkel, *Die Bewegung Bündnisfreier Staaten: Genese, Organisation und Politik (1927–1992)* (Berlin: de Gruyter, 2015).

5. Thomas Borstelmann, *Apartheid's Reluctant Uncle: The United States and Southern Africa in the Early Cold War* (New York: Oxford University Press, 1993), esp. 166–92.

6. See Odd Arne Westad, *The Global Cold War: Third World Interventions and the Making of Our Times* (Cambridge: Cambridge University Press, 2005), 316–30; Vijay Prashad, *The Darker Nations: A People's History of the Third World* (New York: New Press, 2007); see also many insightful remarks in Michael Mann, *The Sources of Social Power*, vol. 4: *Globalizations, 1945–2011* (Cambridge: Cambridge University Press, 2013).

7. Marika Sherwood, "India at the Founding of the United Nations," *International Studies* 33 (1996): 407–28; Leslie James, *George Padmore and Decolonization from Below: Pan-Africanism, the Cold War, and the End of Empire* (Basingstoke: Palgrave Macmillan, 2014), 58–68.

8. Robert J. McMahon, *The Limits of Empire: The United States and Southeast Asia since World War II* (New York: Columbia University Press, 1999), 26–28.

9. See S. C. M. Paine, *The Wars for Asia, 1911–1949* (Cambridge: Cambridge University Press, 2012); also Bayly and Harper, *Forgotten Armies*, 462.

10. On the Korean war and its significance, see Michael H. Hunt and Steven I. Levine, *Arc of Empire: America's Wars in Asia from the Philippines to Vietnam* (Chapel Hill: University of North Carolina Press, 2012), 120–84.

11. Hugues Tertrais, *Le piastre et le fusil: Le coût de la guerre d'Indochine 1945–1954* (Paris: Ministère de l'économie, des finances et de l'industrie, Comité pour l'histoire économique et financière de la France, 2002), 270.

12. Wm. Roger Louis and Ronald Robinson, "Empire Preserv'd: How the Americans Put Anti-Communism before Anti-Imperialism," in Duara, *Decolonization*, 152–61, quote at 152. For a fuller treatment: Wm. Roger Louis, *Ends of British Imperialism: The Scramble for Empire, Suez and Decolonization* (London: I. B. Tauris, 2006), 451–502.

13. John Kent, "The United States and the Decolonization of Black Africa, 1945–63," in David Ryan and Victor Pungong (eds.), *The United States and Decolonization: Power and Freedom* (Basingstoke: Palgrave Macmillan, 2000), 174–75.

14. Salim Yaqub, *Containing Arab Nationalism: The Eisenhower Doctrine and the Middle East* (Chapel Hill: University of North Carolina Press, 2004), 83–84; comprehensively, Douglas Little, *American Orientalism: The United States and the Middle East since 1945*, 2nd ed. (Chapel Hill: University of North Carolina Press, 2008); Stephen P. Cohen, *Beyond America's Grasp: A Century of Failed Diplomacy in the Middle East* (New York: Farrar, Straus and Giroux, 2009).

15. P. L. Pham, *Ending "East of Suez": The British Decision to Withdraw from Malaysia and Singapore, 1964–1968* (Oxford: Oxford University Press, 2010), 238–39.

16. Initially, the United States was interested most of all in the Congo: Gerhard Th. Mollin, *Die USA und der Kolonialismus: Amerika als Partner und Nachfolger der belgischen Macht in Afrika, 1939–1965* (Berlin: Akademie Verlag, 1996); for an overview, see Michael E. Latham, "The Cold War in the Third World," in Leffler and Westad, *Cambridge History of the Cold War*, vol. 2, 258–80.

17. Jeffrey James Byrne, "The Cold War in Africa," in Kalinovsky and Daigle, *Routledge Handbook of the Cold War*, 149–62, esp. 153.

18. Paul Nugent, *Africa since Independence: A Comparative History*, 2nd ed. (Basingstoke: Palgrave Macmillan, 2004), 246–49.

19. Mark Kramer, "The Decline of Soviet Arms Transfers to the Third World, 1986–1991: Political, Economic, and Military Dimensions," in Artemy M. Kalinovsky and Sergey Radchenko (eds.), *The End of the Cold War and the Third World: New Perspectives on Regional Conflict* (London: Routledge, 2011), 46–100, at 46.

20. Piero Gleijeses, *Conflicting Missions: Havana, Washington, and Africa, 1959–1976* (Chapel Hill: University of North Carolina Press, 2002); Christine Hatzky, *Kubaner in Angola: Süd-Süd-Kooperation und Bildungstransfer 1967–1991* (Munich: Oldenbourg, 2012).

21. By way of summary, see Elizabeth Schmidt, *Foreign Intervention in Africa: From the Cold War to the War on Terror* (Cambridge: Cambridge University Press, 2013), chaps. 4–5.

22. Stephen L. Weigert, *Angola: A Modern Military History, 1961–2002* (Basingstoke: Palgrave Macmillan, 2011); on another trouble spot, the Horn of Africa, see Fred Marte, *Political Cycles in International Relations: The Cold War and Africa 1945–1990* (Amsterdam: VU University Press, 1994), 197–269.

23. Westad, *Global Cold War*, 316–30; Artemy M. Kalinovsky, *A Long Goodbye: The Soviet Withdrawal from Afghanistan* (Cambridge, MA: Harvard University Press, 2011).

24. Emphasizing imperial plans, see Mark Mazower, *No Enchanted Palace: The End of Empire and the Ideological Origins of the United Nations* (Princeton, NJ: Princeton University Press, 2009).

25. See the case study by John D. Kelly and Martha Kaplan, *Represented Communities: Fiji and World Decolonisation* (Chicago: University of Chicago Press, 2001).

26. "Declaration on the Granting of Independence to Colonial Countries and Peoples," UN.org, accessed February 29, 2016. http://www.un.org/en/decolonization/declaration.shtml.

27. See the influential study by Matthew Connelly, *A Diplomatic Revolution: Algeria's Fight for Independence and the Origins of the Post–Cold War Era* (Oxford: Oxford University Press, 2002).

28. Thomas Borstelmann, *The 1970s: A New Global History from Civil Rights to Economic Inequality* (Princeton, NJ: Princeton University Press, 2011), 14–15, 295.

29. Stefan-Ludwig Hoffmann (ed.), *Human Rights in the Twentieth Century* (Cambridge: Cambridge University Press, 2011); Roland Burke, *Decolonization and the Evolution of International Human Rights* (Philadelphia: University of Pennsylvania Press, 2010); Jan Eckel, *Die Ambivalenz des Guten: Menschenrechte in der internationalen Politik seit den 1940ern*, 2nd ed. (Göttingen: Vandenhoeck & Ruprecht, 2015), esp. chap. 5; also important were legal developments in individual colonies as described in Charles O. H. Parkinson, *Bills of Rights and Decolonization: The Emergence of Domestic Human Rights Instruments in Britain's Overseas Territories* (Oxford: Oxford University Press, 2007).

30. A. W. Brian Simpson, *Human Rights and the End of Empire: Britain and the Genesis of the European Convention* (Oxford: Oxford University Press, 2001), 89–90.

31. Fisch, *Selbstbestimmungsrecht*; Bradley R. Simpson, "Self-Determination, Human Rights and the End of Empire in the 1970s," *Humanity* 4 (2013): 239–60; on the longer history of ideas, see Eric D. Weitz, "Self-Determination: How a German Enlightenment Idea became the Slogan of National Liberation and a Human Right," *American Historical Review* 120 (2015): 462–96.

6. IDEAS AND PROGRAMS

1. *The Collected Works of Mahatma Gandhi*, 100 vols. (New Delhi: Ministry of Information and Broadcasting, 1958–1997), including 3 volumes of index.

2. Raymond F. Betts, *Decolonization*, 2nd ed. (New York: Routledge, 2004), 38.

3. Osterhammel and Jansen, *Kolonialismus*, 112–17.

4. Sun Yat-sen (1866–1925) was mainly an anti-Manchu activist for much of his revolutionary career. He only turned against the Western powers during the last years of his life when he gained the support of the Soviet Union.

5. Bassam Tibi, "Politische Ideen in der 'Dritten Welt' während der Dekolonisation," in Iring Fetscher and Herfried Münkler (eds.), *Pipers Handbuch der politischen Ideen*, vol. 5 (Munich: Piper, 1987), 361–402; on Asia, see Pankaj Mishra, *From the Ruins of Empire: The Intellectuals Who Remade Asia* (New York: Farrar, Straus and Giroux, 2012). A wide-ranging survey is Bikhu Parekh, "Non-Western Political Thought," in Terence Ball and Richard Bellamy (eds.), *The Cambridge History of Twentieth-Century Political Thought* (Cambridge: Cambridge University Press, 2003), 553–78.

6. For a related approach from a political science perspective, see Margaret Kohn and Keally McBride, *Political Theories of Decolonization: Postcolonialism and the Problem of Foundations* (Oxford: Oxford University Press, 2011).

7. See, for Asia, Mishra, *Ruins of Empire*.

8. A standard work on the following is Todd Shepard, *The Invention of Decolonization: The Algerian War and the Remaking of France* (Ithaca, NY: Cornell University Press, 2006), esp. 55–100. See also Paul Clay Sorum, *Intellectuals and Decolonization in France* (Chapel Hill: University of North Carolina Press, 1977); and James D. Le Sueur, *Uncivil War: Intellectuals and Identity Politics during the Decolonization of Algeria*, 2nd ed. (Lincoln: University of Nebraska Press, 2005).

9. Shepard, *Invention of Decolonization*, 82–83. See also Ward, "European Provenance," 259.

10. Harold Macmillan, "Address to Both Houses of the Parliament of the Union of South Africa, Cape Town, February 3, 1960," in Ronald Hyam and Wm. Roger Louis (eds.), *British Documents on the End of Empire*, series A, vol. 3: *The Conservative Government and the End of Empire, 1957–1964*, part 1 (London: Stationery Office, 2000), 167–74. On the history of this speech, see Larry J. Butler and Sarah Stockwell (eds.), *The Wind of Change: Harold Macmillan and British Decolonization* (Basingstoke: Palgrave Macmillan, 2013).

11. The term "panacea" is from Hyam, *Britain's Declining Empire*, 9, 165–66. See also Cooper, *Citizenship*; Michael Collins, "Decolonisation and the 'Federal Moment'," *Diplomacy and Statecraft* 24 (2013): 21–40.

12. Cooper, *Colonialism in Question*, 11. On the same same topic, see Wolfgang Reinhard (ed.), *Verstaatlichung der Welt? Europäische Staatsmodelle und außereuropäische Machtprozesse* (Munich: Oldenbourg, 1999).

13. Charter of the Organization of African Unity (25 May 1963), Article III, 2–3.

14. Andreas Eckert, "Anti-Western Doctrines of Nationalism," in Breuilly, *Handbook of the History of Nationalism*, 56–74, quote at 70. On the relationship of anticolonialism to nationalism, see also chapter 2 of this book.

15. Georges Balandier, "The Colonial Situation: A Theoretical Approach (1951)," in Immanuel Wallerstein (ed.), *Social Change: The Colonial Situation* (New York: John Wiley, 1966), 34–61. On the context and reception of Balandier's article, see Jean Copans (ed.), "Georges Balandier, lecture et re-lecture," special issue of *Cahiers Internationaux de Sociologie* 110 (2001); Marie-Claude Smouts (ed.), *La situation postcoloniale: Les postcolonial studies dans le débat français* (Paris: Presses de Sciences Po, 2007). For Balandier's anticolonial working context, see Gregory Mann, "Anti-Colonialism and Social Science: Georges Balandier, Madeira Keita, and 'the Colonial Situation' in French Africa," *Comparative Studies in Society and History* 55 (2013): 92–119.

16. Aimé Césaire, *Discourse on Colonialism* (New York: Monthly Review Press, 1972), 13, 19–20, 61. The original French version came out in 1950.

17. Albert Memmi, *The Colonizer and the Colonized* (New York: Orion Press, 1965); Octave Mannoni, *Psychologie de la colonisation* (Paris: Editions du Seuil, 1950). Memmi's book originally appeared in French in 1957. Mannoni's work was severely criticized by anticolonial thinkers such as Fanon for the use of colonialist clichés such as the preexisting inferiority of the colonized.

18. Frantz Fanon, *Black Skin, White Masks*, new ed. (New York: Grove Press, 2008). The original French edition was published in 1952.

19. Frantz Fanon, *The Wretched of the Earth*, new ed. (New York: Grove Press, 2004), esp. 1–52. The original French edition was published in 1961.

20. On the origins and development of the concept, see Mark T. Berger, "After the Third World? History, Destiny and the Fate of Third Worldism," *Third World Quarterly* 25 (2004): 9–39; Christoph Kalter, *Die Entdeckung der Dritten Welt: Dekolonisierung und neue radikale Linke in Frankreich* (Frankfurt: Campus, 2011), 44–80.

21. There are more levels of meaning distinguished by Jennifer Wenzel, "Remembering the Past's Future: Anti-Imperialist Nostalgia and Some Versions of the Third World," *Cultural Critique* 62 (2006): 1–32.

22. Prashad, *Darker Nations*, xv.

23. Robert Malley, *The Call from Algeria: Third Worldism, Revolution, and the Turn to Islam* (Berkeley: University of California Press, 1996), 112.

24. Prasenjit Duara, "The Discourse of Civilization and Decolonization," *Journal of World History* 15 (2004): 1–5, quote at 3.

25. Mohamed Chérif Sahli, *Décoloniser l'histoire: Introduction à l'histoire du Maghreb* (Paris: Maspero, 1965); Ngũgĩ wa Thiong'o, *Decolonising the Mind: The Politics of Language in African Literature* (London: Currey, 1986). Most recently, for example, Amy Allen, *The End of Progress: Decolonizing the Normative Foundations of Critical Theory* (New York: Columbia University Press, 2016). See also Cooper, *Africa*, 187–89.

26. For overviews putting the emergence of postcolonialism in historical perspective, see Robert J. C. Young, *Postcolonialism: An Historical Introduction* (Oxford: Blackwell, 2001); María do Mar Castro Varela and Nikita Dhawan, *Postkoloniale Theorie: Eine kritische Einführung*, 2nd ed. (Bielefeld: Transcript, 2015).

27. See Neil Lazarus, *The Postcolonial Unconscious* (Cambridge: Cambridge University Press, 2011), 33–34.

28. Robert J. C. Young, *Empire, Colony, Postcolony* (Oxford: Wiley Blackwell, 2015), 149.

29. For a different position, see Young, *Postcolonialism*.

30. For an early and a more recent critical appreciation, see Dane Kennedy, "Imperial History and Post-Colonial Theory," *Journal of Imperial and Commonwealth History* 24 (1996): 345–63; Sebastian Conrad, *What Is Global History?* (Princeton, NJ: Princeton University Press, 2016), 53–57.

7. LEGACIES AND MEMORIES

1. *New York Times*, August 8, 2015.

2. Vanessa Ogle, *The Global Transformation of Time, 1870–1950* (Cambridge, MA: Harvard University Press, 2015), 94–95 (Japanese-Korean case).

3. Betts, *Decolonization*, 1.

4. Randall Hansen, *Citizenship and Immigration in Post-War Britain: The Institutional Origins of a Multicultural Nation* (Oxford: Oxford University Press, 2000); Weil, *How to Be French*, chap. 6; Hans van Amersfoort and Mies van Niekerk, "Immigration as a Colonial Inheritance: Post-Colonial Immigration in the Netherlands, 1945–2002" *Journal of Ethnic and Migration Studies* 32 (2006): 323–46. In comparative perspective: Imke Sturm-Martin, *Zuwanderungspolitik in Großbritannien und Frankreich: Ein historischer Vergleich (1945–1962)* (Frankfurt: Campus, 2001).

5. Matthew Lange and Andrew Dawson, "Dividing and Ruling the World? A Statistical Test of the Effects of Colonialism on Postcolonial Civil Violence," *Social Forces* 88 (2009): 785–818.

6. See the series of field studies in different parts of the world by William F. S. Miles, *Scars of Partition: Postcolonial Legacies in French and British Borderlands* (Lincoln: University of Nebraska Press, 2014).

7. For a subtle discussion of such mechanisms of transmission, see Jean-François Bayart and Romain Bertrand, "De quel 'legs colonial' parle-t-on?" *Esprit* 12 (2006): 134–60.

8. See, for example, the long and inconclusive debate among political scientists about the specific nature of the African postcolonial state and the weight of the colonial legacy, e.g., Jean-François Bayart, *The State in Africa: The Politics of the Belly*, 2nd ed. (Cambridge, MA: Polity, 2009); Mahmood Mamdani, *Citizen and Subject: Contemporary Africa and the Legacy of Late Colonialism* (Princeton, NJ: Princeton University Press, 1996); Achille Mbembe, *On the Postcolony* (Berkeley: University of California Press, 2001); Crawford Young, *The Post-Colonial State in Africa: Fifty Years of Independence, 1960–2010* (Madison: University of Wisconsin Press, 2012).

9. According to Michel Foucher, *Fronts et frontières: Un tour du monde géopolitique*, 2nd ed. (Paris: Fayard, 1991), 49.

10. For a comparison of several cases of successful and failed secessions in postcolonial Africa, see Redie Bereketeab (ed.), *Self-Determination and Secession in Africa: The Post-Colonial State* (London: Routledge, 2015).

11. For a good overview of different types of decolonization migration, see Ian Talbot, "The End of the European Colonial Empires and Forced Migration: Some Comparative Case Studies," in Panikos Panayi and Pippa Virdee (eds.), *Refugees and the End of Empire: Imperial Collapse and Forced Migration in the Twentieth Century* (Basingstoke: Palgrave Macmillan, 2011), 28–50.

12. On Françafrique, see Jean-Pierre Bat, *Le syndrome Foccart: La politique française en Afrique, de 1959 à nos jours* (Paris: Gallimard, 2012).

13. For a more detailed look at this, see Osterhammel and Jansen, *Kolonialismus*, 123–26. The "minimal impact thesis" is formulated in Stuart Ward, "Introduction," in Stuart Ward (ed.), *British Culture and the End of Empire* (Manchester: Manchester University Press, 2001), 1–20, at 4.

14. A still highly informative early attempt at a broad comparison is Hugh Seton-Hall (ed.), "Imperial Hangovers," special issue of *Journal of Contemporary History* 15 (1980). A balanced discussion of how decolonization affected one metropole is provided by Christoph Kalter and Martin Rempe, "La République décolonisée: Wie die Dekolonisierung Frankreich verändert hat," *Geschichte und Gesellschaft* 37 (2011): 157–97.

15. On the Franco-British comparison, see Kahler, *Decolonization in Britain and France*, chaps. 2–3.

16. Herman Lebovics, *Bringing the Empire Back Home: France in the Global Age* (Durham, NC: Duke University Press, 2004), 58–82.

17. See Martin Rempe, *Decolonization by Europeanization? The Early EEC and the Transformation of French-African Relations* (Berlin: KFG Working Paper Series, 2011), 13–15.

18. The long process leading to British EEC membership is reconstructed by Alex May, "The Commonwealth and Britain's Turn to Europe, 1945–73," *Round Table* 102 (2013): 29–39; the significance of British membership in the EU is discussed by Hyam, *Britain's Declining Empire*, 239, 301–10; and by Darwin, *End of the British Empire*, 47–51.

19. For a survey that also encompasses the cultural consequences, see Elizabeth Buettner, *Europe after Empire: Decolonization, Society, and Culture* (Cambridge: Cambridge University Press, 2016).

20. Overviews and numbers in Bouda Etemad, "Europe and Migration after Decolonization," *Journal of European Economic History* 27 (1998): 457–70; Smith, *Europe's Invisible Migrants*; Jean-Louis Miège and Colette Dubois (eds.), *L'Europe retrouvée: Les migrations de la décolonisa-*

tion (Paris: L'Harmattan, 1994). For a provocative comparison of two often overlooked subgroups, see Michael O. Sharpe, *Postcolonial Citizens and Ethnic Migrants: The Netherlands and Japan in the Age of Globalization* (Basingstoke: Palgrave Macmillan, 2014).

21. Lori Watt, *When Empire Comes Home: Repatriation and Reintegration in Postwar Japan* (Cambridge, MA: Harvard University Press, 2009).

22. On the concept of the "postcolonial bonus," see Gert Oostindie, *Postcolonial Netherlands: Sixty-Five Years of Forgetting, Commemorating, Silencing* (Amsterdam: Amsterdam University Press, 2011), 15–16. The French case has been thoroughly studied by Yann Scioldo-Zürcher, *Devenir métropolitain: Politique d'intégration et parcours de rapatriés d'Algérie en métropole (1954–2005)* (Paris: EHESS, 2010); for comparative perspectives on the French repatriates: Manuel Borutta and Jan C. Jansen (eds.), *Vertriebene and Pieds-Noirs in Postwar Germany and France: Comparative Perspectives* (Basingstoke: Palgrave Macmillan, 2016).

23. On these processes, see Hansen, *Citizenship*; Amelia H. Lyons, "French or Foreign? The Algerian Migrants' Status at the End of Empire (1962–1968)," *Journal of Modern European History* 12 (2014): 126–44. For the early beginnings of the end of imperial citizenship, with regard to India and Pakistan, see Sarah Ansari, "Subjects or Citizens? India, Pakistan and the 1948 British Nationality Act," *Journal of Imperial and Commonwealth History* 41 (2013): 285–312.

24. Jordanna Bailkin, *The Afterlife of Empire* (Berkeley: University of California Press, 2012), quote at 237.

25. See Kalter and Rempe, "République décolonisée," 182.

26. For a recent collection with a metropolitan focus, see Ruth Craggs and Claire Wintle (eds.), *Cultures of Decolonization: Transnational Productions and Practices, 1945–1970* (Manchester: Manchester University Press, 2016). A case study on the changing context of one art style is Daniel J. Sherman, *French Primitivism and the Ends of Empire, 1947–1975* (Chicago: University of Chicago Press, 2011).

27. John M. MacKenzie, "The Persistence of Empire in Metropolitan Culture," in Ward, *British Culture and the End of Empire*, 21–36.

28. See, from an extensive literature, Paul Gilroy, *There Ain't No Black in the Union Jack: The Cultural Politics of Race and Nation* (London: Hutchinson, 1987); Pascal Blanchard and Nicolas Bancel, *De l'indigène à l'immigré* (Paris: Gallimard, 1998).

29. Also on the following cases from sub-Saharan Africa, see Yves-André Fauré, "Célébrations officielles et pouvoirs africains: Symbolique et construction de l'Etat," *Canadian Journal of African Studies* 12 (1978): 383–404.

30. Maria Misra, "From Nehruvian Neglect to Bollywood Heroes: The Memory of the Raj in Post-War India," in Dominic Geppert and Frank Lorenz Müller (eds.), *Sites of Imperial Memory: Commemorating Colonial Rule in the Nineteenth and Twentieth Centuries* (Manchester: Manchester University Press, 2015), 187–206.

31. Jan C. Jansen, *Erobern und Erinnern: Symbolpolitik, öffentlicher Raum und französischer Kolonialismus in Algerien, 1830–1950* (Munich: Oldenbourg, 2013), 477–88; Jansen, "Creating National Heroes: Colonial Rule, Anticolonial Politics, and Conflicting Memories of Emir 'Abd al-Qadir in Algeria, 1900–1960s," *History and Memory* 28 (2016): 3–46.

32. See, e.g., the case study provided by Eric Jennings, "From *Indochine* to *Indochic*: The Lang Bian/Dalat Palace Hotel and French Colonial Leisure, Power and Culture," *Modern Asian Studies* 37 (2003): 159–94.

33. On these semicentennial celebrations, see the comparisons in Carola Lentz and Godiwn Kornes (eds.), *Staatsinszenierung, Erinnerungsmarathon und Volksfest: Afrika feiert 50 Jahre Unabhängigkeit* (Frankfurt: Brandes & Apsel, 2011).

34. This contrast is developed by Bruce Cumings, "Colonial Formations and Deformations: Korea, Taiwan and Vietnam," in Duara, *Decolonization*, 276–98.

35. On Great Britain, see John Darwin, *Britain and Decolonisation: The Retreat from Empire in the Post-war World* (Basingstoke: Macmillan Education, 1988), 20, 94–95.

36. On this, see James J. Orr, *The Victim as Hero: Ideologies of Peace and National Identity in Postwar Japan* (Honolulu: University of Hawai'i Press, 2001).

37. Comparative perspectives in Olivier Dard and Daniel Lefeuvre (eds.), *L'Europe face à son passé colonial* (Paris: Riveneuve, 2008); Dietmar Rothermund (ed.), *Memories of Post-Imperial Nations: The Aftermath of Decolonization, 1945–2013* (Cambridge: Cambridge University Press, 2015).

38. For a survey, see Jan C. Jansen, "Memory Lobbying and the Shaping of 'Colonial Memories' in France since the 1990s: The Local, the Na-

tional, and the International," in Borutta and Jansen, *Vertriebene and Pieds-Noirs*, 252–71; Romain Bertrand, *Mémoires d'empire: La controverse autour du "fait colonial"* (Bellecombe-en-Bauge: Croquant, 2006).

39. Sebastian Conrad, "The Dialectics of Remembrance: Memories of Empire in Cold War Japan," *Comparative Studies in Society and History* 56 (2014): 4–33.

40. Christian Meier, *Das Gebot zu vergessen und die Unabweisbarkeit des Erinnerns: Vom öffentlichen Umgang mit schlimmer Vergangenheit* (Munich: Siedler, 2010).

SELECT READINGS

THEORIZING DECOLONIZATION

Aldrich, Robert, and Stuart Ward, "Ends of Empire: Decolonizing the Nation in British and French Historiography," in Stefan Berger and Chris Lorenz (eds.), *Nationalizing the Past: Historians as Nation Builders in Modern Europe* (Basingstoke: Palgrave Macmillan, 2010), 259–81.

Betts, Raymond F., "Decolonization: A Brief History of the Word," in Els Bogaerts and Remco Raben (eds.), *Beyond Empire and Nation: The Decolonization of African and Asian Societies, 1930s–1960s* (Leiden: KITLV Press, 2012), 23–37.

Darwin, John, *The End of the British Empire: The Historical Debate* (Oxford: Blackwell, 1991).

Hopkins, Antony G., "Rethinking Decolonization," *Past and Present* 200 (2008): 211–47.

Howe, Stephen, "When—if Ever—Did Empire End? Recent Studies of Imperialism and Decolonization," *Journal of Contemporary History* 40 (2005): 585–99.

Louis, Wm. Roger, and Ronald Robinson, "The Imperialism of Decolonization," *Journal of Imperial and Commonwealth History* 22 (1994): 462–511.

Osterhammel, Jürgen, *Colonialism: A Theoretical Overview*, 2nd ed. (Princeton, NJ: Markus Wiener, 2005).

Spruyt, Hendrik, *Ending Empire: Contested Sovereignty and Territorial Partition* (Ithaca, NY: Cornell University Press, 2005).

Thomas, Martin, and Andrew Thompson, "Empire and Globalisation: From 'High Imperialism' to Decolonisation," *International History Review* 36 (2014): 142–70.

GENERAL AND COMPARATIVE SURVEYS

Albertini, Rudolf von, *Decolonization: The Administration and Future of the Colonies, 1919–1960* (Garden City, NY: Doubleday, 1971). German original published in 1966.

Betts, Raymond F., *Decolonization*, 2nd ed. (New York: Routledge, 2004).

Bogaerts, Els, and Remco Raben (eds.), *Beyond Empire and Nation: The Decolonization of African and Asian Societies, 1930s–1960s* (Leiden: KITLV Press, 2012).

Borstelmann, Thomas, *The 1970s: A New Global History from Civil Rights to Economic Inequality* (Princeton, NJ: Princeton University Press, 2011).

Brocheux, Pierre, Samia El Mechat, Marc Frey, Karl Hack, Arnaud Nanta, Solofo Randrianja, and Jean-Marc Regnault, *Les décolonisations au XXe siècle: La fin des empires européens et japonais* (Paris: A. Colin, 2012).

Burbank, Jane, and Frederick Cooper, *Empires in World History: Power and the Politics of Difference* (Princeton, NJ: Princeton University Press, 2010).

Duara, Prasenjit (ed.), *Decolonization: Perspectives from Now and Then: Rewriting Histories*, 2nd ed. (London: Routledge, 2004).

Dülffer, Jost, and Mark Frey (eds.), *Elites and Decolonization in the Twentieth Century* (Basingstoke: Palgrave Macmillan, 2011).

Holland, Robert, *European Decolonization, 1918–1981: An Introductory Survey* (Basingstoke: Palgrave Macmillan, 1985).

———(ed.), *Emergencies and Disorder in the European Empires after 1945* (London: Routledge, 1993).

Jerónimo, Miguel Bandeira, and António Costa Pinto (eds.), *The Ends of European Colonial Empires: Cases and Comparisons* (Basingstoke: Palgrave Macmillan, 2015).

Kennedy, Dane, *Decolonization: A Very Short Introduction* (Oxford: Oxford University Press, 2016).

Le Sueur, James D. (ed.), *The Decolonization Reader* (London: Routledge, 2003).

Mazower, Mark, Jessica Reinisch, and David Feldman (eds.), *Post-war Reconstruction in Europe: International Perspectives, 1945–1949* (Oxford: Oxford University Press, 2011).

Peyroulou, Jean-Pierre, and Fabrice Le Goff, *Atlas des décolonisations: Une histoire inachevée* (Paris: Autrement, 2014).

Rothermund, Dietmar, *The Routledge Companion to Decolonization* (London: Routledge, 2006).

Shepard, Todd, *Voices of Decolonization: A Brief History with Documents* (Boston: Bedford/St. Martin's, 2014).

Shipway, Martin, *Decolonization and Its Impact: A Comparative Approach to the End of the Colonial Empires* (Malden, MA: Blackwell, 2008).

Springhall, John, *Decolonization since 1945: The Collapse of European Overseas Empires* (Basingstoke: Palgrave Macmillan, 2001).

Thomas, Martin, *Fight or Flight: Britain, France, and Their Roads from Empire* (Oxford: Oxford University Press, 2014).

Thomas, Martin, Larry J. Butler, and Bob Moore, *Crises of Empire: Decolonization and Europe's Imperial States, 1918–1975*, 2nd ed. (London: Bloomsbury Academic Publishing, 2015).

Wesseling, Henk L., *Colonialisme, impérialisme, décolonisation: Contributions à l'histoire de l'expansion européenne* (Paris: L'Harmattan, 2013).

DECOLONIZATION BY EMPIRE

British Empire

Bayly, Christopher, and Tim Harper, *Forgotten Armies: The Fall of British Asia, 1941–1945* (Cambridge, MA: Belknap Press, 2006).

Butler, Larry J., *Britain and Empire: Adjusting to a Post-Imperial World* (London: I. B. Tauris, 2002).

Darwin, John, *Britain and Decolonization: The Retreat from Empire in the Post-War World* (Basingstoke: Palgrave Macmillan, 1988).

———, *The Empire Project: The Rise and Fall of the British World-System, 1830–1970* (Cambridge: Cambridge University Press, 2009).

French, David, *Army, Empire, and Cold War: The British Army and Military Policy, 1945–1971* (Oxford: Oxford University Press, 2012).

Holland, Robert, *Blue-Water Empire: The British in the Mediterranean since 1800* (London: Allen Lane, 2012).

Hughes, Matthew (ed.), *British Ways of Counter-Insurgency: A Historical Perspective* (London: Routledge, 2013).

Hyam, Ronald, *Britain's Declining Empire: The Road to Decolonisation, 1918–1968* (Cambridge: Cambridge University Press, 2006).

Louis, Wm. Roger, *Ends of British Imperialism: The Scramble for Empire, Suez, and Decolonization* (London: I. B. Tauris, 2006).

Low, D. A., *Eclipse of Empire* (Cambridge: Cambridge University Press, 1993).

Lynn, Martin (ed.), *The British Empire in the 1950s: Retreat or Revival?* (Basingstoke: Palgrave Macmillan, 2006).

MacIntyre, William David, *British Decolonization, 1946–1997: When, Why and How Did the British Empire Fall?* (London: Macmillan, 1998).

Murphy, Philip, *Monarchy and the End of Empire: The House of Windsor, the British Government, and the Postwar Commonwealth* (Oxford: Oxford University Press, 2013).

Porter, Bernard, *The Lion's Share: A History of British Imperialism 1850–2011*, 5th ed. (London: Routledge, 2012).

Stockwell, Sarah E., "Ends of Empire," in Stockwell (ed.), *The British Empire: Themes and Perspectives* (Oxford: Blackwell, 2008), 269–93.

White, Nicholas J., *Decolonisation: The British Experience since 1945*, 2nd ed. (London: Routledge, 2014).

Other Empires

Ageron, Charles-Robert, *La décolonisation française*, 2nd ed. (Paris: A. Colin, 1994).

Beasley, William G., *Japanese Imperialism, 1894–1945* (Oxford: Clarendon Press, 1987).

Betts, Raymond F., *France and Decolonisation, 1900–1960* (Basingstoke: Palgrave Macmillan, 1991).

Clayton, Anthony, *The Wars of French Decolonization* (London: Longman, 1994).

Cooper, Frederick, *Citizenship between Empire and Nation: Remaking France and French Africa, 1945–1960* (Princeton, NJ: Princeton University Press, 2014).

MacQueen, Norrie, *The Decolonization of Portuguese Africa: Metropolitan Revolution and the Dissolution of Empire* (London: Longman, 1997).

Shepard, Todd, *The Invention of Decolonization: The Algerian War and the Remaking of France* (Ithaca, NY: Cornell University Press, 2006).

van den Doel, Wim, *Afscheid van Indië: De val van het Nederlands imperium in Azië* (Amsterdam: Prometheus, 2001).

DECOLONIZATION BY COUNTRY OR REGION

South Asia

Bates, Crispin, *Subalterns and Raj: South Asia Since 1600* (London: Routledge, 2007).

Hasan, Mushirul (ed.), *India's Partition: Process, Strategy and Mobilization*, 6th ed. (Delhi: Oxford University Press, 2001).

Khan, Yasmin, *The Great Partition: The Making of India and Pakistan* (New Haven: Yale University Press, 2007).

Marston, Daniel, *The Indian Army and the End of the Raj* (Cambridge: Cambridge University Press, 2014).

Peebles, Patrick, *The History of Sri Lanka* (Westport, CT: Greenwood Press, 2006).

Talbot, Ian, and Gurharpal Singh, *The Partition of India* (Cambridge: Cambridge University Press, 2009).

Wolpert, Stanley A., *Shameful Flight: The Last Years of the British Empire in India* (Oxford: Oxford University Press, 2006).

Southeast and East Asia

Andaya, Barbara Watson, and Leonard Y. Andaya, *A History of Malaysia*, 2nd ed. (Basingstoke: Palgrave Macmillan, 2001).

Bayly, Christopher A., and Tim Harper, *Forgotten Wars: Freedom and Revolution in Southeast Asia* (Cambridge, MA: Harvard University Press, 2007).

Bradley, Mark Philip, *Vietnam at War* (Oxford: Oxford University Press, 2009).

Brocheux, Pierre, *Ho Chi Minh: A Biography* (Cambridge: Cambridge University Press, 2007).

Charney, Michael W., *A History of Modern Burma* (Cambridge: Cambridge University Press, 2009).

Dalloz, Jacques, *La guerre d'Indochine, 1945–1954* (Paris: Editions du Seuil, 1987).

Elson, R. E., *The Idea of Indonesia: A History* (Cambridge: Cambridge University Press, 2008).

Frey, Marc, Ronald W. Pruessen, and Tai Yong Tan (eds.), *The Transformation of Southeast Asia: International Perspectives on Decolonization* (Armonk, NY: M. E. Sharpe, 2003).

Goscha, Christopher E. (ed.), *Connecting Histories: Decolonization and the Cold War in Southeast Asia, 1945–1962* (Washington, DC: Woodrow Wilson Center Press, 2009).

Goscha, Christopher E., *Vietnam: A New History* (New York: Basic Books, 2016).

Luttikhuis, Bart, and A. Dirk Moses (eds.), *Colonial Counterinsurgency and Mass Violence: The Dutch Empire in Indonesia* (London: Routledge, 2014).

McMahon, Robert J., *The Limits of Empire: The United States and Southeast Asia since World War II* (New York: Columbia University Press, 1999).

Owen, Norman G. (ed.), *The Emergence of Modern Southeast Asia: A New History* (Honolulu: University of Hawai'i Press, 2005).

Reid, Anthony, *Imperial Alchemy: Nationalism and Political Identity in Southeast Asia* (Cambridge: Cambridge University Press, 2010).

Ricklefs, M. C., *History of Modern Indonesia since c. 1200*, 4th ed. (Basingstoke: Palgrave Macmillan, 2008).

Tsang, Steve, *A Modern History of Hong Kong* (London: I. B. Tauris, 2007).

Vickers, Adrian, *A History of Modern Indonesia*, 2nd ed. (Cambridge: Cambridge University Press, 2013).

Middle East, North Africa, and Mediterranean

Cleveland, William L., and Martin P. Bunton, *A History of the Modern Middle East*, 5th ed. (Boulder, CO: Westview Press, 2013).

Evans, Martin, *Algeria: France's Undeclared War* (Oxford: Oxford University Press, 2012).

Gelvin, James L., *The Modern Middle East: A History*, 3rd ed. (Oxford: Oxford University Press, 2011).

Holland, Robert, *Britain and the Revolt in Cyprus, 1954–1959* (Oxford: Clarendon Press, 1998).

Jankowski, James P., and Israel Gershoni (eds.), *Rethinking Nationalism in the Arab Middle East* (New York: Columbia University Press, 1997).

Louis, Wm. Roger, and Roger Owen (eds.), *Suez 1956: The Crisis and Its Consequences* (Oxford: Clarendon Press, 1989).

Louis, Wm. Roger, and Robert W. Stookey (eds.), *The End of the Palestine Mandate* (London: I. B. Tauris, 1986).

Miller, Susan Gilson, *A History of Modern Morocco* (Cambridge: Cambridge University Press, 2013).

Naylor, Phillip C., *France and Algeria: A History of Decolonization and Transformation* (Gainesville: University Press of Florida, 2000).

Pelt, Adrian, *Libyan Independence and the United Nations: A Case of Planned Decolonization* (New Haven: Yale University Press, 1970).

Perkins, Kenneth J., *A History of Modern Tunisia*, 2nd ed. (Cambridge: Cambridge University Press, 2013).

Schayegh, Cyrus, and Andrew Arsan (eds.), *The Routledge Handbook of the History of the Middle East Mandates* (London: Routledge, 2015).

Sluglett, Peter, *Britain in Iraq: Contriving King and Country*, 2nd ed. (London: I. B. Tauris, 2007).

Thénault, Sylvie, *Histoire de la guerre d'indépendance algérienne* (Paris: Flammarion, 2005).

Tripp, Charles, *A History of Iraq*, 3rd ed. (Cambridge: Cambridge University Press, 2007).

Vandewalle, Dirk J., *A History of Modern Libya*, 2nd ed. (Cambridge: Cambridge University Press, 2012).

Wilson, Mary C., *King Abdullah, Britain, and the Making of Jordan* (Cambridge: Cambridge University Press, 1987).

Southern Africa

Anderson, David, *Histories of the Hanged: The Dirty War in Kenya and the End of Empire* (New York: W. W. Norton, 2005).

Austin, Dennis, *Politics in Ghana, 1946–1960*, 2nd ed. (London: Oxford University Press, 1970).

Bayart, Jean-François, *The State in Africa: The Politics of the Belly*, 2nd ed. (Cambridge, MA: Polity, 2009).

Beinart, William, *Twentieth-Century South Africa*, 2nd ed. (Oxford: Oxford University Press, 2001).

Birmingham, David, *The Decolonization of Africa* (London: University College London Press, 1995).

Branch, Daniel, *Defeating Mau Mau, Creating Kenya: Counterinsurgency, Civil War, and Decolonization* (Cambridge: Cambridge University Press, 2009).

Chafer, Tony, *The End of Empire in French West Africa: France's Successful Decolonization?* (Oxford: Berg, 2002).

Cooper, Frederick, *Africa since 1940: The Past of the Present* (Cambridge: Cambridge University Press, 2002).

———, *Decolonization and African Society: The Labor Question in French and British Africa* (Cambridge: Cambridge University Press, 1996).

Falola, Toyin, and Matthew M. Heaton, *A History of Nigeria* (Cambridge: Cambridge University Press, 2008).

Gifford, Prosser, and Wm. Roger Louis (eds.), *Decolonization and African Independence: The Transfers of Power, 1960–1980* (New Haven: Yale University Press, 1988).

———(eds.), *The Transfer of Power in Africa: Decolonization, 1940–1960*, 2nd ed. (New Haven: Yale University Press, 1982).

Hargreaves, John D., *Decolonization in Africa*, 2nd ed. (London: Longman, 1996).

Joseph, Richard A., *Radical Nationalism in Cameroun: Social Origins of the UPC Rebellion* (Oxford: Clarendon Press, 1977).

Kent, John, *The Internationalization of Colonialism: Britain, France, and Black Africa, 1939–1956* (Oxford: Clarendon Press, 1992).

Schmidt, Elizabeth, *Cold War and Decolonization in Guinea, 1946–1958* (Athens, OH: Ohio University Press, 2007).

Vanthemsche, Guy, *Belgium and the Congo, 1885–1980* (Cambridge: Cambridge University Press, 2012).

Weigert, Stephen L., *Angola: A Modern Military History, 1961–2002* (Basingstoke: Palgrave Macmillan, 2011).

Caribbean, Pacific, and Indian Ocean

Aldrich, Robert, and John Connell, *France's Overseas Frontier: Départements et territoires d'outre-mer* (Cambridge: Cambridge University Press, 2006).

Brereton, Bridget, and Teresita Martinez-Vergne (eds.), *General History of the Caribbean*, vol. 5: *The Caribbean in the Twentieth Century* (Paris/Basingstoke: UNESCO/Palgrave Macmillan, 2004).

Gardner, Helen, and Christopher Waters (eds.), "Decolonisation in Melanesia: Global, National, and Local Histories," special issue, *Journal of Pacific History* 48 (2013).

Higman, Barry W., *A Concise History of the Caribbean* (Cambridge: Cambridge University Press, 2011).

Knight, Franklin W., *The Caribbean: The Genesis of a Fragmented Nationalism*, 3rd ed. (Oxford: Oxford University Press, 2012).

MacIntyre, William David, *Winding Up the British Empire in the Pacific Islands* (Oxford: Oxford University Press, 2014).

Oostindie, Gert, and Inge Klinkers, *Decolonising the Caribbean: Dutch Policies in a Comparative Perspective* (Amsterdam: Amsterdam University Press, 2003).

THEMES AND PERSPECTIVES

Anticolonialism and Nationalism

Aydin, Cemil, *The Politics of Anti-Westernism in Asia: Visions of World Order in Pan-Islamic and Pan-Asian Thought* (New York: Columbia University Press, 2007).

Breuilly, John (ed.), *The Oxford Handbook of the History of Nationalism* (Oxford: Oxford University Press, 2013).

Eckert, Andreas, "Bringing the 'Black Atlantic' into Global History: The Project of Pan-Africanism," in Sebastian Conrad and Dominic Sachsenmaier (eds.), *Competing Visions of World Order: Global Moments and Movements, 1880s–1930s* (Basingstoke: Palgrave Macmillan, 2007), 237–57.

Gallagher, John, "Nationalism and the Crisis of Empire 1919–1922," *Modern Asian Studies* 15 (1981): 355–68.

James, Leslie, *George Padmore and Decolonization from Below: Pan-Africanism, the Cold War, and the End of Empire* (Basingstoke: Palgrave Macmillan, 2014).

Lawrence, Adria K., *Imperial Rule and the Politics of Nationalism: Anti-Colonial Protest in the French Empire* (Cambridge: Cambridge University Press, 2013).

Liauzu, Claude, *Histoire de l'anticolonialisme en France du XVIe siècle à nos jours* (Paris: A. Colin, 2007).

Manela, Erez, *The Wilsonian Moment: Self-Determination and the International Origins of Anticolonial Nationalism* (Oxford: Oxford University Press, 2007).

World Politics, International Law, and Development

Akita, Shigeru, Gerold Krozewski, and Shoichi Watanabe (eds.), *The Transformation of the International Order of Asia: Decolonization, the Cold War, and the Colombo Plan* (London: Routledge, 2015).

Burke, Roland, *Decolonization and the Evolution of International Human Rights* (Philadelphia: University of Pennsylvania Press, 2010).

Connelly, Matthew, *A Diplomatic Revolution: Algeria's Fight for Independence and the Origins of the Post–Cold War Era* (Oxford: Oxford University Press, 2002).

Cooper, Frederick, and Randall Packard (eds.), *International Development and the Social Sciences* (Berkeley: University of California Press, 1997).

Fedorowich, Kent, and Martin Thomas (eds.), *International Diplomacy and Colonial Retreat* (London: Routledge, 2001).

Irwin, Ryan M., "Decolonization and the Cold War," in Artemy M. Kalinovsky and Craig Daigle (eds.), *The Routledge Handbook of the Cold War* (London: Routledge, 2014), 91–104.

———, *Gordian Knot: Apartheid and the Unmaking of the Liberal World Order* (Oxford: Oxford University Press, 2012).

James, Leslie, and Elisabeth Leake (eds.), *Decolonization and the Cold War: Negotiating Independence* (London: Bloomsbury Academic Publishing, 2015).

Latham, Michael E., "The Cold War in the Third World," in Melvyn P. Leffler and Odd Arne Westad (eds.), *The Cambridge History of the Cold War*, vol. 2 (Cambridge: Cambridge University Press, 2010), 258–80.

Lee, Christopher James (ed.), *Making a World after Empire: The Bandung Moment and Its Political Afterlives* (Athens, OH: Ohio University Press, 2010).

Mazower, Mark, *No Enchanted Palace: The End of Empire and the Ideological Origins of the United Nations* (Princeton, NJ: Princeton University Press, 2009).

Pedersen, Susan, *The Guardians: The League of Nations and the Crisis of Empire* (Oxford: Oxford University Press, 2015).

Ryan, David, and Victor Pungong (eds.), *The United States and Decoloniza-tion: Power and Freedom* (Basingstoke: Palgrave Macmillan, 2000).

Tan, See Seng, and Amitav Acharya (eds.), *Bandung Revisited: The Legacy of the 1955 Asian-African Conference for International Order* (Singapore: NUS Press, 2008).

Westad, Odd Arne, *The Global Cold War: Third World Interventions and the Making of Our Times* (Cambridge: Cambridge University Press, 2005).

Economy

Fieldhouse, David K., *Black Africa, 1945–1980: Economic Decolonization and Arrested Development* (London: Routledge, 2012).

———, *Merchant Capital and Economic Decolonization: The United Africa Company, 1929–1987* (Oxford: Clarendon Press, 1994).

Hodeir, Catherine, *Stratégies d'empire: Le grand patronat colonial face à la décolonisation* (Paris: Belin, 2003).

Krozewski, Gerold, *Money and the End of Empire: British International Eco-nomic Policy and the Colonies, 1947–58* (Basingstoke: Palgrave Macmil-lan, 2001).

Lindblad, J. Thomas, *Bridges to New Business: The Economic Decolonization of Indonesia* (Leiden: KITLV Press, 2008).

Marseille, Jaques, *Empire colonial et capitalisme français: Histoire d'un di-vorce*, 2nd ed. (Paris: A. Michel, 2005).

Tignor, Robert L., *Capitalism and Nationalism at the End of Empire: State and Business in Decolonizing Egypt, Nigeria, and Kenya, 1945–1963* (Princeton, NJ: Princeton University Press, 1998).

White, Nicholas J., *British Business in Post-Colonial Malaysia, 1957–70: "Neo-colonialism" or "Disengagement"?* (London: RoutledgeCurzon, 2004).

Ideas

Hall, Ian, "The Revolt against the West: Decolonisation and Its Repercus-sions in British International Thought, 1945–75," *International History Review* 33 (2011): 43–64.

Lazarus, Neil (ed.), *The Cambridge Companion to Postcolonial Literary Stud-ies* (Cambridge: Cambridge University Press, 2004).

Le Sueur, James D., *Uncivil War: Intellectuals and Identity Politics during the Decolonization of Algeria*, 2nd ed. (Lincoln: University of Nebraska Press, 2005).

Mishra, Pankaj, *From the Ruins of Empire: The Intellectuals Who Remade Asia* (New York: Farrar, Straus & Giroux, 2012).

Philpott, Daniel, *Revolutions in Sovereignty: How Ideas Shaped Modern International Relations* (Princeton, NJ: Princeton University Press, 2001).

Young, Robert J. C., *Postcolonialism: An Historical Introduction* (Oxford: Blackwell, 2001).

Repercussions and Aftermath

Aldrich, Robert, *Vestiges of the Colonial Empire in France: Monuments, Museums and Colonial Memories* (Basingstoke: Palgrave Macmillan, 2005).

Aldrich, Robert, and John Connell, *The Last Colonies* (Cambridge: Cambridge University Press, 1998).

Buettner, Elizabeth, *Europe after Empire: Decolonization, Society, and Culture* (Cambridge: Cambridge University Press, 2016).

Kahler, Miles, *Decolonization in Britain and France: The Domestic Consequences of International Relations* (Princeton, NJ: Princeton University Press, 1984).

Miles, William F., *Scars of Partition: Postcolonial Legacies in French and British Borderlands* (Lincoln: University of Nebraska Press, 2014).

Oostindie, Gert, *Postcolonial Netherlands: Sixty-Five Years of Forgetting, Commemorating, Silencing* (Amsterdam: Amsterdam University Press, 2012).

Rothermund, Dietmar (ed.), *Memories of Post-Imperial Nations: The Aftermath of Decolonization, 1945–2013* (Cambridge: Cambridge University Press, 2015).

Smith, Andrea L., (ed.), *Europe's Invisible Migrants* (Amsterdam: Amsterdam University Press, 2003).

Thompson, Andrew (ed.), *Britain's Experience of Empire in the Twentieth Century* (Oxford: Oxford University Press, 2011).

Ward, Stuart (ed.), *British Culture and the End of Empire* (Manchester: Manchester University Press, 2001).

INDEX

Abyssinia. *See* Ethiopia
acceleration, of decolonization processes, 4, 78, 95–97, 101–3, 148
Aden, 95
Al-Afghani, Jamal al-Din, 158
Afghanistan, 39, 153
Africa: and Cold War, 150–51; decolonization of, 96–118, 150; economic development in, 135; nationalism in, 44–45; political voice of, 10; state building in, 63. *See also* North Africa; southern Africa
Africanization, 136
African National Congress (ANC), 44, 117
agency, in decolonizations, 31–32
agriculture, 61, 120, 123–24, 128–29, 134, 182

Algeria: colonial reform in, 41, 69; economic transitions in, 129; ethnic conflicts in, 50; governance of, 58; independence of, 100; memories of colonialism in, 188, 189; migration from, 184, 185; nationalism in, 39, 44, 46, 52, 69, 98; settlers' influence in, 123; violence in, 5, 50, 70, 97–98
Algerian war (1954–62), 96–100, 154, 159–60; memory of, 189, 190
American Revolution, as a reference, 21–22, 85
Angola: colonization of, 8, 63, 112–13; independence of, 114; migration from, 184; migration to, 113; proxy wars in, 113, 152;

Angola (*continued*)
   rivalries in, 46, 113; violence in,
   5, 52, 113, 152
anticolonialism: conflicts and
   rivalries in, 46–52; elites and,
   45–46, 48; in and after First
   World War, 38–39, 42–53; forms
   of, 45; gender issues in, 50–51;
   intellectual underpinnings
   of, 158, 164–65; international
   elements in, 52–53; mass-elite
   tensions in, 50; means em-
   ployed in, 47–48; nationalism
   in relation to, 46–47, 162–63;
   self-determination as central
   principle of, 40; varieties of,
   48, 52–53
apartheid, 8, 20–21; end of, 72,
   117–18
Arab nationalism, 43, 50, 93
Arabs: broken First World War
   promises to, 42; and decolonization, 92–93; mass-elite
   tensions among, 50
arms and arms trade, 94, 123, 151
Asia: political voice of, 10–11;
   United States and, 147–48
Asian-African Conference (1955),
   141
Atlantic Charter (1941), 68
Attlee, Clement, 77–78
Aung San, 84
Australia: in British Empire, 7; as
   dominion, 8, 20; formation of,
   11; as mandate power, 38
authenticity, 162, 167, 188

Baghdad Pact, 93
Balandier, Georges, 163–64
Bandung Conference. *See*
   Asian-African Conference
Bangladesh, 177
Barbados, 115
Belgian Congo: and Cold War,
   150–51; decolonization of, 106–7;
   private economic interests in,
   126; and Second World War, 67;
   violence in, 52. *See also* Congo
Belgium: and colonial politics, 58;
   and Congo, 106–7; empire of,
   8; and First World War, 37
Berber population, 50
Betts, Raymond, 173
Bhabha, Homi K., 168
Biafra, 104
Bonn, Moritz Julius, 3
borders: sanctity of, 162, 177; state,
   15, 22, 27, 47, 161, 177–79
Bourguiba, Habib, 44, 49, 97
boycotts, 43, 117, 125, 138
British Empire: anticolonialism in,
   39; and Central Africa decolonization, 108–11; and colonial
   politics, 56–58, 60; decline of,
   149; and decolonization, 4, 181;
   development practices of, 61;
   dominions of, 7–8, 21, 22, 41,
   54–55, 67; and East African
   decolonization, 108–10; and
   economic transitions, 129–31;
   and Egypt, 90, 93–94; and First
   World War, 36–37; after First
   World War, 54; history of

changes in, 9, 73; influence of colonial interests on, 125–26; and the League of Nations, 10; mandates of, 38, 43; scope of, 7, 73, 146; and Second World War, 67, 75–76; and southern African decolonization, 100–102; transfers of power in, 13–14, 21–22, 29, 76–77; and West African decolonization, 102–3

British Nationality Act (1948), 173

Brunei, 152

Burma, 47, 66, 73, 84, 126, 162

business interests. *See* private economic interests

Cambodia, 149, 203n16

Cameroon, 106, 108–9

Canada: confessional conflicts in, 39; as dominion, 8, 20; formation of, 11; nationalism in, 46

Caribbean: colonization of, 8; decolonization of, 72, 115–16; labor struggle in, 44, 47

Cartier, Raymond, 132

Cartierism, 132

Castro, Fidel, 146

Central Africa: decolonization of, 104; labor struggle in, 44

Central African Federation, 110–11, 126

Central America, 7. *See also* Latin America

Central Intelligence Agency (CIA), 108

Césaire, Aimé, 45, 156, 164

Ceylon, 57, 73, 80–81, 130, 162

Chávez, Hugo, 127

Chiang Kai-shek, 147

China: anticolonialism in, 39; in Cold War years, 141–42; colonization of, 8; criticized as colonialist, 154; empire of, 16–17; and French politics, 58; and Hong Kong, 118; Japan and, 65–66; and Korean War, 148; private economic interests in, 126; Soviet relations with, 141, 147; U.S. relations with, 147

Chinese civil war (1946–49), 147, 154

Churchill, Winston, 68, 77, 141–42

citizenship: after colonialism, 15, 27, 159–60, 184; expansion of, 41, 58; imperial, 59–60, 173

civil wars, 5, 92, 175, 176; internationalized, 152

Cold War: Africa and, 112, 150–51; Asia and, 146–49; Biafra and, 104; Congo and, 108; decolonization in relation to, 31, 101, 144–46, 151–52; as East-West conflict, 139–42; and international development, 133–34; South Africa's value in, 118; Suez crisis and, 93. *See also* global Cold War

collaboration, 23, 30, 84, 91, 100, 109, 183; anticolonialism and, 46, 47; elite, 45, 81

Colonial Development and Welfare Fund, 61

colonial situation (concept), 163–64
colonialism: disappearance of,
    12–13; economic effects of,
    119–22; First World War and,
    36–42; as historical situation,
    163–65; internationalization
    of, 39–40; legacies/remnants of,
    171–72, 174–76; legitimation and
    delegitimization of, 1, 36, 38,
    42, 62, 112, 153, 191; memories
    of, 186–92; private economic
    interests in, 120–21; reforms of,
    41–42, 55–56; as term of oppro-
    brium, 154, 191–92; unrest
    aimed at, 38–39. *See also*
    empires; imperialism; late
    colonialism
colonies, remaining, 6, 116–17
Comintern. *See* Third
    International
Common Agricultural Policy
    (Europe), 182
Common Market (Europe), 182
Commonwealth of Nations, 27, 77,
    80, 84, 89, 90, 114, 144, 174, 182,
    185
communism: and anticolonialism,
    43, 82, 88, 98, 115, 144; interna-
    tional, 53, 87; settler regimes
    against, 151; U.S. fear of, 108,
    148–50
complexe hollandais, 132
Congo, 5, 8, 107–8. *See also* Belgian
    Congo
Congo crisis. *See* Belgian Congo.
Congo Free State, 53
Congo-Zaire, 152, 187–88

constitution, 10, 27, 105, 108, 175;
    constitutional reform, 21–22,
    55, 56–60, 103–4, 109–10
consumerism, 138, 175
Corfu, 7
counterinsurgency warfare. *See*
    emergency/emergency laws
Cuba, 8, 140; intervention in
    Africa 113, 152; missile crisis,
    146; revolution in, 116, 146, 149
Cuban missile crisis, 146
culture, decolonization and, 167,
    185–86
currency, 28, 54, 132–33. *See also*
    sterling area
Cyprus, 7, 49, 95–96

Damas, Léon, 45
Darwin, John, 130
debt, 67, 77, 127–28, 135
decolonization: actual processes
    of, 4–5, 15, 27, 173; analytical
    perspectives on, 22–28; char-
    acteristics of late-colonial era
    and, 25–26; consequences of,
    6–7, 27–28, 33–34, 181–86; core
    period of, 3–4, 35, 71; cultural
    and intellectual outcomes of,
    167, 185–86; definition of, 1–2;
    "discovery" of, 159; economic,
    137; explanatory models of,
    28–32; external conditions for,
    26–27; failures of, 84, 180; First
    World War and, 36–42; global
    developments connected with,
    15–16; history of, 3, 7–9, 14–21,
    35–42; late decolonizations,

111–18; legacies of, 167, 174, 176–80; meanings of, 1–3, 6, 13, 159–60; memory and remembrance associated with, 186–92; as multidimensional process, 2, 172–73; and normative change, 2, 12–13, 153–55; political, 137; precursors of, 20–21; reform movements and, 46–47; sovereignty as result of, 9; Soviet Union and, 18; statistics of, 10; temporalities associated with, 13–17, 32–33; terminology related to, 3–4, 160; themes of, 158–67; timing of, 2–3, 35–36, 71–72, 172–173; transfers of power in, 13–14, 21–22, 29

De Gaulle, Charles, 68, 69, 100, 126

democracy/democratization: in colonies 7, 56–58, 102–3; in India, 80; postcolonial, 84, 114, 181

Democratic Republic of the Congo, 152

Département d'outre-mer (DOM), 59, 116,

dependency theory, 166

development and development policy: in Africa, 131; in Algeria, 99; business strategies associated with, 133–135; late colonialism and, 54–63, 105, 109; postcolonial, 120, 157

Diagne, Blaise, 41

dominions, 7–8, 21, 22, 41, 54–55

domino effect, 72, 101

Duara, Prasenjit, 2

Dutch East Indies, 43, 122, 123, 127

East Africa, 64

East Indies, 55

East Timor, 154

East-West conflict. *See* Cold War.

ecology, 63, 119, 135, 175

economy, 119–38; colonial empires after First World War, 54; colonies' grievances against, 138; colonies seen as burden on, 132; decolonization's effects on, 182; development and business strategies, 133–38; economic planning, 48, 61, 120, 131, 134–35; goals for, 119–20; liberation strategies for, 126–27, 137; private interests in, 120–27, 135–37; transitions in, 127–33. *See also* development and development policy

Eden, Anthony, 94

education, 26, 51, 62, 104, 107, 113, 151, 175, 184; educated elites, 45, 52, 56, 102, 103, 105, 135,

Egypt: anticolonialism in, 39, 43; British relations with, 90, 93–94; coup in, 93; and federalism, 162; nationalism in, 43, 47; and Second World War, 69

Eisenhower, Dwight D., 148, 150

elections, 27, 56–58, 91, 102–6, 114, 117, 179

elites: and anticolonialism, 45–46, 48; conflicts between masses and, 50; exposure of, to foreign

elites (*continued*)
    ideas, 52; modernist, 45, 48;
    in southern Africa, 101–2;
    traditionalist, 45, 48
emergency/emergency laws, 16, 69,
    88, 99, 109–10, 111
empires: end of, 6–7, 12–13, 16–20;
    First World War and, 36–42;
    formation of, 7; imperialism
    after, 33; informal, 8, 89, 124;
    late colonialism, 54–63; Second
    World War and, 63–70; shrink-
    ing or disappearance of, 11;
    spatial perspective on, 17;
    theories of, 32. *See also*
    colonialism
equality, campaigns for, 46–47
Eritrea, 162
Ethiopia: 70, 162, 178; Italian war
    against, 48, 64, 190
ethnicity: conflicts based on,
    49–50, 88–89, 104, 108, 137,
    175–76, 178–79; multiethnicity,
    47, 151, 177–79. *See also* multi-
    racialism; religion
Eurafrica, 161
Europe, consequences of decoloni-
    zation for, 6–7, 33, 173–74,
    181–86
European Economic Community
    (EEC). *See* European
    integration
European integration, 6–7, 116, 132,
    181, 182
European Union (EU). *See*
    European integration
exhibitions, colonial, 55

explanation, models of. *See*
    decolonization: explanatory
    models of
expropriation, 27, 125, 126, 127. *See
    also* nationalization

Falklands Islands, 116
Fanon, Frantz, 158, 160, 164–65, 168,
    217n17
federation, 102–4, 110–11, 115, 126;
    imperial federalism, 47, 106,
    161–62, 180; national, 87, 104
feminism/women's emancipation,
    51, 169
Fiji, 116
First World War (1914–18), 8, 36–42;
    as war of empires, 36–37. *See
    also* Paris peace conference and
    treaties
FLN. *See* Front de Libération
    Nationale
forced migration, 5, 16, 23–24, 65,
    79–80, 88, 99, 109, 129, 188
Fourteen Points, 39–40
Françafrique, 179
France: anticolonial unrest against,
    43, 44; and Central Africa
    decolonization, 108–9; and
    colonial politics, 58–60, 69, 70;
    colonial reforms of, 41, 58–60;
    and decolonization, 4, 116, 173,
    181; and East African decoloni-
    zation, 108–9; and economic
    transitions, 128–29, 132; empire
    of, 8, 9, 11, 54; Fifth Republic,
    100, 105; and First World War,
    36–37; Fourth Republic, 59, 100;

and imperial integration, 58–59, 60 104–6, 116, 161; influence of colonial interests on, 125–26; mandates of, 38; migration to, 184, 185; and North African decolonization, 96–100; and responsibility for colonialism, 190; and Second World War, 67–68; and southern African decolonization, 100–101; and Vietnam, 85–87, 149; and West African decolonization, 102–6

Franco, Francisco, 114

Free French forces, 68, 69, 91

French Community, 105

French Equatorial Africa (AEF), 68, 102, 104–6

French Polynesia, 116–17

French Sudan. *See* Mali

French Union, 59, 104–5

French West Africa (AOF), 37, 39, 41, 50, 59, 67, 102, 104–6, 108, 129, 161, 185

Front de Libération Nationale (FLN), 98–100, 154, 165

Furnivall, John S., 55

Al-Gaddafi, Muammar, 95

Gambia, 104

Gandhi, Mohandas K. ("Mahatma"), 42–43, 48–49, 53, 74, 78, 138, 156–57

Garvey, Marcus, 158

gender, 50–51

Germany: colonial empire of, 8–9; and colonial revisionism, 64–65; and First World War,

37; formation of, 11; and Second World War, 63–65

Ghana, 104, 162. *See also* Gold Coast

Gibraltar, 6

global Cold War, 19, 21, 142

global public, 16, 24, 26, 95, 99, 143, 153

global South, 53, 133, 142–46, 153, 165–66. *See also* Third World

globalization, 3; de-globalization, 54; of the nation-state model, 162

Gold Coast, 101–4. *See also* Ghana

Great Britain: migration to, 185; and responsibility for colonialism, 190; U.S. relations with, 150. *See also* British Empire

Great Depression, 16, 42, 55

Guadeloupe, 59, 116

guerrilla war, 46, 99, 113–14, 86. *See also* emergency/emergency laws

Guiana, 59, 116

Guinea, 105–6, 113, 162

Guinea-Bissau, 113

Guomindang, 147

Guyana, 115

Habsburg monarchy, 11, 37

Haiti, 20, 34

Hausa, 178

Hawaii, 60

Ho Chi Minh, 21, 52, 85, 149, 158

Hong Kong, 12, 118

Houphouët-Boigny, Félix, 105

Huk rebellion, 82

human rights, 16, 154–55
Hussein (sharif of Mecca), 42

ideas, role of, 156–57, 159
impact on metropoles. *See* decolonization; Europe; metropoles
imperialism: after empire, 33; theories of, 32. *See also* colonialism; empires
independence: days, 14, 171, 187; declaration of, 21, 85, 111, 114
India: anticolonialism in, 39; colonial reform in, 41; conflict with Pakistan, 80, 178; as creditor of British Empire, 128; governance of, 56–57, 68–69, 76–78, 80; independence of, 52, 73–78, 144; labor struggle in, 47; and League of Nations, 10; memories of colonialism in, 187; military contributions in world wars, 37, 67, 77; modernism vs. traditionalism in, 48–49; Muslim-Hindu relations in, 76, 78–79; nationalism in, 42–43, 78; as nonaligned state, 141; partition of, 5, 74, 79–80, 178; religion in, 49; and Second World War, 75–76; violence in, 75, 79
Indian National Army, 76
Indian National Congress (INC), 43, 68–69, 75–79
Indochina, 5, 67, 128, 149. *See also* Vietnam
Indonesia: border disputes involving, 178; colonization of, 8;
criticized as colonialist, 154; decolonization of, 125; economic transitions in, 127–28; governance of, 57–58; independence of, 71, 85–87, 148; Japan and, 66–67; mass-elite tensions in, 50; migration from, 184; nationalism in, 46; private economic interests in, 126; regional conflicts in, 49; violence in, 5, 50
industry/industrialization, 47, 60–61, 122, 129, 135
informal empire, 8, 89, 124
infrastructure, 47, 55, 60, 61, 119, 122, 175
integration: imperial, 58–60, 104–6, 116, 161; social, 18, 184, 185, 190; supranational, 6–7, 161–62, 180. *See also* European integration; federation
international law, 2, 9–10, 12–13, 154
International Olympic Committee, 11
international organizations, 10, 16, 24, 134. *See also* League of Nations; Organization for African Unity; United Nations; World Bank
investments: in colonies, 54, 60–61, 113, 122, 125; foreign, 127, 136, 179
Iran, 69, 126, 141
Iraq: anticolonialism in, 39; coup in, 95; decolonization of, 90–91; nationalism in, 43; neocolonial-

ism in, 179; and Second World War, 69; United States and, 154
Ireland, 7, 39, 73
Israel, 43, 92, 94, 183
Israeli-Palestinian conflict, 92, 154, 178
Italy, 8, 11, 19, 63–64

Jamaica, 57, 115
Japan: and Cold War, 140; and colonial politics, 58; consequences of decolonization for, 33, 182–83; empire of, 9, 19, 56; and Korea, 171; memories of colonialism in, 191; migration to, 183; modernization policy of, 61; pan-Asianism as propagated by, 66, 162; and Second World War, 63, 65–67, 76; U.S. relations with, 146, 148
Jefferson, Thomas, 21
Jinnah, Muhammad Ali, 74, 78, 80
Jordan, 90–91, 178

Katanga, 107–8, 126
Kat Angelino, A.D.A. de, 55
Kenya: decolonization of, 109–10; independence of, 101, 110; settler influence in, 124; violence in, 5, 34, 50, 109–10. See also Mau Mau uprising
Kenyatta, Jomo, 110, 156
Al-Khattabi, Abd al-Karim, 44
Korea, 39, 61, 65, 172, 181. See also North Korea; South Korea

Korean war (1950–52), 5, 148
Kurds, 178

labor: forced 59–60, 63, 67, 69; migration, 184–85; struggle and unrest, 44, 47, 136. See also trade unions
Labour Party (Great Britain), 77
land reform, 83, 109, 134
language, 28, 167, 175, 184
Laos, 149, 203n16
La Réunion, 59, 116
late colonialism, 54–63; characteristics of, 55; development, 60–63; and the economy, 54; political reforms, 56–60; the repressive state in, 63; scholarly research on, 54–55; and state building, 63. See also colonialism; modernization
Latin America, 8, 10, 20, 135, 146, 165, 168. See also Central America; South America
League against Imperialism, 53
League of Nations, 10, 34, 37–38, 40–41, 64
Lebanon: decolonization of, 70, 91; religion in, 49, 179; violence in, 69
legacies: of colonialism, 33, 167–68, 171–172, 174–176; of decolonization, 80, 134, 157, 167, 176–86. See also memory
legitimation. See colonialism: legitimation and delegitimization of
Lenin, V. I., 40

Leopold II, 53

Libya, 8, 64, 95, 194n15

lobby groups, 26, 42, 98, 113, 124, 145, 190. *See also* private economic interests

loi-cadre (framework law), 105

Lumumba, Patrice, 107–8, 150, 190

Macmillan, Harold, 101, 160

Madagascar, 47, 67–68, 106, 109; ethnic conflicts in, 50; uprising in, 5, 109

Maghreb: anticolonialism in, 44; decolonization of, 96–100; nationalism in, 47. *See also* North Africa

Malaya: decolonization of, 88–89; economic development in, 136; economic transitions in, 131; ethnic conflicts in, 50; independence of, 89; insurgency in, 150; Japan and, 66

Malayan Communist Party, 88

Malayan emergency, 88

Malaysia. *See* Malaya

Mali, 106, 162

Malta, 7, 59

Manchuria, 61, 65

mandate/mandate system, 37, 40–41

Mandela, Nelson, 117

Mannoni, Octave, 164, 217n17

Martinique, 59, 116, 165

Marxism, 32, 151, 152, 165, 168

Mau Mau uprising (1950s), 5, 109, 154, 189; memories of, 189. *See also* Kenya

Mauretania, 114

Mauritius, 115, 179

Mayotte, 116

Memmi, Albert, 164

memory, 186–92; conflicts over 187, 190; in former colonies, 187–89; in former metropoles, 189–90; international dimensions of, 190–91; recent upsurge in, 190–92; of violence, 5–6, 80, 190

Mendès-France, Pierre, 126

metropoles: as centers of colonial systems, 7, 12, 23, 54; colonial elites' intellectual formation in, 52; colonialism's effect on, 180–81; colonies' relationship with, 59–60, 115, 173; decolonization's effect on, 23, 6–7, 33, 173–74, 181–86; economic benefits of colonialism for, 81, 122, 133; economic flows to, 122; knowledge of colonies in, 55; memories of colonialism in, 189–90; migration to, 183–84; as remainders of colonial systems, 11, 174; settlers' influence in, 124

Middle East: anticolonialism in, 42, 43; colonization of, 69; decolonization of, 72, 89–95; informal empire in, 72, 89–91; mass-elite tensions in, 50; nationalism in, 47

migration, 183–85; triggered by decolonization 24, 178, 183–84, 190. *See also* forced migration military bases, 9, 27, 81, 83, 90, 91, 95–96, 116, 140

minorities, in postcolonial states, 50, 78–79, 81, 109, 125, 137, 183

mobility, late colonialism and increase of, 173

Mobutu, Joseph-Désiré (Mobutu Sese Seko), 107, 108, 152

modernist elites, 45, 48

modernization, 60–63, 120, 131, 134–35; theory of, 16, 166; and violence, 63, 99, 113. *See also* development and development policy; late colonialism.

multiracialism, 109, 110

Morocco: border disputes involving, 178; ethnic conflicts in, 50; independence of, 96–97; nationalism in, 44, 47, 69, 97; violence in, 114

Mossadegh, Mohammad, 126

Mountbatten, Louis, 78, 80

Mozambique: colonization of, 8, 63, 112–13; migration from, 184; violence in, 5, 113

multinational corporations, 136

multiracialism, 109, 110

Muslim Brotherhood, 43

Muslim League, 78–79

Myanmar. *See* Burma

Namibia, 12, 117

Nasser, Gamal Abdel, 93–95, 150, 162

nationalism: anticolonialism in relation to, 46–47, 162–63; Arab, 43, 50, 93; competing ideologies for, 51–52, 160–62; critiques of, 161; economic, 127, 137, 138; and economic development, 134–35; after First World War, 42–52; gender issues in, 51; and imperial solidarity, 46; in nineteenth century, 7; rivalries in, 46. *See also* federation; integration

nationalization, 94, 127, 129. *See also* expropriation

national liberation, as explanatory model, 30

nation-building: decolonization and West European, 173–74, 189; memory and, 188

nation-state model, 10, 12, 47, 162, 177

NATO. *See* North Atlantic Treaty Organization

Nauru, 11

Negritude, 45, 161, 165

Nehru, Jawaharlal, 49, 80, 158

neocolonialism, 87, 161, 179; as explanatory model, 30, 32, 170

Netherlands: anticolonial unrest against, 43; and colonial politics, 60; and decolonization, 115–16, 148; economic benefits of colonialism for, 122, 125; and economic transitions, 127, 132; empire of, 8, 9, 55; and First World War, 37; and Indonesia, 85–86; migration to, 184; and responsibility for colonialism, 190

Netherlands Antilles, 60, 115

New Caledonia, 116
New Hebrides, 116
New Zealand, 7, 8, 20
Niger, 106
Nigeria, 5, 52, 104, 179
Nkrumah, Kwame, 103–4, 162
nonaligned movement, 26, 141.
    See also Third World
non-self-governing territories, 6,
    117
norms/normative change, 9–13,
    153–55
North Africa: anticolonialism in,
    42, 43; colonization of, 8, 69;
    decolonization of, 72, 89,
    95–100; Italy and, 64; pro-
    German sentiment in, 39;
    religion in, 49; and Second
    World War, 67–68. *See also*
    Maghreb
North Atlantic Treaty Organiza-
    tion (NATO), 140, 150
Northern Rhodesia, 110–11
North Korea, 34, 140, 148, 171. *See
    also* Korea
North-South conflict, 134, 142–46,
    191. *See also* world politics
nuclear weapons, 140, 145, 148, 150
Nyasaland, 110–11

October Revolution, 17
oil shocks, 135
Opium War, 17
Organization for African Unity,
    162
Organization of Petroleum Ex-
    porting Countries (OPEC), 143

Ottoman Empire, 11, 17, 37
Outer Mongolia, 140

Pakistan, 74–75, 79–80; conflict
    with India, 80, 178
Palestine: Arab revolt in, 43;
    dissolution of mandate in,
    91–92; partition of, 92, 178, 183;
    religion in, 49; violence in, 69,
    92
Palestine Liberation Organization
    (PLO), 153
pan-Africanism, 44–45, 47, 53, 156,
    160, 162
pan-Arabism, 47, 93, 160, 162
pan-Asianism, 66, 162
Paris peace conference and
    treaties, 37–39, 54, 145, 177
parliamentarism, 57, 58, 78, 80, 84,
    104, 121
Philippines: and Cold War, 140,
    146; decolonization of, 147;
    development in, 62; governance
    of, 57; independence of, 60, 71,
    82–83; neocolonialism in, 87,
    179; Spain's loss of, 8
politics. *See* world politics
Polynesia, 8, 116–17
Portugal: and colonial politics,
    58–60; and decolonization, 9,
    102, 112–14, 152, 173, 181–82;
    empire of, 8; and First World
    War, 37; migration to, 184;
    revolution in, 114, 181–82; and
    settlers, 124
postcolonial studies/theory, 33,
    167–70

private economic interests, 120–27, 135–37
psychology of colonialism, 164–65
Puerto Rico, 116

race and racism: and African nationalism, 45; colonialism and, 164, 186; colonial troops, 37; decolonization in relation to, 1, 13, 20–21, 112; international ostracism of racism, 151, 154; settlers' attitude on, 123; South Africa and, 102, 117–18, 141
raw materials and natural resources, 15, 61, 66, 67, 77, 100, 108, 112, 121, 125, 126, 129, 134, 138, 143
reform. *See* colonialism: reforms of; late colonialism: political reforms
religion: conflicts based on, 27, 29, 49, 76, 78–80, 81, 176; in relation to anticolonialism and nationalism 49, 51, 160
repatriates. *See* migration
repercussions, of decolonization on the metropoles. *See* decolonization; Europe; metropoles
resettlement. *See* forced migration
revolution: decolonization as, 3, 20, 85, 95, 114, 116, 128, 165, 181–82; social, 48, 83; Third World and, 166
Rhodesia, 12, 46, 111–12, 114, 124
Rif rebellion (1921–26), 44

Romania, 141
Roosevelt, Franklin D., 68, 147
Rothermund, Dietmar, 6
Russian Empire, 37
Russian Federation, 11
Russo-Japanese war (1904–5), 38

Said, Edward, 167, 168
Saint-Domingue, 20
Salazar, Oliveira, 112
Sarraut, Albert, 55
secession: from empire, 20, 21, 111; from postcolonial states, 104, 107–8, 126, 177–78
Second World War, 61, 63–70, 75–76; as war of empires, 64
self-determination, 3, 13, 22, 33, 40, 68, 155, 178
self-government, 7, 21–22, 47, 103, 137, 149
Senegal, 41, 58, 106, 162
Senghor, Léopold, 45, 105, 106, 156, 158, 161
settlers: Algeria as colony of, 44, 58, 98, 100; and anticommunism, 151; characterization of, 123; economic interests of, 123; as obstacles to decolonization, 109–14; political influence of, 124; revolts of, 21; and second colonial occupation of Africa, 63
Sierra Leone, 104
Singapore, 66, 81, 89, 146, 152
social engineering, 16, 151
social sciences, 16, 166
socialism, 48, 93, 120, 134, 151

social welfare, 16, 62, 105, 129, 134, 185

Somalia, 178

South Africa: apartheid in, 8, 20–21, 72, 102, 117–18, 141; in Cold War years, 141; decolonization of, 111–12; as dominion, 8, 73; during First World War, 39; labor struggle in, 44, 47; as mandate power, 38; Truth and Reconciliation Commission in, 191

South America, 7. *See also* Latin America

South Asia: colonization of, 69; decolonization of, 71, 73–81

Southeast Asia: colonization of, 8, 11, 70; decolonization of, 71, 81–89; Japan and, 65

southern Africa: anticolonialism in, 44; decolonization of 72, 100–114, 117–18; development in, 61–62; Marxist regimes in, 152; nationalism in, 44, 47; post–Second World War colonization of, 63; religion in, 49

Southern Rhodesia, 21, 63, 110–11. *See also* Rhodesia

South Korea, 34, 83, 140, 171. *See also* Korea

South Sudan, 178

Southwest Africa. *See* Namibia

sovereignty: alternatives to, 47, 160–62; characteristics of, 9–10; dimensions of, 179; incomplete, 12, 163, 179; layered, 47; nation-state model of, 12, 162, 177; as result of decolonization, 9; United Nations and, 153; varieties of, 160–63

Soviet Union: and Afghanistan, 153; Chinese relations with, 141, 147; and Cold War, 139–42, 144–46; dissolution of, 11, 18–19; and imperialism, 53; as successor of Russian empire, 17; and Third World, 151

Spain: anticolonial unrest against, 44; and colonial politics, 59; and decolonization, 9, 97, 102, 114; empire of, 8

Spivak, Gayatri Chakravorty, 168

Sri Lanka. *See* Ceylon

Stalin, Joseph, 144

statehood. *See* nation-state model; norms/normative change; sovereignty

Statute of Westminster, 10

sterling area, 130

strikes, 102, 117, 125, 138

structural adjustment programs, 135

sub-Saharan Africa. *See* southern Africa

Sudan, 93

Suez Canal and Suez crisis, 72, 90, 93–95, 150, 182

Sukarno, 43, 50, 85, 156

Sun Yat-sen, 158, 216n4

superpowers, 139–40, 145

Suriname, 60, 115–16

symbolism, of decolonization, 14, 172, 187–88

Syria: anticolonialism in, 39; coup in, 93; decolonization of, 70, 91; and federalism, 162; nationalism in, 43, 93; and Second World War, 68; violence in, 69

Tagore, Rabindranath, 160
Taiwan: and Cold War, 140; development in, 61; Japan and, 65; land reform in, 83
Tanganyika, 104
Tanzania, 34
Thailand, 140, 146
Third International (Comintern), 53, 144
Third World: concept of 133, 143, 150, 151, 165–67; solidarity in, 166. See also global South; non-aligned movement; North-South conflict
Tibet, 154
time zones, 171–72
Togo, 105, 106
Touré, Sékou, 105
trade unions, 44, 47, 97, 102, 115, 117
traditionalism, 49, 51, 62, 84, 97, 162–63
traditionalist elites, 45, 48, 52
transfer of power, 29
Transjordan. See Jordan
transnational corporations, 32, 77, 122, 136–37
Trinidad and Tobago, 115, 152
Truman, Harry S., 147, 148
Tshombe, Moïse, 108
Tuareg, 178

Tunisia: independence of, 96–97; labor struggle in, 47; nationalism in, 44, 47, 69; regional conflicts in, 49; religion in, 49; and Second World War, 69; women's rights in, 51
Turkey, 11

Uganda, 104
United Nations: admission of states to, 2, 152; and the Congo, 107; and decolonization, 6, 12–13, 24, 153; and federalism, 162; founding of, 10; membership of, 10–11; and North-South conflict, 143; and Palestine, 92; postcolonial states' influence in, 134; and sovereignty, 153; and Suez crisis, 94; trusteeships of, 34; and world politics, 145. See also nation-state model; norms/normative change; sovereignty
United States: American Revolution as model of decolonization, 21–22; anticolonialism of, 68; and Asia, 147–48; British relations with, 150; Chinese relations with, 147; and Cold War, 139–42, 144–49; and colonial politics, 60; communism regarded as threat by, 148–50; criticized as colonialist, 154; and decolonization, 9, 116; development practices of, 62; and empire, 56; formation of, 11, 20; Japanese relations with, 146, 148; and Philippines, 60,

United States (*continued*)
62, 82–83, 146; and world
politics, 146
urban-rural relations, 49–50
utopian moment, of decolonization, 20, 166–67, 180

Venezuela, 127
Venice, 17
Vietnam: anticolonialism in, 43;
economic transitions in, 128;
Japan and, 66, 82; nationalism
in, 46, 47; struggle for independence in, 21, 34, 46, 85–88
Vietnam wars (1946–54, 1964–73),
5, 34, 85–88, 143, 149
violence: associated with decolonization, 5–6; consequences of,
34; memories of, 188; and
modernization, 63, 99, 113;
resulting from border disputes, 178. *See also* emergency/
emergency laws
Virgin Islands, 116

Warsaw Pact, 140
Washington, George, 21
West Africa: colonization of, 8;
decolonization of, 102–6;

economic transitions in, 129;
and French politics, 59; labor
struggle in, 44, 47; mass-elite
tensions in, 50; and Second
World War, 67
West Bank, 154
Western New Guinea, 154
Western Sahara, 114
West Indies. *See* Caribbean
West Indies Federation, 115, 161
Wilson, Woodrow, 39–40
Wilsonian moment, 40, 145
women. *See* feminism/women's
emancipation
World Bank, 134
world politics, 24, 31; Cold War,
139–42, 144–52; East/West
divide in, 139–46, 152; and a
new order, 153–55, 178; North/
South divide in, 142–46

Youssef, Mohammed ben, 97
Yugoslavia, 11, 18, 141

Zaire, 152, 162, 187–88. *See also*
Congo
Zimbabwe, 12, 114. *See also*
Rhodesia
Zionism, 43, 91–92